Prentice Hall Studies in Writing and Culture

———— *Series Editor* ————
Nancy Sommers
Harvard University

PRENTICE HALL STUDIES IN WRITING AND CULTURE captures the excitement of an emerging discipline that is finally coming into its own. The writers in this series are challenging basic assumptions, asking new questions, trying to broaden the inquiry about writing and the teaching of writing. They not only raise challenging questions about the classroom—about teaching and building communities of writers—they also investigate subjects as far ranging as the nature of knowledge and the role that culture plays in shaping pedagogy. Writers in the series are particularly concerned about the interplay between language and culture, about how considerations of gender, race, and audience shape our writing and our teaching. Early volumes will be devoted to the essay, audience, autobiography, and how writers teach writing. Other studies will appear over time as we explore matters that are critical to teaching writing.

Nancy Sommers is Associate Director of the Expository Writing Program at Harvard. She has also directed the composition program at the University of Oklahoma and has taught in the English Department of Rutgers University where she was a Henry Rutgers research fellow. She has published widely on the theory and practice of teaching writing. She has received the National Council of Teachers of English Promising Research Award for her work on revision and the Richard Braddock Award for her work on responding to student writing.

Books in this Series

James E. Porter, *Audience and Rhetoric*
Kurt Spellmeyer, *Common Ground: Dialogue, Understanding, and the Teaching of Composition*

How Writers
Teach Writing

Edited by **Nancy Kline**
Director of the Writing Project
Barnard College

Prentice Hall, Englewood Cliffs, New Jersey 07632

Library of Congress Cataloging-in-Publication Data

How writers teach writing / edited by Nancy Kline.
      p.   cm. -- (Prentice Hall studies in writing and culture)
   Includes bibliographical references   and index.
   ISBN 0-13-425224-1 (cas)   -- ISBN 0-13-425232-2 (paper)

   1. English language--Rhetoric--Study and teaching.   I. Kline,
Nancy E.   II. Series.
PE1404.H69   1992
808'.042'07--dc20   91-3463
                                                          CIP

Acquisitions Editor: Tracy Augustine
Editorial/production supervision and interior design: Penelope Linskey
Copy Editor: Joyce Perkins
Cover Designer: Marianne Frasco
Prepress Buyer: Herb Klein
Manufacturing Buyer: Patrice Fraccio

© 1992 by Prentice-Hall, Inc.
A Simon & Schuster Company
Englewood Cliffs, New Jersey 07632

Printed in the United States of America
10 9 8 7 6 5 4 3 2 1

ISBN 0-13-425224-1 C

ISBN 0-13-425232-2 P

Prentice-Hall International (UK) Limited, *London*
Prentice-Hall of Australia Pty. Limited, *Sydney*
Prentice-Hall Canada Inc., *Toronto*
Prentice-Hall Hispanoamericana, S.A., *Mexico*
Prentice-Hall of India Private Limited, *New Delhi*
Prentice-Hall of Japan, Inc., *Tokyo*
Simon & Schuster Asia Pte. Ltd., *Singapore*
Editora Prentice-Hall do Brasil, Ltda., *Rio de Janeiro*

For
Amelie Ratliff
her book

🐌 *Contents*

🐝 *Editor's Preface*

The distinct, articulate, passionate voices in these pages transport me straight back to the photocopier room at Expos (as the Expository Writing Program at Harvard is called). When we instructors weren't in class or conference with students, that room was where we lived, frequently on our knees. We seemed to spend more hours fishing evil shreds of blackened crumpled paper from the belly of the beast than we did in our own homes. And during all those hours on the carpet, when we weren't cursing, we were talking to each other. We wanted to hear what our colleagues were teaching and how, we wanted to steal it for our own use, we wanted to tell them what we'd just discovered about writing, and about communicating it to students, we wanted to know how their own work was going and how their student's essays were, we took the good news home to fuel us at our solitary tables.

Like that room, this book is a communal space. Some of the people in it still teach at Harvard, others of us have moved on, to write fulltime or to teach elsewhere—at Simmons, Barnard, Suffolk, MIT, the Borough of Manhattan Community College. We had come to Expos from just as disparate a group of schools: from West Point and BU, Emory and Tufts, big state universities like Michigan, the University of California-San Diego, Tennessee. The student populations we had known were as varied as we, and we brought this variety with us. What we also brought, as professional, publishing writers—and what was immeasurably enriched by our intense ongoing dialogue with each other and with our students—was our love of writing and the teaching of writing. That is what this book is about.

Our premise here is that writers who teach expository writing have a certain inside-out take on the subject that will prove useful to other expository writing teachers, as well as to aspiring writers and to instructors in other disciplines who are interested in integrating writing into their own pedagogy. We are not composition theorists, although we have read composition theory. We are novelists, essayists, poets, historians, translators, anthropologists, journalists, playwrights—people "whose most absorbed and passionate hours are spent arranging words on paper" (Didion, 20). It seems to us that professional writers have two things in particular to share with their colleagues and their students: the first is a passionate engagement with the act of writing, and the second is the fact that they write to an audience. We believe that caring about words and about their reception can be taught.

We believe too that, as Richard Marius puts it, "writing is the supreme tool for learning" and can—and should—be used to deepen the education of our students, in every discipline, at every level of instruction. For writing *is* thinking, *is* learning. The essay begins—began, four centuries ago—with the question *Que sais-je?* ("What do I know?"). It is by asking this question and working out an answer to it on the page that we truly take possession of our knowledge. Writing offers our students, as it offers us, "the pleasure of making connections: ruminating on a subject, seeing patterns emerge, watching an argument evolve, evidence cohere. In short, that glorious territoriality of staking and claiming a subject as [our] own" (Johnson).

How, then, do we go about it? How do writers teach writing?

The Writer as Reader

To begin with, by teaching our students to read.

Not so easy a task at this moment in time, when "we are rapidly and remorselessly leaving behind the age of the book—of the printed page, the written record—and are entering upon something that might be designated 'the media age.' . . . A massive collective rewiring is underway" (Birkerts).

Yet as writers we are persuaded "that learning to write and learning to read are inextricably bound up with one another" (Kline), "that one cannot write well if one does not read" (Birkerts).

As Alex Gold observes,

> It's easy to forget that good writing is a communal project, easy to overlook how much of what a writer can do derives from what she's read and how she has read it. . . . A high goal for anyone who teaches writing in any form, I think, is to encourage, to help, to lead our students to read, by any means whatever. We know that reading itself is under siege now, and any student

who lets it slip away will lose a great deal more than the escapist pleasures of a few leisure hours.

"*Read, read, read* some more. . . . *Read everything,*" exhorts Maxine Rodburg.

And our essays themselves underline the exhortation, both by modeling close readings (see Birkerts on Orwell, Pei on Welty, Marchant on William Carlos Williams, Burg on Shakespeare) and by suggesting how close readings of a wide variety of texts might serve us in the classroom: the Lincoln penny and the diaries of Columbus (Simon), Karl Popper on "testability" (Farrell), Stephen Jay Gould on Mickey Mouse (Cohen).

We teach our students to read in the hope that someday they'll be "culturally literate" and in the belief that if they are really able to explicate a poem or a piece of prose they will be better readers of the outside world, better able to "[explicate] the complex cultural signs that surround them" (Marchant). We teach our students to read so that they will have access to other people's knowledge, other people's lives, and other people's subjectivities—the last of which Lowry Pei calls the "inner inside" of each of us. But above all we teach our students to read so that they will write better. And thus our emphasis in class falls as much (or more) on the "how" of a text as on the "what" of it, on *how the text works*, on the choices made by any given writer and how these choices will affect the reader.

We want our students to focus on their role as readers, to pay attention to their own reactions to a text: "[We] ask them to try to look at their own minds and the poem working therein" (Merchant). We want to teach them that reading is a creative act, that "one is completing the creation of the story as one reads" (Pei), that readers like writers make meaning. We want them to slow down, to value reading, to love it as much as we do:

> For reading is stillness, absorption, the forging and sustaining of mental perspectives; it is active, difficult; it opens upon density and diversity. And it is also listening: to voices, sounds, rhythms, and articulations of otherness. To read is to situate oneself in some relation to a heritage; to watch is to surrender passively to a churning of images. (Birkerts)

But how shall we get our students to turn off MTV, to "stop at words" (Simon) and step into this other world, of stillness and absorption? How can they be made to care?

The answer offered again and again in the pages of this book, implicitly and explicitly, is that we must bring our own passion for language into the classroom. We must lead our students through close reading, real reading—of professional texts and of their own texts. We must bring our students' work into class and conference and pay it just as much attention as we do the texts of published authors.

Students need to have a real experience of reading and to know the privilege of being read.

The Writer's Readers

That it is a privilege, and not a punishment, we have to tell them. And then they have to find that out themselves.

The very thought that they might have an audience is an epiphany for many students. There comes a crucial instant each semester in the writing class when we suggest to them that one of their jobs as writers is to *interest their readers*. They are astonished. No one ever told them in high school that their writing should be *interesting*. Clear, perhaps, well structured. But no one ever bothered to explain that clarity and structure are, among other things, more interesting than unintelligible chaos. And yet, as any writer knows, the reader must be won. She is not yours for the asking. "The poem is always married to someone," writes the poet René Char (159).

Indeed, and writing is the courtship.

Why is it such hard work to read student papers? asks Richard Marius. Because, he answers, we often simply do not know what our students are talking about.

The corollary: our students have not been taught to use the page to talk to anyone. They simply do not know that there is anybody out there listening. "As we know and our students need to learn," writes Victor Kantor Burg, "the difference between a rough draft and a reworked version of it is usually that the former speaks primarily to its author, while the latter turns outward to address its audience."

Students need—and like—to learn this; they are genuinely interested to think that what they have to say might interest others. They are interested in writing well, they want to take command of written English. And once they recognize that texts need readers to complete them—once they see that there are people seated in the orchestra who might applaud, or might get up and leave—even facets of their writing they'd considered trivial and annoying (punctuation, spelling) start to make some sense. When I receive a student essay that has obviously not been proofread, often the first of the semester, I suggest in the margins that this is the equivalent of going on a heavy date without bothering to change your socks. I usually get clean copy from then on.

As Maxine Rodburg comments in her essay on writing workshops, students welcome the idea of audience:

> My students of composition or expository writing are often surprised to consider that writing is not only self-expression but also an implicit relationship between writer and reader. But for years they have themselves been puzzled, wearied, angered by enforced reading of texts that do not seem to consider them. For years they have received back from their teachers writing that has been evaluated, graded, checked, or marked according to a set of standards that too often seems to vary year by year, as the student proceeds through the school system. So they quickly embrace the idea that audience is crucial. They like to be able [in the workshop] to hear the hosannas or see the thumbs down. They like being reminded that writers and readers are human.

They like the sense of the writing class as a community, in which the instructor participates—and not just as a reader, but also as a fellow writer.

Rodburg is quick to point out that there is no such thing as a true democracy: the instructor has read more, written more, gives the grades. But still, if students feel that their teacher has fought deadlines just as they do, has had her own experience of writer's block, has struggled through first drafts and revisions, has known the agony and the ecstasy of being read, is just as prone to crazy rites and rituals when it comes to writing as they are (see Alex Johnson's "Why Isaac Bashevis Singer, Truman Capote, Joseph Conrad and Virginia Woolf [Among Others] Were Having a Bad Morning"), the act of writing gets demystified, becomes less threatening, more possible. The writer's solitude is a reality, but so is the possibility of community.

And so is the possibility of owning your own work.

The Writer's Authority

If they are to write effectively and creatively—not to mention plea-surably—if their writing is to become an effective means of thinking and articulating that thinking, then our students must somehow be persuaded that they have the capacity to be writers (authors, authorities), that they themselves can in fact make meaningful texts, that they can "impose the unity of mind on the diversity of things" (Sartre/Simon), that they have something to say. Richard Marius suggests that one of the problems with student writing is that our students do not know very much, and certainly one of the jobs of the university is to provide them with information. However, what this book as a whole suggests is that our job as writing instructors (but why just writing instructors, why not instructors in every discipline?) is to provide students with something else: namely, the tools with which to shape that information—and with which to find it in the first place; the means to organize what they know and then synthesize it , to make sense of it, to explore and go beyond it, to come into full possession of their own knowledge. Deprived of these tools, our students risk "sinking into narcotic passivity during their college years" (Marius), settling for "the idea that education is accumulation: of facts, of information, of the defini-tions of key terms, of the memorization of names and dates" (Simon). They risk becoming, like the mindlessly fact-crammed Gargantua under the tute-lage of Maitre Thubal Holoferne, "foolish, dreamy, inane, stupefied boo-bies" (Rabelais 49). For, to quote Cardinal Newman, as he is quoted by Pat Hoy, "it is not mere application, however exemplary, which introduces the mind to truth, nor the reading many books, nor the getting up many subjects, nor the witnessing many experiments, nor the attending many lectures. All this is short of enough; a man may have done it all, yet be lingering in the vestibule of knowledge . . . ."

One way to get out of the vestibule of knowledge and into the living room is to write. And it is up to us to escort our students on the journey, to help them reach that place where their thought becomes their own, and they know it, and they know how to say it. Every writing instructor, at every level, must confront the problem of how to empower students as writers, how to help them believe in and exercise their own authority in the page.

Traditionally, instructors have assigned the personal essay as a text in which students may experience themselves as authorities. And indeed Pat Hoy would have us begin just there, in our writing courses. But from the very outset Hoy makes it clear that what he's after is an impersonalizing of the personal, an imaginative reconstruction that "turns images of experience into the impersonal stuff from which good essays are made." What Hoy asserts is that there is a real and demonstrable connection between personal essays and all the other writing our students will do in the university and that "the complexity involved in the ordering of experience belies the claim of those composition theorists who dismiss personal essays because they are merely *expressive*."

This dismissive attitude elides the fact that "'*personal*' has another, shiftier side," to quote Robert Atwan, in his preface to *Best American Essays of 1989*: "Its roots reach back to the Latin '*persona*,' a literal term for 'mask' and, by metonymic extension, a theatrical character (*dramatis persona*)" (ix). Which is to say that the "I" in a personal essay is a mask, a contrivance, a rhetorical device as separate from its author as is the "I" in a first-person fiction. This may not be obvious to students, but it can be taught. By telling them, for instance, that George Orwell never shot an elephant; by taking them through Joan Didion's "Why I Write" and pointing out the modulation from the "I" of her first paragraph to the "I" on her last page; by studying the contrivance in any number of first-person texts; by suggesting to them that the instant I write I on paper, there are two of us, and we are not the same. Hoy writes:

> I find that if I can get [students] to separate themselves from their own experiences—to reflect on themselves, to create an "I" in their texts who is different from the writer creating the texts, if I can do that at the beginning of a composition sequence, everything else falls into place, more or less naturally. Students will never again be so naive as to believe that they have disappeared from even their most objective texts or that the "I" in their most personal essay actually accounts for the many other "I's" they could have created but didn't.

Artists know about this. They know how powerful the personal impersonalized can be. In fact this is the fundamental alchemy of art: the private rendered other (as in Rimbaud's "*Je est un autre*"—"I is another"). The act of translating the personal into the impersonal allows us to communicate our otherwise incommunicable "inner inside." This is what makes fiction, which is purely that, seem "real." And why Lowry Pei can insist, in his essay on writing about short stories, that we must "study the contrivance, the technique, the artifice of fiction in order to become a better co-creator, better able to enter the world of the dream—to become fully awake, as the writer is, inside the dream."

The poet René Char writes, "Poetry's aim being to grant sovereignty by impersonalizing us, in the poem we touch the fullness of what was only partial or deformed by the boastings of the individual" (359). And the composer John Cage is referring to that same transcendency when he says to the painter Philip Guston:

"When you start working, everybody is in your studio—the past, your friends, enemies, the art world, and above all, your own ideas—all are there. But as you continue painting, they start leaving, one by one, and you are left completely alone. Then, if you're lucky, even you leave." (in Mayer, 171–2)

But of course you're still there too, in the canvas, in the composition, in the words. And in the research paper also, even there. Every successful essay is personal, and impersonal; every research paper or literary analysis, like every novel, is somehow rooted in the self.

A personal story:

The summer I got divorced, I had an essay to write for the MLA on Guillaume Apollinaire's fiction. I'd written my master's thesis on the subject and was hoping to cull some usable material from that dry document. It was no use, there was nothing there that caught my eye. So during the summer I reread the fiction, all of it, and what struck me most forcibly was a leitmotif I hadn't even noticed years earlier, in my thesis: namely, the prevalence of amputations in Apollinaire's work. They were everywhere. I couldn't understand how I had missed them. For my session at the MLA I wrote "Fragments of a Discourse on Apollinaire's Fiction: Amputation/Remembrance/Ubiquity." When was it I figured out that my heavily footnoted, deconstructive, Lacanian, textual analysis was a personal essay?

In "Confronting Social and Ethical Issues," Judith Beth Cohen discusses precisely this connection between the subjective and the objective, the highly charged personal topic and the intellectually sound paper that may result from it. Cohen leads us through a series of sequenced assignments designed to help her students move "from the narrative of a personal issue to a closely reasoned argument about the social implications of that same issue." She takes as her starting point a paradox: "if our students are to transcend privatism, they must begin with what is private to them. In order to take their subjectivity and transform it into a means of understanding the human condition, they must begin within that subjectivity. . . . If they are to develop a voice capable of speaking for others as well as themselves, they must first learn to speak with their own voice." But by the end of her essay—and of her writing course—her students' voices have been joined by many others: those of their fellow students, their teacher, the experts they have interviewed, the books and articles they've read. "After reflecting on the many voices they have heard," writes Cohen, "after revising their thinking and their essays, students leave this course knowing how to research an issue, how to critique their own ethical assumptions, and, most importantly, how to see their own story as a living piece of the larger human story."

This does not seem so very different from Alex Gold's conclusion to a very different essay, "The Man in the Tweed Cap: Quotation, Illusion and Identity." Gold's subject is the rhetorical connections between fiction and nonfiction, the use of fictional techniques in the writing of essays; and he focuses specifically on the technique of quotation. This of course leads him into a discussion of voice(s). He opens his conclusion as follows:

> But we have gone so far, I suspect, in encouraging in our students the personal, the private, the merely self-expressive and the narrowly original, that we scarcely let them know how communal, public, and splendidly derivative good writing truly is. Teachers often tell students to give their own ideas, not to hide behind other writers' opinions. I think we need to show them how to give their own ideas in the *presence* of other people's voices and opinions.

The writer must speak in her own voice, but in the presence of others. Writing is at once a solitary and a communal act. This is the news we bring our students. This is why they must read; this is why they must write with clarity and elegance—so that they can be read. The self is where writing originates, but the self is surrounded by others, and they speak in the text that is spoken by the self. Nor is that text complete until the writer has detached from it and sent it out to meet its readers. And only if the writer assumes full authority can she commence and carry out the complex business of writing, the shaping of her material to make it *mean*.

Yet, as Linda Simon observes in her essay on the writing of history:

> Students rarely see their task as that of imposing order on any material they confront. Instead, when asked why they write papers, students reveal that writing is another kind of test-taking. They are persuaded that in the act of writing it is not they who have any authority but rather the instructor and the experts upon whom they rely for their information. They write not out of a need to speak in a distinctive voice but rather out of a desire to merge their voices with so many others. They write not because they want to, but because we, the instructors, ask them to.

As an antidote to our students' shaky (or nonexistent) sense of authority in essays other than the personal essay, Simon proposes that we disabuse them of the notion that Truth exists, that there is one Answer they must find. "Once the illusion of certainty is lost," she writes, "the writer no longer tests his work against an absolute Truth but against his own sense of logic, his own priorities of importance, his own way of shaping reality. . . . Authority is gained even as illusions are lost."

An observation seconded by Maxine Rodburg, who suggests that as the student gains authority, the teacher relinquishes hers, fruitfully:

> Freed of the traditional authoritarian role, the teacher may respond as a human being to student work: as writer to writer. Acknowledging our human fallibility—the fact that each of us is one voice only, with no hotline to "The Truth"—encourages students to trust us at the same time it teaches them to depend more and more on their own critical abilities: to serve as their own teachers, critics and editors.

Simon's and Rodburg's suggestion that we acknowledge—even that we base our teaching on—uncertainty, ambiguity, open questions rather than final solutions, exploration rather than certitude, is echoed again and again, in essay after essay, throughout this book.

Thus, playwright Victor Kantor Burg asks: "What student's mind— what writer's mind—has not begun to write without knowing really where it will go, only to learn at the end where it meant to start?" Thus, writing about the explication of poetry, Fred Marchant remarks: " Behind all my suggestions is my sense that the explication need not be a tearing apart of the poem but rather could be a charting of the student's own exploratory progress in the making of meaning within and with the text." Thus, in my own essay "Writing as Translation," I suggest that language's capacity to be opaque sometimes yields, quite suddenly, "to let us into places we did not even know were there. There is so much to be explored, uncovered, in the act of writing itself. Might it not by our job to guide students beyond formulas, toward the essay as exploration?"

Cynthia Ozick has written, "Nearly every essay, like every story, is an experiment, not a credo" (x). I believe every writer in this book would agree. And I believe we would all agree with Linda Simon's contention that the student's sense of authority is strengthened precisely to the degree that he recognizes the tentative nature of reality or at least the tentative nature of our knowledge of reality. "Students are timid, of course, about asserting their authority," writes Simon, "but they relax visibly when they believe that they are required only to *essay*, to try, in their writing, rather than to complete and conclude."

So, the writing of history.

But what about authority in the writing of science?

How are we to relate the pedagogy of ambiguity, the essay as exploration, the uses of personal narrative, the personal impersonalized, to undergraduate writing about physics or chemistry?

"Science values objectivity," writes anthropologist Eileen Farrell. "It rules out of court precisely the kind of subjective experience that gives us leverage in the personal narrative. Authority in science comes from observing a new thing, not from observing a familiar thing from a uniquely personal perspective." Scientists write to announce a discovery. They are experts writing to peers. They have something urgent to communicate. Where does this leave a first-year student, who has no major scientific breakthrough to announce? How can anyone short of a postdoc possibly write with any sense of authority at all in science?

That there is a need for writers who are, precisely, not postdocs to write about science becomes clearer every day. Ours is a world ruled by technology. How are those of us who don't know calculus to understand what's going on? We need interpreters. Add to our need the fact that students stand to learn more science—or, at the very least, different science—if they write about it (see, among other books, William Zinsser's *Writing to Learn*), and it will be evident that an undergraduate course in science-writing is no empty academic exercise.

The solution Farrell offers to the problem of the writer's authority in writing about science is to transform the student into a "comparative expert" and the instructor into a "needy reader" (this in the place of "hapless defendant" and "hanging judge"). Farrell offers certain specific ways to effect this transformation in her course, such as "designing assignments that ask the student to choose a concept from the assigned reading and apply it to a topic of his choice." Since the instructor has not researched the student's specific topic, the latter becomes a comparative authority on it, capable of writing a paper from which his reader will actually learn something.

This transformative experience, proposed by Farrell as the goal of her particular course, has implications for all of us, I think, no matter what our discipline. Because instructors do know more about their subject than students. Because chances are excellent that I know more about irony and allusion in the short stories of Flannery O'Connor than the beginning writers in my class, but still I can say to them, and mean it: "If you have just written an essay analyzing narrative voice in "A Good Man Is Hard to Find," you know that text and that particular aspect of it better than I do. You are a comparative expert. You have things to teach me. You can speak with authority."

What precisely does it do for our students' writing to find themselves in this position of authority, suddenly confronted with a needy reader—or a roomful of them, as in a writing workshop? "My students look around the table," writes Rodburg, "and realize something crucial: people have read what they wrote. Real people, with needs—the needs of real readers to understand the writer's intentions."

And so, and then? What Eileen Farrell suggests, straightfaced, is that the writer's realization of his readers' needs (for clarity) actually causes him to write better (that is, more clearly), for it forces him to give up the comforting fantasy of his audience as "mind-reader[s] akin to the mother of infancy, who is expected to sense empathetically what the infant means by his inarticulate cries." The preverbal essay disappears. What Vygotsky calls "inner speech" gives way to public discourse. The student takes responsibility for his text.

The Writer's Text

In the place of inarticulate cries, what is it we hope to find in our students' essays?

"Evidence that the writer is thinking, reasoning, reflecting, and not merely reporting information collected from other sources" (Marius).

The "clarity, precision, structure, shape and careful strategy" that good nonfiction shares with fiction (Rodburg).

"Artful persuasion" (Hoy); "elaboration of meanings" (Farrell); "engagement, development, suspense, embodiment, and illusion" (Gold); "intricacy and detail" (Birkerts).

"The kind of communication that makes community possible" (Pei).

Good stories. And the distinctive voice with which to tell them (Simon, Cohen, and just about everyone else in this book).

Texts that enter into conversation with their readers (Marchant).

Texts that go exploring, that take risks (Kline, Johnson, Hoy, Marchant, Burg, Simon).

If I've attributed the thoughts above to specific writers in this book, that doesn't mean the same or similar thoughts are not to be found in other essays by other writers in these pages. We seem to be remarkably unanimous in what we look for in our students' work, no matter what the subject we ask them to write about. And, too, we resemble one another in our teaching methods (of which there is much discussion in our individual essays). The subject that is always on the table, for all of us, in the classroom, in our offices, whether we are scrutinizing published authors' texts or student drafts, is how the written text comes into being. As writers teaching writing, our emphasis lies always on the process of writing itself.

The Writer's Process

We've seen how Eileen Farrell calls for changed relationships between instructors and beginning writers. And along with this she seeks another crucial transformation: between the writer and her "internal censor," that powerful inside player who, just like the external audience, must cease to be a "hanging judge" and turn into a "needy reader," if any coherent writing at all is to occur. This character appears in many guises in many of the essays in this book—she is known to all of us. But our in-house expert is Alex Johnson.

In "Why Isaac Bashevis Singer, Truman Capote, Joseph Conrad and Virginia Woolf (Among Others) Were Having a Bad Morning," Johnson asks and attempts to answer everything students always wanted to know about the writing process but were afraid to ask: "Why is writing so hard?

Why does it take me so long? Why do I need to do so many drafts? Why can't I do them faster? Will the process ever be less agonizing?" She takes us on a tour of the recorded agonies of a series of professional writers, thereby strengthening our sense (as she does her students') that writing is a community where we can really learn from one another, or at least take comfort in each other's struggles, despite our separate solitudes.

It seems to me that this sense of writing as shared struggle and shared risk is a real gift we can offer to students. As I suggest in "Writing as Translation: The Great Between," they need to know that

> Always in the dialectic of writing there is the source and the target, and in the space between them—here—deep in inner space, is the writer, here is where the writer spins, writes, must remain, suspended, till the work is completed.
> This is just as true of expository prose as it is of fiction. And it is just as true of student writing as it is of professional writing. The student essay, like any translation, comes into existence in the dizzying, spacy *between*. Not a comfortable location, though it is exciting. This weightlessness, this lack of gravity is unnerving. And so is the solitude. . . . When student writers find themselves afloat like this, they think there's been some terrible mistake. This can't be right, this galactic (oceanic) ambiguity. This suspension in the eternal silence of infinite space.

But anyone who writes has necessarily been there, has necessarily been "Lost," as Fred Marchant (by way of David Wagoner) would say, and this is information that apprentice writers need to have. They need to know they must

> Stand still. The trees ahead and the bushes beside you
> Are not lost. Wherever you are is called Here,
> And you must treat it as a powerful stranger,
> Must ask permission to know it and be known. . . .
>
> > (Wagoner/Marchant)

Students need to learn to sit with their writing in disarray around them, to tolerate ambiguity, to seek what Nancy Sommers calls "the dissonance of discovery" (Sommers, 127). They need to be taught these things and anything else that we can teach them about how writing really works. And this Alex Johnson does, with humor and precision.

She names the inner villains we want to help our students tame: The Internal Critic, The Saboteur, The Procrastinator, The Perfectionist. She discusses writer's block and where it comes from, and proposes to students a five-stage writing process—which is not prescriptive, she hastens to add, for "just as the writer makes a subject his own, so must he with his own writing process. It is as individual as writers themselves."

One of the most helpful thoughts she has to offer to our students is "that writing happens long before [we] ever type a word; the [our] best thinking and writing will happen before and after the first draft, but not necessarily during it." And she completes the thought with her emphasis on revision, an emphasis shared by all of us.

Writers know that writing is revision, that "in terms of the writing process, revision is where the best work, specifically, the writing gets done" (Johnson). We know this in our bones—that we "must note, write, rewrite: rehearse, rehearse, rethink, run through it still another time" (Burg). We know that writing never really stops, that texts are never really finished, just abandoned. That "finding meaning is a slow process, despite the exigencies of college courses, where meaning must be found in two weeks" (Simon). We write revisions into our syllabus, persuaded no good writing can occur without them and that our students must be taught this—by experiencing it, as often as possible, in their writing courses. We hope they will internalize it, for they are unlikely to experience it anywhere else. If we can teach them to begin their papers, even in our absence, sufficiently ahead of time so they'll be able to revise them, we will have gone a long way toward teaching them how to write.

As Johnson points out, it is when our students are revising that "at last . . . the internal critic has his place. If the creative, the intuitive work has been done beforehand, let the internal critic loose with his gleaming machete." Now is when we need him. Writes Maxine Rodburg, "Most students leaving the composition classroom rarely will be back to take another writing course; yet they will be writing for the rest of their college careers, often for the rest of their professional careers. We must give them their own internalized teachers, critics, editors." These we model for them in the classroom and the conference, as well as in our assignment sheets and our comments on their papers.

One of the most crucial dialogues in any writing class is, obviously, the written one between instructor and student: assignment sheet–first draft–comments–revision–comments–and so on, through however many drafts the student writes. Eileen Farrell observes that students "need to receive comments that are not negative or vaguely encouraging but stimulating—responses designed to elicit further explanation or suggest fruitful new lines of thought." To this observation I would add that students need to receive comments that are well written—not in the sense of being polished prose but in the sense of being articulate, thoughtful, clear and personal. In the sense of really saying something. Most of the writing we instructors do in the composition class consists of these comments. If we can show our students how we think about their writing by writing a response to it, then we will reinforce for them the fact that writing actually communicates, that papers (like books) are one half of a conversation, and that there is someone listening on the other end of the line.

In the course of the semester, my colleague Lowry Pei extends the written dialogue with his students by writing mini-essays to them (some half a page, some not so mini), in which he ruminates on whatever aspect of writing he's thinking about that day. When he and I both taught at Expos, I was always finding copies of these ruminations in my mailbox and passing them along to my own classes. Pei's essay "Why Fiction, Why Criticize?"

may serve as an example of this kind of caring disquisition from teacher to student, which testifies to his belief that "an important part of the enterprise [of teaching writing], as of any kind of teaching, is to tell the students why it is worth doing."

We cannot take for granted that they'll know this. Our students may think that learning to read and learning to write are irrelevant. We know they are essential. We know that language and our opposable thumbs, which permit us to hold a pencil, are what make us human. Let us teach our students that. Let us teach them to articulate and thereby reinforce their knowledge of the world and of themselves. Our students need to be able to make sense of things, they need to be able to make things, to make meanings. Let us use our own textual power and our deep pleasure in the text to help our students locate theirs. Let us share with them our love of language, our respect for words, our sense of play and our dead seriousness as writers and as teachers. Let us offer them our belief in the astonishing human act of writing.

Nancy Kline

Works Cited

Atwan, Robert. *Best American Essays of 1989.* New York: Ticknor & Fields, 1989.

Char, René. *Oeuvres complètes.* Paris: Gallimard, 1983.

Didion, Joan. "Why I Write." *The Writer on Her Work,* ed. Janet Sternburg. New York: Norton, 1980.

Mayer, Musa. *Night Studio.* New York: Knopf, 1988.

Ozick, Cynthia. *Metaphor & Memory.* New York: Knopf, 1989.

Rabelais. *Oeuvres complètes.* Paris: Gallimard, 1955.

Sommers, Nancy. "Revision Strategies of Student Writers and Experienced Adult Writers." *The Writing Teacher's Sourcebook,* eds. Gary Tate & Edward P. J. Corbett. New York: Oxford, 1988.

Vygotsky, L.S. *Thought and Language.* Trans. Eugenia Hanfmann and Gertrude Vakar. Cambridge, MA: MIT, 1962.

Zinsser, William. *Writing to Learn.* New York: Harper & Row, 1988.

A word on the organization of this book. Our essays can be read in any order. The connections between them are multiple. I have grouped them as follows: the first five discuss reading, at some length; the next four explore the writer's authority; a shift then occurs, in Eileen Farrell's pivotal essay, into questions of audience and of certain reconceptualizations in the teaching of writing. Within this arrangement, those seven essays that might be headed "what to write about" are grouped together at the center of the book.

His evolution as writing teacher

Sven Birkerts

❧ *Reading, Then Writing: The Arithmetic*

The assumption that I operate under in this piece is a sad one, to me at least. It is that we are rapidly and remorselessly leaving behind the age of the book—of the printed page, the written record—and are entering upon something that might be designated "the media age."

I have been teaching one of the required writing courses to Harvard freshmen for five years now (and similar courses elsewhere before that). I have been present to watch a tendency start to turn into a condition. At first a few students, then some, then most. My syntax accelerates the momentum of the change, but never mind. Let me try to explain what I mean.

To begin with, I would emphasize that I am in no way disputing the brightness or seriousness of my students. No, one has only to step into the classroom on the first day of school to feel their keenness. Fifteen sets of eyes flash to the door to check out the new teacher. They are alert, curious, ready to begin. Sometimes it seems that everything else moves and changes over the years—that only those eyes remain constant. Certainly they are an important part of what teaching is all about.

But if the eyes are changeless, then what is different? It has to be something there *behind* that bright display of energy—the cognitive make-up, the fundamental relation to the world and to history. In these students I find a whole new set of aptitudes and responses, an altered dispositional alignment. I'll try to describe it. For starters, one can't help but notice that these kids are quicker—more restless in posture and demeanor, more neu-

1

ral. Certain of their reflexes have been honed to a disconcerting pitch of readiness. They have been programmed to perform and they can scarcely wait to begin. At the same time, they seem blanker, shallower than their predecessors. And while I'm sure that 17- and 18-year-olds have always been oriented toward the present—in their lives, in the culture—the extent to which they are cut off from the past, from an encompassing sense of history, is startling. Indeed, I would say that the scope of their ignorance proves the prophet false—it *is* something new under the sun.

What am I saying? That these young people are all dressed up with no place to go. That they are formidably trained and "psyched," but that they have little knowledge or understanding to put to use. The engine is sophisticated, but the tank is nearly empty. Choose your own metaphor. The point is that they are appallingly without the kinds of context required for any significant exchange of ideas.

This recognition overtakes me every term, usually right away. For it is my habit to stop and ask for explanations whenever certain words, names or references come up. I watch as those clear, focused gazes cloud over, again and again. "Can anyone tell me who Sigmund Freud was?" Pause. You can almost *feel* the urgent ransacking of 15 memory banks. When was the French Revolution? *What* was the French Revolution? Who was Karl Marx? And so on. They just don't know. Most of them, that is. And if they do have some inkling, then they have a hard time formulating a coherent answer. They lack the means, the language. "He's the guy . . . you know, Freudian slip?"

I realize that this gripe has a familiar, even fashionable, sound to it. All of a sudden everybody is talking about "cultural literacy," about shared information, about the woeful inadequacy of high school curricula, etc. And I, too, have been reading E. D. Hirsch's book. But I do not think that this is mainly, centrally, a curriculum-related problem. In fact, it is something much larger, and much more difficult to remedy. What Hirsch has identified is just one of the consequences of this profound cultural shift—the shift from print as a cognitive base to one shaped by a range of electronic media. A massive collective rewiring is underway.

Hirsch is, of course, right to be alarmed. The problems are very real and very pressing. Americans *are* increasingly isolated from one another because they lack a common set of associations, of usable cultural counters. But where Hirsch's analysis stops the crisis begins. What would people communicate about once they had these common references? The Gettysburg Address? Carbon dioxide? Would the discourse of the nation become a grand game of Trivial Pursuit? The real point is that we lack the substance *behind* those names, dates, and tag lines. We have lost a sense of the past, a historical grounding; we are without a working knowledge of ideas and philosophies; we have lost our feeling for language as a living, supple, delighting, and generative entity. And no fiddling with curricula is going to restore these things to us.

I was most struck in my reading of Hirsch by how little he discussed reading and how seldom he mentioned TV. Television was brought up only twice in his text, and then just in passing. Yet I would argue that these two activities—their essentially inverse relation to one another—must form the very axis of the debate. Not in a simplistic way. Not in the sense that time spent watching is seen merely as time spent away from books. No, more in the sense that TV (I use TV here as a shorthand for a whole set of new technologies, including VCR movies, video games, portable cassette players, word processors programmed to check spelling and do God knows what else . . .) works to create an ambiance, a new synaptic patterning, a persuasive sense of a collectively shared "now," all of which cut against reading and what it represents. For reading is stillness, absorption, the forging and sustaining of mental perspectives; it is active, difficult; it opens upon density and diversity. And it is also listening: to voices, sounds, rhythms, and articulations of otherness. To read is to situate oneself in some relation to a heritage; to watch is to surrender passively to a churning of images.

I'm not saying that my students do nothing but watch TV, listen to tapes, and play video games. But I do believe that their inner dispositions, their sensibilities, have been formed—more than those of any generation in human history—by those activities, those forces. They are at large in our culture. One doesn't have to watch television to be affected by its ubiquity. The fact of it, the fact that our obscure but omnipresent Zeitgeist is conditioned by it and everywhere alludes to it, makes it harder than ever to venture the independent act of reading a book. Reading becomes a struggle because the prevailing attitude is that it is an odd, asocial activity. An eccentricity. I don't mean reading for school, and I don't mean "beach" reading. I mean the serious, private, self-generated interaction with books that forms the main path toward inner cultivation.

Almost none of my students read independently. I know this because I ask them. On the first day of class I request written answers to certain questions. About their backgrounds, their experience with high school English. And about their reading. How much they read outside of school, what they read, their favorite books, and so on. The responses are heartbreaking. Nearly every student admits—some of them sheepishly, others not—that reading is a problem. "Too busy." "I wish I had the time!" "I've always had a hard time with books that are supposed to be good for me." And then, proudly: "If I have the time, I like to relax with Stephen King." I can't tell you how many of my best and brightest have written that sentence. Stephen King, Stephen King, Stephen King. How rarely will someone cite a reputable "serious" book—by Milan Kundera, Vladimir

Nabokov, Walker Percy, Ann Tyler, *any*one. Nonfiction—history, politics, social history, psychology—is a *terra incognita*. But there they have an excuse: they will have to *study* the stuff.

Fine, so kids don't read anymore. Will the world of the future be different, worse, because people can't pass the time discussing Eudora Welty and Heinrich Böll? Well, yes. I fear it will be much worse. Not because certain plots, characters, inventions, or themes won't be assessed. To focus on those elements overlooks the other, perhaps *deeper*, functions of reading. I mean the way that the reading of serious books teaches one constantly (often unconsciously) about the world. The reader cross-references information about everything from dates and places to speech patterns to social mores. We are more apt to know about the French Revolution from having come across references to it in a dozen contexts than from having studied a textbook back in the tenth grade. But even more important is the way that reading keeps the language alive in us. Not just words and their uses but a feeling for the syntactic masonry required by different kinds of expression. Exposure to language on the page—the kind of hearing that goes on over thousands and thousands of pages—enlarges the inner reach. It teaches what can be expressed and how it can be expressed. It gives a feeling for the growth and movement of ideas and alerts us to the full range of positions, tones, and possibilities. The reader learns a healthy distrust of appearances—for what are most novels but penetrations and reversals of our preconceptions about character and situation? He learns, too, to search out the opacities and secrets of other lives and to hold complex orders of experience in his head. Will the world be different if people stop reading? Very likely it will once again be flat.

So much for students and their reading habits. The fact remains that my course (Expository Writing: Literature) is supposed to teach them to *write*. Clearly and expressively; subtly, and with depth and dimension. I have 11 or 12 weeks, two 50-minute classes a week, plus three private conferences. Where to begin?

I believe—as must be obvious—that one cannot write well if one does not read. Or, at very least, if one does not have the soul, the inner resources, of a reader. I believe that writing that is clear and varied, capable of sustained exposition as well as of detail and discrimination, cannot happen where there is not a sensibility equipped to generate it. And such a sensibility cannot exist without the kind of auditory inwardness that reading cultivates. For writing is so much more than just the transmission of ideas or information. Writing—effective, memorable writing—depends on the writer hearing the language. One balances sounds, their values and meanings; one holds in readiness clauses and word chains; one speeds up and slows down according to the needs of the expression. The ear does the brain's fingertip work—it joins and adjusts, adds and subtracts. It hears the rightness of a phrase, rejects a dissonance. If you can't hear words and their arrangements—the music that accompanies and enforces meaning—then you can't write. Certainly not well.

But as I have indicated, these students are not eager readers. The printed page taxes and wearies them; they find little pleasure there. What hope does a teacher have for getting them to write well? Initially, I confess, I always despair. I read through their first papers—so neatly word-processed, so proudly titled with the bold-faced curliques that the technology makes possible—and my heart sinks. The writing is almost always flat, monotonous, built up of simple units. Immigrant prose. But no, immigrant prose, clumsy though it may be, is often alert to the textures and imagistic possibilities of the language. This writing is bland and slippery, unpressurized by mind. It shows, if anything, the influence of rhetoric and televised banality. "The controversy surrounding the use of steroids is a heated one. Should an athlete be allowed to take drugs to improve performance? Or should these drugs be outlawed? The recent case of Olympic athlete Ben Johnson . . . ." Simple units. Where there is a compound sentence it is, more often than not, a creation made up of two short declarations joined by a comma or a conjunction. "These drugs must be outlawed and athletes must follow the law." The prose has little or no musicality and lacks any depth of field; it is casually associative in movement, syntactically inert, and barren of interesting reference. Complexity is nonexistent. Some sort of communication has been ventured, but only a paid reader—that is, a teacher—would read more than a few lines. If I exaggerate, it's only slightly.

The problem is immediately obvious. There is, however, no real dilemma. I must do what I can in the time I have to change this state of affairs. As I cannot undo the effects of years and years of not reading, I must do the next best thing. I must teach them to listen, to make hearing the core of their writing process. I must give them a good solid dose of close reading.

Close reading, as I understand it, is really nothing more than paying attention to a text. The difficulties are not in the conception but in the doing. To close-read a page of prose, a poem, anything, is to create a receptivity, a silence in yourself so that the work can leave an impression. Just as you cannot race past a painting in a museum and call that "seeing" the art, so you cannot move your eyes rapidly over a page and imagine that you have "read" it. The goal of close reading might be stated as follows: to hear the language on the page as intensely as the writer heard it in the process of composition and to feel its rhythms, hesitations, and pauses. The only talent required is a talent for focus and deceleration. To read anything in a meaningful way, you must push through the shallow-field perceptual mode that modern life makes habitual. The operation is not nearly as simple as it sounds. The eye has been taught to speed across word clusters. The sound in the ear, which lags behind the eye, is usually a noise, like the garbling that comes when tape gets dragged across the magnetic heads.

That garble has to be slowed, at very least to normal speech tempo. The harder it is for a reader to slow the pace, the more vital it is that he learn how to.

What procedure I have for teaching my writing course has been slow to evolve. For while I sensed the nature of the problem early on, it took me a good long time to plant my response at the core of my pedagogy. At first I was busy obeying what I saw as the three-part requirement of the course: I assigned a variety of readings in the anthology, careful to provide examples of the main literary genres (short story, essay, poetry, and drama); I asked for a set number of papers, most of which were to deal with themes from the reading; and I arranged a schedule of private conferences. Conference time was used for going over finished work. I would point out mistakes, make suggestions for the future. And, I have to say, my students did improve. Their work at the end of the course was always more polished and confident than it had been at the start.

But something was wrong. I could sense it. The kinds of improvements that were being registered were of degree, not kind. The prose was better, but most of the progress was attributable to practice, to the fact that they were writing on a weekly schedule. The fundamental flaws—stylistic simplicity, glibness, and so on—were all still there. I was sending these students out with a nod and a good grade, but I did not have the feeling that I had really made a difference to their writing.

The first breakthrough came with the decision to make one of their assignments a personal essay. It seemed like a natural way to break the monotony of literary topic papers and it sorted well with the essay portion of the course. After all, we were reading Annie Dillard, George Orwell, Loren Eiseley, and others—why not get them to try something in a similar vein? I was startled by the results. Not only were the essays themselves more interesting than anything I had received before, but the writing was better. Dramatically so. I suddenly found stylistic variety, precision, a willingness to be expressive. I kept shaking my head. What could I conclude but that when the topic was something that concerned them—a person, an activity, an episode from their lives—they cared much more about how their prose sounded. They *wanted* to get something across; they wanted it to be interesting. What's more, they knew their subject—its details and intricacies—and they felt more confident about making use of what they knew. The potential, in other words, was there.

It was not long before I followed this lead and started to experiment. For one thing, I positioned the personal essay assignment closer to the beginning of the course (before, it had been a reward, a chance for release given late in the term). I reasoned that if the students could feel the satisfactions of depth, detail, and stylistic care, then they might try to achieve similar results in their nonpersonal writing. Here I met with disappointment. The students saw the personal essay as a "fun" assignment—once the fun was over, the drudgery could begin. I could not sell them on the notion that the other assignments offered kindred pleasures.

Possibly for this reason—I can't remember now—I decided to build on the personal essay assignment. Under the new dispensation, I treated the first submission as a rough draft (without telling the students this beforehand: the words "rough draft" are the kiss of death in a writing class). I then based a full 30- to 40-minute conference on a discussion of the piece. "Discussion" is not quite apt. The meetings were more like cheerful police interrogations. I cast myself in the role of their ideal—if bullying—listener; I questioned them relentlessly, flattering, wheedling, pushing for data. "But what was it *like* to be six years old and studying the violin? Where did you stand? How long? How did you hold the thing? Can you remember what you played, how it sounded? Did you hate your parents for making you do this? *Why* did they make you do this?" Whatever their topic, I pressed. And of course there was always much more to be learned. As often as not, the student arrived by himself at the core of interest, at the real topic that the first version had somehow masked. "Well, why didn't you say *that*? That's the most interesting thing you've said. If you were making an all-night confession to your best friend, how would you describe what happened? Would you pick these same details?"

My goal was to get the student to leave the conference with a clear sense of what was interesting about his subject—indeed, with a clear sense that I was interested in hearing every last detail. I filled them up with question marks and then turned them loose.

And the writing improved further. I started getting wonderfully evocative—and searching and hilarious—essays on every topic under the sun. I could scarcely believe the change I was seeing. When they wrote for themselves, about themselves, they *listened*. And they took pains to make their prose sound good.

Still, this was a writing course in literature, and the question remained. Could I get them to transfer these skills, if not the enthusiasm, to subjects they deemed less exciting or relevant? I would be lying if I said yes. Some difference was felt, sure. Now there was an extra measure of confidence, a kind of self-momentum that carried over. But I could not rely on it. And several years later, I still cannot. Personal writing by itself is not a magic solution. But it points the way to a valuable tactic that I had long overlooked.

My experience with teaching the personal essay—especially with the now obligatory interrogatory conference—showed me something that holds out genuine hope for the cause. It is, in fact, what decided me on writing this piece. To put it simply, I discovered that my students were not only tolerant, or patient, with detail—they were fascinated by it. And I don't just mean details and sense memories from their own lives. I mean detail for itself, as a category of magnitude. It was as if the general principles that they were forced to master in high school—combined with the fact that most of them had never given reading a chance—had left them with an enormous cognitive vacuum. They were so obviously avid for brass tacks, for concrete instances and precise distinctions. I had long assumed the opposite, that nothing was so boring to them as "nitpicking," or going over a text or a topic with attentive care. I was wrong. They loved it. And this extended not only to the fine points of essays and stories but also to the subtleties of writing styles—their own and those of others. What an eye-opening discovery—that here, in an era of rhetoric and appearances, in a climate characterized by the evanescent images on the TV screen and the impatient pulsing of the personal computer, was a desire, a positive *relish*, for intricacy and detail. How to explain it? Was it that the world of the daily news was just too much with them; does an overwhelmingly complex macroreality make them crave what they can manipulate and master? I don't know. But this recognition changed my teaching completely.

Where formerly I rushed from genre to genre, basing nearly all in-class discussion around themes and concepts—because I thought this would keep them interested and that if they were interested they would write better—now I've all but thrown the switch into reverse. If we used to cover four genres, we now cover two, with maybe just a nod toward a third. Instead of discussing four short stories, we're lucky to finish with two. But what a difference! At times now I feel like we're a team of mechanics working on an engine. The engagement is intense; the give-and-take is focused, often excited. I don't flatter myself that I'm some sort of super-teacher, nor do I believe that the gods keep sending me the very best students. I think I know what's making the change. These students are getting a taste of what reading—and writing—really are, many of them for the first time ever. They're finding out how much a text can hold—and be.

A typical session might go something like this. Let's say that I've asked everyone to read George Orwell's essay "On Shooting An Elephant." In giving the assignment I've done nothing more than stress that they should read slowly and carefully. Now we begin.

The first thing I do, always, is to ask them to keep their books closed and listen while I read the opening, in this case the first paragraph:

> In Moulmein, in Lower Burma, I was hated by large numbers of people—the only time in my life that I have been important enough for this to happen to me. I was subdivisional police officer of the town, and in an aimless, petty kind of way antiEuropean feeling was very bitter. No one had the guts to raise a riot, but if a European woman went through the bazaar alone somebody would probably spit betel juice over her dress. As a police officer I was an obvious target and was baited whenever it seemed safe to do so. When a nimble Burman tripped me up on the football field and the referee (another Burman) looked the other way, the crowd yelled with hideous laughter. This happened more than once. In the end the sneering yellow faces of the young men that met me everywhere, the insults hooted after me when I was at a safe

distance, got badly on my nerves. The young Buddhist priests were the worst of all. There were several thousands of them in the town and none of them seemed to have anything to do except stand on street corners and jeer at Europeans.

I stop. I've tried to read slowly and expressively. When I've let the word-sounds die off, when I'm certain of the attention of my students, I start to ask questions. Simple, factual questions. For if I've learned anything from teaching literature, it's this: assume nothing. We'll get nowhere so long as individuals in the class have blind spots and unanswered questions.

First things first. Where is Burma? Many blank looks. But one or two hands go up and we establish the geographical site. Now, what is Orwell, the presumed narrator, doing there? That is, why is he a subdivisional police officer? When? The same thing happens—slowly. But by degrees, as they pool their remembered facts, the overall context is set out. British imperialism. The Raj. The Empire on which the sun never sets . . . And what is betel juice—where does it come from, what color is it? Football? No, he means soccer, of course. And who knows anything about Buddhism? Okay . . . what is a bazaar?

At this point, I'm still insisting that they keep their books closed. I read the passage again. But the questions I ask afterward are of a different sort. I say, "If you had nothing but this passage to go by, what could you tell me about the person who is speaking? Age, personality, anything. Do you like him or dislike him? Do you trust his perspective? Why?" There are long silences. With only their memories to check, they are not sure what to say at first. But opinions do begin to surface. Assertions and counterassertions. Inevitable disagreements. I have to keep punctuating these with my stock "Why do you say that? Where do you get that?" What emerges from the process is finally this: that they have retained nearly all of the information; that most of them can give at least some part of the passage verbatim. I push at this, and they are intrigued enough to oblige. In a matter of minutes, working together, we have pretty much reconstituted the order of the sentences, a good deal of the wording. They have astonished themselves.

Now we switch again. I ask them to account for what happens to them when they read. Do they see pictures in their minds, do they hear a voice? They nod: pictures. We talk about whether these are clear or blurry; general or precise. Depends, they say. I ask them which images are vivid, and why. Then I reframe the question: "If you had to open a film on the basis of this first paragraph—remaining faithful to what has been given—how would you do it?" Here is a question they can respond to. They like to think in terms of film—they grasp the problematic instantly. I get sophisticated suggestions about close-ups, cuts, camera movements, and so on. But when this threatens to become a separate game, I force another change of subject. "If we had nothing but the first paragraph to go by, what would we guess that the essay will be about?" I allow them to open their books. They comb the sentences looking for clues. As they already know where the essay will go, they are gratified to find the oppositions and tensions spelled out right on top of the narrative surface. Combining these hints with what we've already determined about the character and attitude of the narrator, they make good progress reconstructing the moral resolution.

I've touched on the avidness that these students display for detail. Let me add to this. I have noticed, for one thing, that the impulse, or aptitude, comes to life most quickly when the task can be posed as a challenge, a detection problem. Can anyone find . . . ? If they believe that there is an answer to be gotten, they will exercise remarkable ingenuity in searching—and they appear to enjoy the process. My second observation—or suggestion—is that the close-reading process never be allowed to overwhelm everything else. The students respond well to sudden changes in magnitude. I like to switch from the most microscopic of inspections—comparing sentence rhythms, say—to the most broadly thematic questions. Like: How do these very subtle contrasts find their way into the big picture? Why would an author expend so much care on his prose? What is he trying to communicate that is so important?

As you can see, there is enough in one opening paragraph to claim the best energies of a class for a whole hour. But what then? Obviously we cannot work through the rest of the piece with the same diligence. I have several follow-up strategies. Sometimes I let *them* choose the focal zone. I simply ask, If you imagine your attention as a kind of gauge, at what point does the needle shoot up most dramatically? Where is the uranium deposit? Different passages are named, and in each case there are opinions about why. Is it the subject matter? The imagery? The use of language? My job is to keep pushing, to get them to make finer and finer discriminations.

Or else I will pluck a particularly well-written section and ask the students to locate the subtlest of its language devices. Again, once they believe that there is an answer waiting at the far end of their search, they will filter the words and sentences through the finest of meshes. For example:

> When I pulled the trigger I did not hear the bang or feel the kick—one never does when a shot goes home—but I heard the devilish roar of glee that went up from the crowd. In that instant, in too short a time, one would have thought, even for the bullet to get there, a mysterious, terrible change had come over the elephant. He neither stirred nor fell, but every line of his body had altered. He looked suddenly stricken, immensely old, as though the frightful impact of the bullet had paralysed him without knocking him down. At last, after what seemed a long time—it might have been five seconds, I dare say—he sagged flabbily to his knees. His mouth slobbered.

In minutes they are bringing forward their trophies. How the inset phrase of the first sentence enacts the sensation of recoil. How the second sentence builds tension by contrasting the speed of the bullet with the slow, almost viscous movement of the narrator's voice. How the s's in the third and fourth sentences contribute to a jagged impression of impact and imminent collapse. How "sagged flabbily" sketches a movement using sound and rhythm (' ' - -). And so on. They are happy to keep going.

And the good of all this close reading? Well, to begin with, it gets them interested in prose. As a medium, as an object of study. They see value in reading it carefully. And they have a new respect for its possibilities. The realization dawns that writing technique—style—is something more than just clear exposition. Syntax and word sounds, they see, can be manipulated for effect. It's suddenly obvious that reading involves a lot more than moving the eyes back and forth over clusters of key words; that there are instances where every least phrase deserves to be heard and weighed.

We don't, of course, spend all our time looking at isolated passages from the prose of the masters. As this is a writing course, it is essential that they transfer some of the benefits derived from this kind of reading to their own practice. And one way to make a beginning at this is to get them to level similar attention at their own prose and the prose of their peers. I do this in two ways. First, with in-class exercises. A typical exercise may be assigned as follows: "Take out a sheet of paper. I want you to find a way to characterize your morning thus far. Give us a story, an episode, a dialogue, whatever you like. But it has to be interesting and it has to win us over. You have 15 minutes." Or, "You are a book reviewer for a nationally syndicated radio program, something on the order of All Things Considered. You have a two-minute slot in which to render your verdict of [say] Eudora Welty's 'Why I Live at the P.O.' You have to convey something of what the story is like and you have to keep your easily bored listeners from switching the dial."

At the end of 15 minutes I collect the papers. I have asked them to work anonymously. I tell them, further, that if they absolutely hate what they have produced, they should write NO on top of the page. Some do. But most are eager to hear their words read aloud.

I then go through the pieces in sequence, reading them and soliciting responses. "Do you want to hear more? Does this work? Is the attention-needle moving, twitching, or is it at rest? Why?" Then, working from memory, they have to specify their reactions. "Why is it dull? The words, the cadences? Why did you laugh there? Can you remember a sentence, an image? How would you change it to make it better?"

A more sustained inspection takes place when student essays are photocopied and passed around (with names excised). As always, they have the option of refusing to have their papers discussed. But most are game. My procedure, then, is to give them ten minutes or so to read the essay and to make notations. In addition, I ask each reader to find the very best passage and mark it off and then to come up with one constructive—and specific—suggestion for the author.

I begin by reading the first paragraph. By now they all know my spiels about how much can be learned from first impressions and about how openings often encode an author's entire agenda. When I have finished reading, I ask for responses based solely on that first paragraph. What is the voice? The subject? Can we tell from these few sentences where it might go? Do we care? If this writer has won your interest—at least provisionally— then how has he/she managed it? If not, why not? Most writing teachers are familiar with the basic workshop mode, and what I do does not vary significantly. We look for good and bad points; I make every effort to get critics to frame their reservations constructively—not just "This is boring," but "This might be more interesting if . . ." The one way that my approach might differ from some others is in the amount of focus directed at an isolated portion of the text, generally the beginning (though the last paragraph can yield wonders as well). I emphasize the notion of organicism. A sentence or paragraph, I say, can be tested like a tissue culture—it can often tell us essential things about the condition of the rest of the body, and so on. One need only remember not to work the technique (or simile) to death. There is always a right time for switching to the big picture, for asking how the parts cohere, for taking a good hard look at what the author is saying and what that's worth. But there will come a time—and this is the benchmark of progress—when students will not be able to talk about the *what* without repeated references to the *how*. And *that* is a writer's perception.

I started this essay by pointing to what I see as a genuinely worrisome situation—that we are now witnessing the emergence of generations of students who are not, and have never been, readers; whose habits and reflexes have been conditioned by the media culture they live in. And I expressed alarm, further, at how this conditioning (or, to reverse it, *lack* of conditioning) impoverished their writing. My awakening to a certain potential for change—finding that they can still learn what reading and paying attention are all about and that this can improve their writing—does not entirely vanquish my alarm. While it's true that I note considerable progress in my students' writing, I feel that it has been a progress initiated, not necessarily secured. I fear the gravity pull of old tendencies and the inevitable incursion of academic jargon. Twelve weeks is simply not enough time to drive the nail home.

The improvements? Mainly, I would say, these students have learned something about the value of attention. They have begun to listen and, to greater or lesser degree, they have begun to hear. They have grasped the idea that prose makes a sound and that the way it sounds matters to its effectiveness. Their work now ventures complexity and stylistic diversity—more concrete nouns, more attempts to pin down exact sensory perceptions. It is also less solipsistic: that is, it reflects consideration for the ear and interest of the potential reader. To be sure, the results are not pure magic. The sow's ear of the given is not yet the silk purse of the desired. But the changes leave me for the first time with a sense of job satisfaction. I could here cite any one of the several dozen passages that have begun to restore my faith, but the context forbids it. For each passage or sentence is part of a long story; to do it honor I would have to track the student through the various stages of composition and critique—subject, I think, for another essay.

Suffice it to say I am not altogether without hope. The wholesale erosion of literacy will not abate, but some of these students will still manage to catch a hint of what it means to read. They will, perhaps, find that there is pleasure to be had in the surmounting of verbal obstacles. Others may discover the peculiar satisfaction that comes as words are fitted together to make meaning and that there is a release of adrenalin in the throes of composition that is like nothing else. There will be those, too, who will never come close to attaining such realizations and for whom writing will always be a battle. But my fantasy is that even the least committed, least attentive student will have absorbed a portion of what I have offered. Not as knowledge, necessarily, or as a set of skills, but in the form of a voice, a superego. I would hope that even such a student would find it unaccountably harder, and more irksome, to fling together just any old words. There would arise in him or her at those moments of temptation, like a dream half-remembered, the image of an expectant but scrupulous reader, one who is just waiting to see what marvels will next be revealed.

Alex Gold

✺ The Man in the Tweed Cap: Quotation, Illusion, and Identity

> When we contemplate any living
> system, or part of it, we
> generally ask, "What does it
> look like?" and "What does it
> do?"
>
> *Erich Harth*

In a recent review of William H. Whyte's *City: Rediscovering the Center*, Brendan Gill describes Whyte as an urban Thoreau, "a seasoned New Yorker, 71 years of age," who's spent much of his life on city streets, "analyzing the way people use parks, plazas, streets, street furniture, side-walks, and even curbstones and window ledges" (99). Gill gives a passage from *City* that shows New York as Whyte sees it; the man in the tweed cap is a "phony pitchman" whom Whyte has watched work the crowds for more than ten years:

> A jaunty fellow with a tweed cap stands beside a small table. On it is a clipboard and writing pad. A sign fixed to the table says SAVE THE PORPOISE! As people go by he says to them, please join the fight and sign the petition for the porpoises. Many people stop. Just sign here, he says, extending a pen. As they sign up, he suggests that a small donation would help. Overhead. Printing expenses. He is giving his time free. Most of those who stop, sign, and most of those who sign, give. (qtd. in Gill, 101)

New York as Whyte sees it, of course, is New York as Whyte *writes* it; and here the writing is so spare and lucid that it all but disappears as the scene takes shape and slips into action. Whyte's style comes close to the contemporary ideal of efficient clarity, an uncluttered stylelessness that can easily seem simply "natural." After all, even the con man writes well: no second draft could improve SAVE THE PORPOISE!

Just one "writerly" element, a little flash of narrative "technique," catches the eye for an instant. It's the instant in which Whyte first renders the man's voice: "As people go by he says to them, please join the fight and sign the petition for the porpoises." Whyte conveys a quietness, a polite solicitude in the "jaunty" pitchman's manner, simply by giving no sign to mark the transition from pure narrative to the "character's" reported words. "Many people stop. Just sign here, he says, extending a pen."

But this instant should be enough to remind us that good writing doesn't fall from the sky. For the truth is that many writers before Whyte worked on this passage, so many that we can read it as a history of narrative technique, a palimpsest of chapters on the course of modern fiction. Whyte relies on the effaced plain-style of Hemingway's "transparent and objective narration" ("On it is a clipboard and a writing pad"), and the fluent immediacy of Flaubert's art of "letting the story tell itself," to unfold an action so seemingly unmediated that the reader falls straight into the scene of the man, the table, the sign, the pen—there seems to be no intervening "Whyte" at all. And we move closer to the *moment* of that scene even than Hemingway did, for we watch and listen in the continuous present of Robbe-Grillet's "school-of-the-look" simultaneous narration ("Many people stop"), a technique that takes the past-as-present "It was now lunch time" of Hemingway's "The Short Happy Life of Francis Macomber" into the simple-present "Now" of Robbe-Grillet's *Jealousy*: "Now the voice of the second driver reaches this central section of the veranda" (115). And we seem to approach *physically* closer to the man at the table than with Robbe-Grillet, through that unmarked melding of pure narration and reported speech—a technique Gérard Génette and Brian McHale have called "free direct discourse," or "immediate speech."[1] This last move, the little touch we first noticed—"Many people stop. Just sign here"—comes from *Ulysses:* "Going down the path of Sycamore street beside the Empire music hall Lenehan showed M'Coy how the whole thing was. One of those manholes like a bloody gaspipe and there was the poor devil stuck down in it, half choked with sewer gas. Down went Tom Rochford anyhow" (191).

Thomas Pavel says that contemporary writing has moved "toward a drastic reduction of fictional distance that brings fictional worlds as close as possible to the beholder"; "frames and conventional borders seem to vanish, and the purpose becomes achievement of immediacy" (146). If that's so, then our nonfictional "urban Thoreau" seems not so much a street-scene Natural Writer as a man with a doctorate in Postmodern prose.

Fanciful imposition? An academic exercise? I don't think so. Of course I don't suppose that Whyte was "influenced" by Joyce or Hemingway in the same sense that Eliot was influenced by Pound, or Conrad by Maupassant.[2] From one perspective Whyte is simply a good writer. He was, Gill tells us, for many years both a writer and an editor for *Fortune* magazine, famous early for his best-selling study of business executives, *The Organization Man* (99). When he came to this street-entrepreneur in the unfolding of *City*, Whyte undoubtedly knew how to handle him without calling Robbe-Grillet on the telephone. But it's easy to forget that good writing is a communal project, easy to overlook how much of what a writer can do derives from what she's read and how she has read it. Every filmmaker understands the power and the use of close-ups; but they understand because they've seen films and learned, and they've all learned finally from D. W. Griffith, who invented them. In exactly this way Whyte's writing ultimately draws its ease and range from the art of fiction, from techniques of narration and embodiment that such writers as Joyce and Flaubert struggled to perfect and then willed to every writer who followed—no distinction made among the company of novelists, short-story writers, essayists, historians, biographers, journalists, critics, reviewers, and editors of *Fortune*.

No distinction made, that is, so long as the writer also reads, and has learned that the quality and range of his writing depends largely on what he does while he's reading. A high goal for anyone who teaches writing in any form, I think, is to encourage, to help, to lead our students to read, by any means whatever. We know that reading itself is under siege now, and any student who lets it slip away will lose a great deal more than the escapist pleasures of a few leisure hours. But those of us who teach fiction as well as writing have a special opportunity. We can lead our students directly into that community of first teachers. We can help them learn to draw directly from novels and short stories what writers like Whyte have learned. Readers who know how to follow not only what Nabokov calls "the boy and girl in the story" but also the making of the story as it unfolds on the page will have portable writing-teachers for the rest of their writing lives.

The ancient Greeks and Romans knew this very well. They drew on great literature—from Homer and Virgil to the lyric poets—for the "rhetoric" to sustain their lives of public debate and political address. It was Quintilian himself who recommended that for the orator "the love of literature and the reading of the poets" should "end only with life itself" (*Institutio oratoria*, I, 8, 12; qtd. in Curtius 67). In our own day, fiction writers are the masters of literary "rhetoric," for it's they who constantly examine and renew, in every province and dialect of our discourse, the powers of persuasion, perspective, originality, and vividness: how to gain assent, how to turn a problem over, how to innovate in language, how to create illusions. It's these powers that we can lead our students to watch, to admire, and to appropriate.

What we call these fictional powers—of engagement, development, suspense, embodiment, and illusion—depends on what we want to do with them. A novelist teaching novel writing (John Gardner in *The Art of Fiction*, for example) includes them under "technique." A novelist teaching literature (Nabokov at Cornell in his *Lectures on Literature*) presents them as elements of "enchantment." A critic who studies the relations between style and culture might call them "imitation" (Erich Auerbach in *Mimesis*). Quintilian would likely see them as aspects of a modern "rhetoric." And all the more tendentious, programmatic, or limited critical approaches—now in such luxuriant proliferation—will have their own sets of terms, from the "irrealizations" of reception theory to the "moods" and "voices" of narratology. This abundance of terminology simply indicates the many directions open to a student who's learned to observe such techniques (to choose the most neutral-seeming term of the lot). And that range of choice makes the study of narrative technique an ideal approach to fiction itself, as well as to any writing that looks beyond the first fundamentals of the college essay.

In a course I've taught often in the Writing Program at Harvard the students read fiction, write analytic essays, and also write some fiction of their own, mostly in the form of short exercises. When the students write fiction, the course emphasizes the technical or the "enchanting"—we try to look at the wizardry that brings scenes and characters, speeches and actions, into vivid life, and the students practice their own versions of the magic as they work on their fiction. When the students write analytic essays, we emphasize the rhetorical—we look for ways to translate fictional powers into expository practice, to learn how linked exploration or a centripetal unfolding, for example, can structure an essay just as strongly as a purely Euclidean progression. The essays take a critical perspective that's loosely "narratological," in the sense that the students always look closely at the linguistic manipulations that construct or generate the illusions of character, action, and place before talking about what those actions mean or who those characters are. (But again, fiction writers themselves talked in simple English about "narratology" long before the word existed: it was William Gass who said, "There are no descriptions in fiction, there are only constructions" [17].)

The conceptual neatness of the course—studying in the short stories elements to imitate in the fiction writing, appropriate in the exposition, and analyze in the criticism—becomes as spurious in practice as the "guiding principles" set out on most university syllabuses—which someone once described as engraved invitations to a mud-wrestling match. But in looking first at what makes fictions so *fictional*—so constitutive, absorbing, and engaging—we reach soon enough the first stage of Nabokov's ideally naive readers: those who are amazed not only at *what* they are reading, but *that* they are reading. And in this context the project of essay writing more easily regains the dignity it deserves; the student not only has things to understand and things to say but also things to steal.

From time to time we isolate an element of expository writing—some aspect of language, construction, argument, exploration, or evidence—to pursue through fictional practice, looking for suggestions. Sometimes our writers provide advice pre-tied, *in propria persona*, as when E. M. Forster unintentionally tells the difference between commentary and argument by telling the difference between story—"The king died and then the queen died"—and plot—"The king died, and then the queen died of grief" (86). But these apothegms rarely reveal as much as the hunt through the works themselves. I'd like now to retrace one of those hunts, not to lecture or conduct a class but simply to show the procedures in more detail. In order to do this economically I'll sweep into a linear narrative elements that in the course appear everywhere: in assignments, class discussions, exercises, and so on. And for my subject I'll return to the smallest rhetorical device, the one that William Whyte used by omission when he introduced his man in the tweed hat: the quotation mark.

To set in mind the most elementary use of the quotation mark in exposition I've taken a sentence from Melvin Konner's *The Tangled Wing: Biological Constraints on the Human Spirit:*

> And another team, led by F. G. Patterson, claims to have taught the infant female gorilla, Koko, more than 400 words, leading Patterson to say, in print, in a distinguished scholarly journal, "language is no longer the exclusive domain of man." (153)

To see a similarly basic use in fiction, we can take a scene from Walker Percy's *The Last Gentleman:*

> "Birmingham? Gadsden?"
> "Halfway between," cried the old man, his eye glittering like an eagle's. "Wait a minute," said he, looking at the engineer with his festive and slightly ironic astonishment. "Don't I know you? Arent' you—" snapping his fingers.
> "Will Barrett. Williston Bibb Barrett."
> "Over in—" he shook his head toward the southwest.
> "Ithaca. In the Mississippi Delta."
> "You're Ed Barrett's boy."
> "Yes sir."
> "Lawyer Barrett. Went to Congress from Mississippi in nineteen and forty." Now it was his turn to do the amazing. "Trained pointers, won at Grand Junction in—"
> "That was my uncle, Fannin Barrett," murmured the engineer. (47)

Konner's sentence of course uses the conventions and devices of written language to convey a meaning. In this case the meaning is both complex and skillfully conveyed, for we learn not only about a gorilla and a scientist but also about "Koko" and "Patterson"—and best of all, we learn something of the writer's opinion of Patterson's opinion, a meaning drawn out of the interrupted rhythms of the long sentence as it approaches, in mild astonishment, "to say, in print, in a distinguished scholarly journal, 'language is no longer the exclusive domain of man.' "

Everyone knows what those quotation marks mean, but it is useful to spell the meaning out. The quotation marks tell us something quite precise—that the words enclosed are identical to words that have been spoken or written somewhere else. Here, that somewhere else is a particular page in a specified journal in an article that appears under the name "Patterson." Quotation marks, that is to say, are like the equals sign (=), only stronger, for they assert not merely an equivalence but an identity. In fact they guarantee that identity; quotation marks are the only punctuation with the force of law.

So much for the sentence. If we return to the scene from *The Last Gentleman* (and keep our language consistent) we'd say that Percy uses the devices of written language to convey meaning, plus something else. That something else is illusion: the illusion that we're listening to two men speak. Every element of this imagined event is illusionary: we aren't listening, no one is speaking, there are no men, and there aren't two of them.

And nowadays we know that we give only the everyday-language or "weak" version of fictional illusion when we say, "listening to two men speak." In fact no reader (or very few) hallucinates the presence of "men" or hears the sound of anybody "speaking." Instead we succumb to a series of much stronger and more remarkable illusionistic propositions: (1) that the words "Don't I know you?" come from an imaginary source that somehow resembles a person; (2) that the words "Will Barrett" come from another such source, which differs from the first in ways that somehow resemble the ways one person differs from another; (3) that these two imaginary sources occupy a space that somehow resembles the world; (4) that reading words in a book while imagining that they're issued by one imaginary source to another imaginary source, in an imaginary space that somehow resembles the world, can provide a real understanding of real people.

When we describe literary illusion in this fashion we can use a now-common terminology and say that we've mentally suspended or "bracketed" not only the "truth claim" but the "meaning claim" of the "discourse." This in no way implies that the discourse has no meaning, or no truth. It simply says that for the moment we're interested in looking at how the implicit claims get made and in what we can learn by seeing when and why we accept variations of those claims. The implicit claim here—that characters in a fiction are very like people—is what Mieke Bal calls "the character-effect" (80). But Hillis Miller has the most elegant phrase: he says fiction creates "powerful phantasms of personalities" (104).

If we want to know there the phantasms come from, we can look again at our scene:

"Birmingham? Gadsden?"
"Halfway between. Wait a minute—Don't I know you? Aren't you—"
"Will Barrett. Williston Bibb Barrett."
"Over in—"
"Ithaca. In the Mississippi Delta."
"You're Ed Barrett's boy."
"Yes sir."
"Lawyer Barrett. Went to Congress from Mississippi in nineteen and forty. Trained pointers, won at Grand Junction in—"
"That was my uncle, Fannin Barrett."

Not *quite* the scene; we can't "see" as much now. But the sense of person-ness, very nearly the full conviction of personal presences, sweeps in at once. We can imagine writing an entire novel in this fashion; as we'll see, William Gaddis has come close to doing so. But for our own scene it's sufficient to say that even without

cried the old man, his eye glittering like an eagle's.
said he, looking at the engineer with his festive and slightly ironic astonishment.
snapping his fingers.
he shook his head toward the southwest.
Now it was his turn to do the amazing.
murmured the engineer.

we still get phantasms. Quoted speech alone invokes them. And "invoke" is the right word; fictional quotation marks call up a presence, like Glendower summoning his spirits from the vasty deep. But when the marks call, the spirits come.

Génette reminds us just how crucial this simple fact seemed to the greatest of the Greek students of persuasive arts, Plato. Génette does this by pointing out that Plato uses the word *mimésis* in a peculiar way. We know that *mimésis,* usually translated "imitation," constitutes for the ancient Greeks the very heart—both the goal and the definition—of literary art. In discussions from the Renaissance to the present day critics regularly use *mimésis* to signify everything we mean by "the imitation of nature," including the "imitation" of ideals beyond the merely natural—Nature instead of nature. Critics frequently discuss *mimésis* among the Greeks as if it always had this range of implication. And we know moreover that Plato respected the power of *mimésis* enough to banish it, as too dangerous a threat to calm morality, from the education of at least some of his ideal citizens. But Génette reminds us that Plato explicitly uses *mimésis* to mean simply "quotation." Plato's *mimésis,* Génette writes, is "an equivalent of *dialogue,* with the sense not of *imitation* but of transcription, or—the most neutral and therefore, the most accurate term—*quotation*" (43).

If we check Génette at Book III of *The Republic,* we see that he's right. "Imitation" is the power in Homer that bothers Socrates so much, the power to influence and persuade through enchantment, and Homer "imitates" only when he quotes: when he "gives a speech as though he were someone else," when he "speaks as though he himself were Chryses and tries as hard as he can to make it seem to us that it's not Homer speaking, but the priest, the old man" (393c,b).

Few nonfiction writers will find much use for such a power in its most fully developed form—most essayists, after all, rarely quote long conversations in their essays. But we ought to take careful note of one writer who did indeed adopt this method—Plato himself. The effect is especially fascinating in the moment when he informs us of the immorality of quotation:

> "Isn't it narrative when he gives all the speeches and also what comes between the speeches?"
> "Of course."
> "But, when he gives a speech as though he were someone else, won't we say that he then likens his own style as much as possible to that of the man he has announced as the speaker?"
> "We'll say that, surely." (393c)

Whatever Plato may think of "quotation," it's clear that he seizes the form for himself, that for the sake of his story's power he "tries as hard as he can to make it seem to us that it's not [Plato] speaking but [Socrates], the old man." And of course it works. We know that Plato wrote all the words, and that Socrates may never have spoken them—at least not in just this fashion. But it's the image—the phantasm—of Socrates that endures with such clarity that it gives to the philosophy the added force of a vividly lived life, an existence in history, in "reality" as well as in words. Homer in Plato's day had much of the force of a religion, and Plato understood that one difference between religions and philosophies is that religions have speaking parts.

Up to this point we've sometimes said that "quotation" has a certain power and sometimes attributed power to the quotation marks themselves. We should ask, though, whether those marks do in fact have any "power" other than as purely transparent functional indicators. A mathematician, after all, would be completely indifferent to substituting (**) for (=) as long as everyone agreed that the meaning remained: the function alone is what counts.

To get an answer from fiction, we can look at a passage from the story "Grace" in James Joyce's *Dubliners:*

> "That was a decent young chap, that medical fellow," he said. "Only for him—"
> "Oh, only for him," said Mr. Power, "it might have been a case of seven days without the option of a fine."
> "Yes, yes," said Mr. Kernan, trying to remember. "I remember now there was a policeman. Decent young fellow, he seemed. How did it happen at all?"

"It happened that you were peloothered, Tom" said Mr. Cunningham gravely. (203)

This is Joyce running in neutral; a conversation in a room, a good cast of characters, but nothing remarkable—just the usual phantasms.

What we hear and see in this passage, though, isn't strictly Joyce. It's the product of an involuntary collaboration between the writer and his printer, a man named Grant Richards. We can find the passage in every edition of *Dubliners* published before 1968, but it's not what Joyce wrote. Here is Joyce as he wanted to appear, and as Robert Scholes restored him:

—That was a decent young chap, that medical fellow, he said. Only for him—
—O, only for him, said Mr. Power, it might have been a case of seven days without the option of a fine.
—Yes, yes, said Mr. Kernan, trying to remember. I remember now there was a policeman. Decent young fellow, he seemed. How did it happen at all?
—It happened that you were peloothered, Tom, said Mr. Cunningham gravely. (Joyce/Scholes, 160)

The first difference we notice, I think, is the sound level: Joyce's version lowers the volume. The Mr.Kernan who says

I remember now there was a policeman.

speaks more softly than the one who says

"I remember now there was a policeman."

And the group of men in Joyce's scene seem more *grouped;* somehow they have gathered themselves more closely. The radius of their circle is smaller, their talk sounds less brisk and spacious, less rhetorical.

Joyce denounced the conventional marks substituted by the printer as an "eyesore"; they gave his work, he said, "an impression of unreality" (Joyce/Scholes, 6). This is an interesting remark: it tells us that somehow the dashes convey, for Joyce, reality—or at least *more* reality than the quotation marks do. If the assumption behind Joyce's remarks is right, then we have a provisional answer to the question we asked: the marks do have a power other than as transparent functional signs. What's more, we can vary that power by playing with the sign.

There's room to disagree in describing the difference in effect made by changing the marks. But every reader, every student, notices that there is indeed a difference, one that goes beyond volume level. In some subtle way the characters themselves change; the change has to do with assertiveness, or forcefulness, or perhaps just the clarity of outline that the characters bear with them. In our quotationed scene each man when he speaks seems to stand or to sit straight up, to deliver his mind with the clarity of a self-possessed utterance:

"That was a decent young chap, that medical fellow," he said.

The strong delineation of the speech-marks gives a definition of outline to the speakers themselves, or rather to our sense of those speakers. Mr. Kernan in quotations has an envelope of identity around him, clean and transparent; Joyce's Mr. Kernan seems almost to fade into the background, or into something:

> —Yes, yes, said Mr. Kernan, trying to remember. I remember now there was a policeman.

When Kernan reenters at *I remember* he emerges just a fraction of a felt instant too slowly from—what? From the voice of the narrator:

trying to remember.
I remember now

That narrating voice holds on to Mr. Kernan for an ambiguous micro-instant, the instant it takes us to decide who is speaking, character or teller. It's the same micro-instant we take at

Kernan, trying

to know for certain that we've shifted from Mr. Kernan to another fellow: the fellow who's telling the story.

For Joyce hasn't simply put dashes where Richards wanted inverted commas. After the introductory dash he gives no mark of closure at all, and no mark to show that a speaker interrupted by the narrator (he said) has begun again to speak. So now Joyce's narrative commentary can drift along in the same plane as the men's talk:
that medical fellow, he said, only for him.

This is something new. Joyce has begun the process of reducing the distance between narrator and character that culminates—at least for now—in Whyte's handling of the man in the tweed cap.

So with a very small change in a peculiarly rarified stratum of fictional art—punctuation style—Joyce sets in motion much larger changes in the nature of fictional worlds. Talk begins to sound quieter, identity begins to seem less clearly outlined, the narrative presence begins to feel less strongly marked.

E. H. Gombrich has said that "art has a history because the illusions of art are not only the fruit but the indispensable tools for the artist's analysis of appearances" (30). The artist, in other words, does not simply create illusions that correspond to his or her vision of the world; he uses those illusions as "indispensable tools" for the "analysis of appearances." Several times in *Dubliners* Joyce uses the altered illusion of the dashes in just this way: to explore elements of character blurred or even hidden by quotation marks. This sounds peculiar; we don't ordinarily think of quotation marks as blurring or hiding anything. But the history of technique in any art is the history of uncovering what previous techniques assumed. It will be worthwhile, I think, to watch such an uncovering as it takes place in *Dubliners*, at the end of "A Little Cloud."

"A Little Cloud" is the story of a little man named Little Chandler:

The half-moons of his nails were perfect and when he smiled you caught a glimpse of a row of childish white teeth.

Little Chandler is a clerk with an infant son. He dreams of being (but not of becoming) a great poet, and he blames the meanness and the pallid drift of his life on the ordinariness of the woman he married, on the trap of a banal domestic life, rather than on his own self-absorption and moral cowardice. He spends an evening with the extravagant, vulgar Ignatious Gallaher, a friend from childhood who has "got on" as a great fellow of the London press and a lord of the Parisian *cocottes*. Little Chandler is 32; he takes leave of Gallaher, goes home, and tries to read:

It was useless. He couldn't read. He couldn't do anything. The wailing of the child pierced the drum of his ear. It was useless, useless! He was a prisoner for life. His arms trembled with anger and suddenly bending to the child's face he shouted:
—Stop!

(The child stops for an instant, then begins to sob convulsively.)

The door was burst open and a young woman ran in, panting.
—What is it? What is it? she cried.
The child, hearing its mother's voice, broke out into a paroxysm of sobbing.
—It's nothing, Annie . . . it's nothing. . . . He began to cry . . . (85)

When we reach

He began to cry

we actually *feel* something peculiar, a flicker of ambiguity about the identity of the speaker, and of the crier; *who* began to cry, Little Chandler or the infant? Do we hear Little Chandler speaking of "the child," or the narrator speaking of Little Chandler? Joyce prepares for that shimmer of ambivalent identities first by having the stupendously self-absorbed Little Chandler think of his son as "the child" and his wife as "a young woman," next by allowing the line,

[The child] broke out into a paroxysm of sobbing

to introduce not the infant's but Little Chandler's paroxysm:

—It's nothing. . . . He . . . he began to cry. . . . I couldn't.

But it's the reader's prior acceptance of the blurs and shifts of the dashed text that make the effect so strong and clear. And in the next instant the sense, the meaning of this identity-shimmer comes home. For now we actually hear Little Chandler change places with his son; then we hear Chandler begin to realize what has happened:

—It's nothing, Annie . . . it's nothing. . . . He began to cry . . .
She flung her parcels on the floor and snatched the child from him.
    —What have you done to him? she cried, glaring into his face.
Little Chandler sustained for one moment the gaze of her eyes and his heart
closed together as he met the hatred in them. He began to stammer:
    —It's nothing. . . . He . . . he began to cry. . . . I couldn't . . . I
didn't do anything. . . . What?
Giving no heed to him she began to walk up and down the room, clasping the
child tightly in her arms and murmuring:
    —My little man! My little mannie! Was 'ou frightened, love? . . . There
now, love! There now! . . . Lambabaun! Mamma's little lamb of the world:
. . . There now!
Little Chandler felt his cheeks suffused with shame and he stood back out of
the lamplight. He listened while the paroxysm of the child's sobbing grew less
and less; and tears of remorse started to his eyes.

Few people grow up in the Dublin of *Dubliners*; when Annie sings in
this passage we get to hear what it's like to listen, at 32, as a longing infant,
to the song sung to you by the mother you've made of your wife. But the
experience of this moment—the moment most crucial to our understanding
of "A Little Cloud"—derives in considerable measure from an effect outside
the words themselves.

I think it's possible to see that when writers change the way they
represent speech, they open up an avenue to alter, in their stories, the sense
of what it feels like to be a person. Changing the "look" of quoted speech
directly addresses the fundamentally visual nature of fiction—everything
that happens when we read, after all, begins with our eyes. We may *imagine*
what a character "looks" like, but we directly register what the character's
speech *looks* like. Changes at this basic level can subtly change our sense of
the very nature of character—or being—itself.

This effect is at least as marked when a writer changes the form of
quoted thinking, rather than quoted speaking. For we should remember
that, in fiction, thinking as well as speaking is usually rendered as a form of
(direct or indirect) speech. And when we change what it feels like to think
thoughts, we've affected perhaps the deepest line of "identification" between readers and characters. Consider for a moment what it feels like to
think as Hester Prynne does:

Sometimes, the red infamy upon her breast would give a sympathetic throb,
as she passed near a venerable minister or magistrate, the model of piety and
justice, to whom that age of antique reverence looked up, as to a mortal man in
fellowship with angels. "What evil thing is at hand?" would Hester say to
herself. (Hawthorne 92)

Thinking for Hester is like making a speech, and listening to it, too. Or
to put it more properly, if we "thought" the way Hester does we might feel
as if we were making a speech to ourselves. Hester's phantasmic reality has
receded a bit for us—she seems to live not only in a world that has an
intrusive narrator in it but also in one that requires her to intrude upon

herself in the same way that he does. In the following passage we get to hear both:

> Or, once more, the electric thrill would give her warning—"Behold, Hester, here is a companion!"—and, looking up, she would detect the eyes of a young maiden glancing at the scarlet letter, shyly and aside, and quickly averted, with a faint, chill crimson in her cheeks; as if her purity were somewhat sullied by that momentary glance. O Fiend, whose talisman was that fatal symbol, wouldst thou leave nothing, whether in youth or age for this poor sinner to revere? (93)

The "O Fiend" may be that meddling narrator, but "Behold!" is Hester. Something in her own mind translates that "electric thrill" into a command that feels as if it's thought *through* her—"Behold, Hester"—rather than by her. She's not as alone in there, it seems, as are the phantasms of our own day. And even when she isn't broken in upon in her thinking, Hester will break in upon herself, as if her mind were a kind of pulpit she could step up to at will. Whenever she has a long thought to think, for example, she asks herself a question in order to gain permission to answer:

> She was terror-stricken by the revelations that were thus made. What were they? Could they be other than the insidious whispers of the bad angel, who would fain have persuaded the struggling woman, as yet only half his victim, that the outward guise of purity was but a lie, and that, if truth were every-where to be shown, a scarlet letter would blaze forth on many a bosom besides Hester Prynne's? (92)

Of course we can't know if thought actually "felt" to Hawthorne as we've described it or if anyone of Hawthorne's own day would characterize the sense of mind in this passage as we do: the conventional nearly always seems simply normal until a new convention makes comparison possible. And we must never forget that illusions gain their force from the context out of which they arise. Hawthorne's readers would not have read Hester as we do, against the backdrop of Molly Bloom and Benny Profane. (And a French reader accustomed to dashes in 19th-century texts might not see them as less "unreal" than quotation marks.) But we can be sure that writers after Hawthorne came to believe that thinking, punctuated in the fashion of *The Scarlet Letter,* didn't feel like *their* thinking. So Flaubert gave Emma Bovary (to take a famous and seminal example) a new way of thinking, a kind of thought that somehow seemed more "real":

> She reflected occasionally that these were, nevertheless, the most beautiful days of life—the honeymoon days, as people called them. To be sure, their sweetness would be best enjoyed far off, in one of those lands with exciting names where the first weeks of marriage can be savored so much more deliciously and languidly! The post-chaise with its blue silk curtains would have climbed slowly up the mountain roads, and the postilion's song would have re-echoed among the cliffs . . . (50)

Emma's thinking emerges so smoothly from whatever else might surround it, whatever else it is that says "she reflected," that we scarcely notice the transition; nothing "tells" us that the thought "the honeymoon days, as people called them," is Emma's rather than the narrator's, but we know it nevertheless. We seem to know this on our own, naturally; nothing intrudes on our reading, or into Emma's mind. We scarcely feel that anything other than her mind even *reports* her mind. Flaubert has found ways —and the effort he took to find them is one of the best-known stories in literature—to represent thinking with such a relative transparency of report that he's left Emma's mind entirely to Emma. So now she's in there alone.

It's as difficult to believe that *Madame Bovary* followed *The Scarlet Letter* by only six years as it is to accept that *Pilgrim's Progress* was written after *Paradise Lost*. For the sensation of Emma's thinking is very much closer to what it feels like to be us: her sense of being is far more like most of ours. And when we go from the bustle and thunderclap interventions of Hester Prynne's mind directly to the quiet solitude of Emma's, we can almost feel that moment—as if it really were just a moment—when identity became secular, private, and resolutely personal.

But thinking in quotation marks disappears relatively early in the history of the novel. In fiction after Hawthorne, thought moves deeper and deeper into indirect discourse, where changes in styles of thought, in the illusions of thinking, occur as explorations in the syntax of indirection. And since our subject at the moment is the printed sign, the mark of quotation itself, we should leave thinking and return to speech proper, where the exploration on the *surface* of the page has an unbroken history throughout our century. Consider for instance the first page of William Gaddis's *JR*, a sort of technical great-grandson to Joyce's dashes:

—Money . . . ? in a voice that rustled.
—Paper, yes.
—And we'd never seen it. Paper money.
—We never saw paper money till we came east.
—It looked so strange the first time we saw it. Lifeless.
—You couldn't believe it was worth a thing.
—Not after Father jingling his change.
—Those were silver dollars.
—And silver halves, yes and quarters, Julia. The ones from his pupils, I can hear him now . . .
Sunlight, pocketed in a cloud, spilled suddenly broken across the floor through the leaves of the trees outside.
—Coming up the veranda, how he jingled when he walked.
—He'd have his pupils rest the quarters that they brought him on the backs of their hands when they did their scales. He charged fifty cents a lesson, you see, Mister . . .
—Coen, without the h. Now if both you ladies . . .

The entire novel—some 700 pages—pours out in this nearly unnarrated fashion, in a mounting rush of more and more voices, a great tumble of talk, often spilling untagged from six or eight different sources that jostle and shove each other aside. Often the babbling is split through with the squawk of a radio, a stereo, an opera on closed circuit TV:

> —Sixth grade Mister Stye, orientationwise . . .
> —Yes, well, gets right to the facts and that visual, nothing pansy about that, the, want to turn that sound down just a little now Dan? The ah, as I was saying . . .
> ————————I am the song the Brahmin sings and when he flies man, I am the . . .
> —Yes that ahm, visual might be misinterpreted . . .
> —As I was saying Stye, this whole Cultural Center project, we're thinking of tying it right in with the school Spring Arts Festival in the spring, expanding it a little with a few remote specials on the itv that will get across the remote capabilities of microwave transmission with a good dependable cable system, get the patriotic theme in there. Whiteback?
> —Yes, the ahm, this boy who turned in all the train tickets where are they yes, about a lost child . . .
> ————————the thing of our company share in America is not just to own but to use, that is the thing of a share as investment capital money works for you all the time by other people do the work of the company you are not even there you just own, how you own is that you . . . (179)

Great chunks of the book reach us by telephone. Helpful narrative tags—"said Mr. Bast"—scarcely exist; making noise is more important than being anybody particular. The world of *JR* is almost literally disembodied; for great stretches there is nothing to see, nothing to smell, nothing to touch. The first few pages of the book seem almost physically intimidating; the reader thinks, How am I supposed to make sense of this? But as we read we begin to realize, with some apprehension, that we do indeed make sense of this chaos. Within the space of a few pages we're reading this madhouse clangor as easily as we read Jane Austen. And exactly this ease, this awful familiarity, constitutes the greatest shock of *JR*. It's true enough that the events of the novel now look almost suspiciously prophetic—a 12-year-old boy operating from the telephone booth outside his junior high school founds and runs an enormous corporation, a corporation that exists only on paper but acquires enough power to bankrupt real people, shut down real plants, and level real towns. But the shock of the novel is not the prescience of the story. The shock is all in the familiarity of the made world, a world in which being, itself, is just talk:

> —not here no, oh it's you Mister Bris . . . not disturbing me not that's all right, Mister Bast's still off on some sort of business . . . oh you are? Didn't realize you and he were business associates Mister Brisboy thought it was more ah . . . no no didn't mean you didn't regard him as a dear friend I . . . just wouldn't get this upset Mister Brisboy I'm sure he wouldn't let that happen, now . . . No I'm sure he wouldn't mind (508)

No one, though, has explored the illusionary force of quotation marks as thoroughly as John Barth in "Menelaiad." For Barth goes beyond the sign itself, to push into the *syntax* of the sign—he writes a story built entirely around the grammar of quotation marks. Here, for example, are two lines from deep within "Menelaiad":

> " ' (")('(("What?"))') (") '
> " ' " ' " 'Why?' I repeated, "I repeated,' I repeated," I repeated,' I repeated," I repeat. (48)

Given out of context, the first line makes no sense at all; it's literally unreadable. But by the time we reach this moment in the story that line does more than make sense; it carries with it a specific and vivid set of mental images, images of scenes which flip through the mind like the moving pictures of a riffle-book animation. The reader can see, in a sort of layered flash, Menelaus in the darkened hall of his castle talking with Telemachus and Peisistratus; also Menelaus with Helen on the poop-deck of his ship off the African coast; also Menelaus confronting his unfaithful wife in her bedchamber the night he helped to burn Troy. In each scene Menelaus is telling a story, the story of his life, to whoever is there with him—exactly this same story that we're hearing even now as we read. And in each setting Menelaus is just now saying, What? Barth achieves all this action, all these *images*, with quotation marks.

Here's how he does it: Barth begins the story with Menelaus alone, thinking to himself:

> Menelaus here, more or less.

Then Menelaus speaks aloud to himself, tells himself a story:

> "Helen," I say: "Helen's responsible for this."

In the story he's telling he comes to a night, years earlier but long after the Trojan War and his voyage home, when Telemachus and Peisistratus came to his castle for visit:

> " 'Telemachus Odysseus'-son,' the lad replied, 'come from goat-girt Ithaca for news of my father, but willing to have his cloak clutched and listen all night to the tale of How You Lost Your Navigator, Wandered Seven Years, Came Ashore at Pharos, Waylaid Eidothea, Tackled Proteus, Learned to Reach Greece by Sailing up the Nile, and Made Love to Your Wife, the most beautiful woman I've ever seen, After an Abstinence of Eighteen Years.'
> " 'Seventeen.' " (129)

In a little while Telemachus will want to hear how Menelaus got home from Troy. So Menalaus must tell another story within a story And in that story another character—Proteus—will in his turn want to know how Menelaus came to be there on the beach at Pharos, wrestling with a god. And so on back to Troy. Each new story moves to another level of embedded quotation. But as the reader moves deeper and deeper into the history of Menelaus's mind the reading eye trains itself to distinguish " ' from " ' " ' about as readily as it distinguishes "Helen" from "Eidothea."

And whenever the eye registers " ' the reader knows that whatever speech appears next comes from the scene of that night at the castle: from Peisistratus, Telemachus, Helen, or Menelaus himself. So here the *number* of marks calls up the scene. And the grammar of embedding allows Barth to flip instantly from any scene—any moment in Menalaus's self-history—to any other:

> " ' " ' "Seasick," she admitted. "Throwing up." To my just query, why she repaid in so close-kneed coin my failure to butcher her in Troy, she answered —'
> " ' " 'Let me guess,' requested Proteus."
> " ' " 'What I said in Troy," said offshore Helen.
> "What I say to you now." '
> " 'Whatever was that?' pressed Peisistratus."
> "Hold on, hold on yet awhile, Menelaus," I advise. (143)

Three characters and two scenes spring up with this:

> " ' "|'"
> " '|'"
> " '!" (138)*

The wonderment of an entire lifetime comes to us in the collapsing of decades between the first line below—what Helen says to Menelaus as he stands over her in burning Troy—and the second line—the ancient Menalus's reaction when he remembers that moment, eons later:

> " ' " ' " ' "Love!" ' " ' " ' "

So in Barth's treatment quotation marks become genuine visual elements, each set carrying with it the image of characters and settings. More than that, though, the multilayered flipping of voices and images from a half-dozen times, moments that span scores of years, creates—or recreates—the sensation of mind as a permeable, time-shot piece of memory-work, an entity that lives more in the no-time of all its own past moments than within the boundary of a simple present. The sensation is distinctly vertiginous and not very comfortable—no more so for us than for Menelaus. He's well aware that telling himself his own story may be most of what holds him together. But Barth holds up for our contemplation not only the tale of Menalaus but the experience of Menelaus's mind—and once again it's those quotation marks that drive and enable this exploration of identity.

But even Barth didn't exhaust the visual variations of quotation marks. Yet another one appeared recently in a story by Brian Kitely, reprinted in *The Best Short Stories 1988*. The story is told in the first person, by a man collecting insect specimens; we come to this passage at the end of the first section of the story:

> "But think of your poor wife up there in Canader," my FDA agent said. "Selling a house. Packing up two kids. Moving to a new country. You're a cruel man." The new job also meant a transfer from Calgary to Minneapolis.

> It's a cruel company, I said. They told me to butter you up, but in good conscience I couldn't. "Good conscience," he roared, slapping me on the back. When shall we meet tomorrow? I asked. (58)

Here is a narrator whose speech is as private as his thoughts. The FDA agent speaks out in the open, in quotation marks; the narrator speaks in private, in there with his silent thinking. And once again the nature of the self has changed. The secular isolation of the sealed, private mind here acquires enough gravitational pull to keep even speech from escaping:

> "Good conscience," he roared, slapping me on the back. When shall we meet tomorrow? I asked.

It does indeed seem a cruel company, in this story titled "Still Life with Insects."

Now that we've carried our quotational tour of fiction from Homer and Chryses to the day before yesterday in a boxcar in Minnesota, perhaps it's time to return to our original question: What can the nonfiction writer learn from looking at the illusions of speech in fiction?

To answer that question let's retrieve our sentence about Koko and Patterson and restore it to the context of its original paragraph, to see how it looks in the light of fictional technique:

> Is it true [that only human beings possess symbolic speech]? It may yet be. But it cannot escape our notice that the last 15 years have seen a frontal assault on this position, launched by people who claim to study our closest animal relatives. At least four different teams in four different universities using widely varying methods claim to have taught chimpanzees the elements of language. And another team, lead by F. G. Patterson, claims to have taught the infant female gorilla, Koko, more than 400 words, leading Patterson to say, in print, in a distinguished scholarly journal, "language is no longer the exclusive domain of man."

As soon as that quotation opens, I think, we feel the paragraph itself open out. "Language is no longer the exclusive domain of man" brings in another *voice*—here not a phantasmic voice with the full vigor of "personality," but a voice nevertheless, with the full guarantee of a separate identity, the full social force of a voice raised up to speaking volume. And all this despite the fact that the quotation comes from "a distinguished scholarly journal," the sort of publication we assume to have a phantasmic temperature approaching absolute zero. What we're hearing, then, is the simple force of the rhetoric of quotation.

Of course we've always known that "quotation" is a rhetorical device. In Konner's paragraph, for example, we can see well enough that the quotation appears in the emphatic position, at the end of the paragraph; that it caps a progression of increasing particularity, from "people who claim" through "four different teams" to the actual words of a specific person; that it acts as a vivid concluding summary in the same way that a brief, striking analogy or a well-chosen metaphorical phrase might work. But we see now, I think, exactly what sort of rhetorical device quotation is. It makes a rhetorical statement about identity; it initiates a verbal community; and it does these things by invoking personal voice. Quotation isn't simply a figure of speech: it's *the* figure of speech.

Here's a small test for the rhetoric of quotation:

1. Joyce wrote *Ulysses* in order to preserve the speech of his father and his father's friends.

2. Joyce says that he wrote *Ulysses* in order to preserve the speech of his father and his father's friends.

3. Joyce says that he wrote *Ulysses* "to preserve the speech of my father and his friends."

To my ear, number 3 not only has greater emotional weight, it's actually more suggestive. The implications of the statement resonate more strongly when I hear it than when I simply know it.

Journalists, of course, understand this phenomenon very well. Newspaper reporters don't always give exact quotations for the sake of accurate reporting or authoritative confirmation. As often as otherwise reporters quote for vividness, for the illusion of "reality," for the grounding in the world that quoted speech brings. On the front page of the *New York Times* of April 10, 1989, for example, there's an article on clashes between police and protestors in Soviet Georgia; the third paragraph is as follows:

> "My God, it is so tragic, so awful and tragic," said Lana Gogoberidze, a Georgian filmmaker who has been involved in the demonstrations. "Young girls and boys are dead. The situation is very dangerous here." (Esther B. Fein)

And the lead article has this third paragraph:

> "We are marching here to ask, Is the Supreme Court going to affirm that women are full citizens and not property, or is the Supreme Court the captive of the extreme right wing?" asked Gloria Steinem, one of many feminist leaders reunited today in the streets of the capital. (Robin Toner)

Neither quotation is necessary to convey the *facts* of either event. But both work to convey the *reality* of the events, through the rhetorical and realistic technique of quotation. Again: quotation is a technique of verisimilitude, a summoning of personal identity.

If we turn back to the passage from *The Tangled Wing* and look at the surrounding context for the Patterson and Koko passage, we see that Konner makes extensive use of this technique. Our paragraph is the fourth in Chapter 8, which is titled "Logos." This chapter, like every other in the book, begins with an epigraph, this one from Joan Didion's *A Book of Common Prayer:*

> The consciousness of the human organism is carried in its grammar.
> Or the unconsciousness of the human organism. (152)

The first paragraph of the chapter gives a quotation from E. O. Wilson's *Sociobiology*, the next paragraph one from the Gospel According to John. There's a kind of gathering of voices going on here, a social movement, so to speak, that we see very often in first-rate writers. (Konner's book was nominated for a National Book Award, he writes often as a medical columnist for *The New York Times*, and he's published both fiction and poetry.) We almost *expect* such gathering movements from many of our best-known essayists. Stephen Jay Gould is one such writer. His frequently reprinted "Freudian Slip," for example, begins by quoting the Marquis de Condorcet, Charles Dickens, and Erasmus Darwin, all in the first two paragraphs.

Nor is this quotational practice limited to soft scientists with a literary bent writing for a wide audience. If I look on my bookshelves for something distinctly unliterary, I might pick *On Strategy: A Critical Analysis of the Vietnam War*. The author is Harry G. Summers, Colonel of Infantry. The book is used as a student text at the Army War College (13). Nevertheless, the first chapter quotes extensively not only from generals, presidents, senators, and army manuals but also from von Clausewitz, Tom Wolfe, and Miss Manners. Col. Summers, no less than Konner and Gould, defines his own identity as a writer partly through his openness to the voices of other speakers and writers and through active use of those voices in his own work.

At the higher levels of writing, this collaborative habit of writing *along with* other speakers and writers constitutes the norm, not the exception. In fact writing as a voice among other voices may well be one of the most distinctive traits of published nonfictional writing. Yet in the teaching of writing quotation is often treated as a minor embellishment. In the otherwise excellent *Oxford Guide to Writing*, for example, all we learn about quotation (except as an element of the "research paper") is that "an occasional apt quotation adds interest to your writing" (25). Nevertheless, the first sentence of the *Oxford Guide* itself, is this: "Writing, it has been said, can be learned but not taught" (xi). Robert Scholes may well be right in characterizing as "pseudo non-literature" the bulk of the writing we call "college composition" (6). But students who practice writing that's open to the company of other voices—by quoting fairly, carefully, and vividly from any texts under analysis, and by quoting freely from the spoken and written world outside those texts—will go a long way toward excising both the pseudo and the non-.

Of course every discipline will have different customs of quotation; students should learn that this is so and should learn to study those quotational conventions in the same way that we've just looked at fictional conventions. A newspaper article that begins with a quotation, for example, announces a different sort of "news" than an article that begins with the traditional "five *W*" summary and reaches its "grounding" quotation-paragraph further down the column. And certainly no student should be encouraged to load down every analysis and exposition with the deadwood of irrelevant imports. Nobody wants to sound like that university president of some years ago, who became so famous for his allusion-larded speeches that other speakers could allude to *him* simply by saying, "As Hegel says, Good evening, ladies and gentlemen."

But we have gone so far, I suspect, in encouraging in our students the personal, the private, the merely self-expressive, and the narrowly original, that we scarcely let them know how communal, public, and splendidly derivative good writing truly is. Teachers often tell students to give their own ideas, not to hide behind other writers' opinions. I think we need to show them how to give their own ideas in the *presence* of other people's voices and opinions. It's right that fiction should explore the narrowing of voice, the privatizing of identity that culminates in a first-person narrator whose own speech seems to stay inside his mind: one of the functions of fictional exploration is to warn us of hidden dangers. But there's no need to encourage in our students the one-mind, one-voice essay, the nonfictional equivalent of a still life in a boxcar. Certainly it's better to hear the bustle of the marketplace: "Isn't it narrative when he gives all the speeches and also what comes between the speeches?" Of course it is. Just sign here.

NOTES

[1] In Génette, *Narrative Discourse Revisited* (Ithaca, New York: Cornell U. P. 1988), p. 56, where Génette adopts the terminology of Brian McHale, "Free Indirect Discourse: A Survey of Recent Accounts," *PTL* 3:3 (April 1978), 259.

[2] For Conrad's "saturation" in Maupassant, see Ian Watt, *Conrad in the Nineteenth Century* (Berkeley: U. of California Press, 1979), p. 49.

Works Cited

Auerbach, Erich. *Mimésis: The Representation of Reality in Western Literature.* Trans. Willard Trask. New York: Doubleday & Company, 1957.

Bal, Mieke. *Introduction to the Theory of Narratology.* Toronto: U. of Toronto P., 1985.

Barth, John. "Menelaiad." *Lost in the Funhouse.* New York: Doubleday, 1968. 127–262.

Curtius, Ernst Robert. *European Literature and the Latin Middle Ages.* Trans. Willard R. Trask. New York: The Bollingen Foundation (1953), Harper & Row, 1963.

Flaubert, Gustave. *Madame Bovary.* Trans. Francis Steegmuller. Franklin Center, PA: The Franklin Library, 1978.

Forster, E. M. *Aspects of the Novel.* New York: Harcourt, Brace & World, 1927, reissued 1954.

Gaddis, William. *JR.* New York: Alfred A. Knopf, 1975.

Gardner, John. *The Art of Fiction.* New York: Alfred A. Knopf, 1984.

Gass, William H. *Fiction and the Figures of Life.* Boston: Nonpareil Books, 1971.

Génette, Gérard. *Narrative Discourse Revisited.* Trans. Jane E. Lewin. Ithaca, NY: Cornell U. P., 1988.

Gill, Brendan. "The Sky Line: Holding the Center." Rev. of William H. Whyte's *City: Rediscovering the Center. The New Yorker,* March 6, 1989. 99–104.

Gombrich, E. H. *Art and Illusion: A Study in the Psychology of Pictorial Representation.* The A. W. Mellon Lectures in the Fine Arts, 1956. Princeton U. P., Bollingen Series XXXV:5, 1960.

Gould, Stephen Jay. "Freudian Slip," rpt. in *The Bread Loaf Anthology of Contemporary American Essays.* Hanover, NH: U. P. of New England, 1989.

Harth, Erich. *Windows on the Mind: Reflections on the Physical Basis of Consciousness.* New York: Quill, 1983.

Hawthorne, Nathaniel. *The Scarlet Letter and Other Writings.* Ed. H. Bruce Franklin. Stanford U. P., 1967.

Joyce, James. *Dubliners.* Intro. by Padraic Colum (1926). New York: Random House (The Modern Library), ND.

———.*Dubliners.* Ed. Robert Scholes. New York: Viking Press, 1968.

———.*Ulysses: The Corrected Text.* Ed. Hans Walter Gabler, with Wolfhard Steppe and Claus Melchior. New York: 1986.

Kane, Thomas S. *The Oxford Guide to Writing.* New York: Oxford U. P., 1983.

Kitely, Brian. "Still Life with Insects." *The Best American Short Stories 1988.* Ed. Mark Helprin, with Shannon Ravenel. Boston: Houghton Mifflin, 1988. 57–63.

Konner, Melvin.*The Tangled Wing.* New York: Holt, Rinehart and Winston, 1982.

Miller, J. Hillis. "The Function of Rhetorical Study at the Present Time." *Teaching Literature: What is Needed Now,* ed. James Engell and David Perkins. Cambridge, MA: Harvard U. P., 1988. 87–110.

Nabokov, Vladimir. *Lectures on Literature.* Ed. Fredson Bowers, intro. by John Updike. New York: Harcourt Brace Jovanovich, 1980.

Pavel, Thomas G. *Fictional Worlds.* Cambridge, MA: Harvard U. P., 1986.

Plato, *The Republic of Plato.* Trans. Allan Bloom. New York: Basic Books, 1968.

Percy, Walker. *The Last Gentleman.* New York: Farrar, Straus and Giroux, 1966. Rpt. Avon Books, 1978.

Robbe-Grillet. *Jealousy.* In *Two Novels by Robbe-Grillet: Jealousy & In the Labyrinth.* Trans. Richard Howard. New York: Grove Press, 1965.

Scholes, Robert. *Textual Power: Literary Theory and the Teaching of English.* New Haven: Yale U. P., 1985.

Summers, Col. Harry G., Jr. *On Strategy: A Critical Analysis of The Vietnam War.* New York: Dell, 1984.

Watt, Ian. *Conrad in the Nineteenth Century.* Berkeley, California: U. of California P., 1979.

Whyte, William H. *City.* New York: Doubleday, 1988.

Lowry Pei

ॐ *Why Fiction, Why Criticize?*

In 1979, in a talk honoring Malcolm Cowley, John Cheever said some-thing that I think can be unfolded into an answer to the old and never-finally-answered question posed by my title. He ended his reminiscences of roughly 50 years of friendship by recalling "Malcolm's role in the great, bloody clash between literature and psychiatry."

Few of you, I am sure [the final section of the talk began], are old enough to remember when people would decline a lunch by saying that they had an appointment with their alienist. An alienist was meant to cure you of that painful sense of alienation that is, so far as I know, the very beginning of perception. . . . I am a prejudiced man, of course, and when I say that I consider literature to be our only enduring proof of civilization, I am speaking untruthfully, provoked by a medical scientist who considers literature an aberration, a perversion, committed by men and women who are incapable of love and incurably addicted to the transports of grain alcohol and sometimes even stronger drugs. All of this can be cured, the doctor tells us. We no longer need suffer the anguish of writing a book or the pain of reading one. . . . But without literature, of course, we would have no knowledge of the meaning of love. Literature is the only history we possess of this overwhelming sen-timent.

. . . my feeling is that literature is a vast universality of memory that is understood not at all but that is manifestly potent. One is translated these days into 12 or 14 languages, not because we possess any secrets of happiness or success but for matters that seem quite inconsequential. Not very long ago in a little mountain village in Bulgaria, a complete stranger embraced me and kissed me and exclaimed in a jumble of languages: "How can I thank you for your memorable description of the thrill of watching autumn leaves stream through the beam of a car's headlights."

Thus may we live happily with one another. (rpt. in *New York Times Book Review*, 28 August 1983, p. 18)

I won't try to argue that literature can cause us to live happily with one another—that burden does not belong on the back of an art form—nor that it is "our only enduring proof of civilization," an assertion that Cheever admits is prejudiced and untrue. Instead I want to ponder the equally outlandish statement, which he offers simply as an assumption, that "without literature . . . we would have no knowledge of the meaning of love."

Much is compacted into that sentence: it says that literature is a way of knowing, and that it conveys, or creates, a kind of knowledge that exists nowhere else; audaciously, Cheever asserts that the knowledge unique to literature is something that I dare say we all feel we can learn for ourselves—"the meaning of love."

The one form that I can discuss with a writer's intimacy is fiction; I don't mention the other forms of literature only because I don't feel able to do justice to them, even though I think Cheever's bold generalization probably applies. About fiction this is my premise: that the crucial illusion it produces is the illusion that we can share another's subjectivity. In life outside of books the feeling that we can share another's subjectivity is called being in love—a condition which, as we all know, doesn't prevail as much of the time as we would like. Inside of books this condition is business as usual. We take for granted that we do know what is in Gurov and Anna's hearts in "The Lady with the Pet Dog"; and though it is expressed in a way that Chekhov would probably have found unreadable, we take for granted the same thing about the protagonist of Donald Barthelme's "The Indian Uprising." As Hemingway demonstrated, it is possible to write a story in which we must guess at the characters' subjective experiences, but the point still is that we do guess, because we assume that fiction is the form in which we will become privy to thoughts and feelings. Often we will know these more clearly than the characters who are having them, without feeling surprised at being offered such knowledge.

Fiction is not only about the inner mechanism of the social being, which other forms of knowing also address, but it is, crucially (as Charles L'Homme, Professor of English at Simmons College, points out), about the existential self, the inner inside that is *not social*. It is able to address the part of us that is stubbornly, inevitably singular, the part that is private and that we vaguely apprehend whenever we try to understand what has connected all of the experiences we have had since birth: behind them all is something indescribable we call the self, or soul, or spirit. Fiction validates that utterly private experience, by letting us know not only that other people have had such experiences, but that we are having them ourselves. It enables us to know our own knowing, which we somehow were not aware of, yet which we encounter in fiction with a feeling of recognition, not discovery, that shows we held this unarticulated knowledge all along.

Not only does fiction perceive this part of the world—this "inner inside" that I believe is the key piece of the human world—but it then orders and makes meaningful a picture of the world that constantly includes this recognition and communication of what is in subjectivity. It is particularly important to emphasize this at a time when other explanations of what we are leave out this dimension of the self. Most psychology is about the inner mechanism of the social being (the "outer inside," so to speak), and behaviorism, going a step further, seems to aspire to do away with consciousness altogether. History shies away from this part of the interior life as speculation, methodologically invalid. Sociobiology seems constructed to undermine it. Economics rests on assumptions about human motivations that economists themselves describe as rules of their form of discourse rather than as knowledge. We live as individuals, yet most of our ways of knowing ourselves study us *en masse*. In short, most disciplines have little or nothing to do with the self, the inner inside, because they possess no technique for investigating it or communicating it. Yet what would life be—life as it is lived, not as a theory—if this dimension were left out? So not only is the self worthy of study (the fact that people don't have to be made to read fiction proves that), but so is the technique, the art form, that makes such study possible.

It is difficult for me to see what a specifically literary criticism could be except the study of the artfulness of the literary work of art. Otherwise literature becomes a source of homilies to be preached to oneself or others, or an amateur way of engaging another discipline: psychology, theology, political theory, philosophy, linguistics . . . it's not difficult to extend the list. We have Marxist criticism, Freudian criticism, structuralist criticism— once upon a time there were historical criticism and biographical criticism—more schools than I need name exist and are coming into being; but in each case the adjective that precedes "criticism" is more important than any text. Marxist or Freudian or anthropological or feminist or Christian thought, the critic takes for granted, is more important than the single work of art. But I want to ask, What happens if we try to focus on literature itself?

I would propose that the study of a piece of fiction begin not with what it says, but with what it is: how a story is different from any other kind of writing, in what characteristic ways a piece of fiction makes meaning, evokes feeling—what effects it works and how it works them, what choices lie behind the performance. How do the first few paragraphs of a story make us care enough to do the work of reading it? How does the narrator engage the reader in a relationship particular to that story—or, in other words, instruct us in how to play our part in the art work? How does a writer go about saying, in Eudora Welty's words, "both what can and what never can be said"? Analytical work on such questions calls forth the faculty of creative reading: that ability to collaborate with the author to bring a story alive which at the same time enlivens the reader. Meaning (not message) is still the goal of such a reading, but it doesn't begin with the question What does this story have to say? Rather it begins with Forget the theme—how does the story work?

A brief look at one short story may help to examplify what I mean, though no one story, or one reading, can capture all that I am trying to suggest. But consider Eudora Welty's "A Worn Path," a story whose frequent appearance in anthologies of short fiction suggests that it works for many readers.

"It was December [the story begins]—a bright frozen day in the early morning. Far out in the country there was an old Negro woman with her head tied in a red rag, coming along a path through the pinewoods." We are with a narrator who places us at once, with special clarity in time (December, early morning), and not quite so clearly in space ("the pinewoods"). Perhaps "the pinewoods" are enough to suggest the South (especially given that we know who the author is); on the other hand, they are vague enough to lend a distinct feeling of being in a story-world. We are not reading history or anthropology; if we were, the pinewoods would be in a specific state and probably a clearly defined region of it. These are the pinewoods of the imagination; a certain freedom inheres in that. We are also at a distance from the one person inhabiting this landscape, looking at an area "far out in the country" through which one bright spot moves: the red headrag of this "old negro woman."

In the next sentence we are radically closer to her: "Her name was Phoenix Jackson." The narrator, we discover, is not an observer scanning the scene impartially; this voice telling the story knows Phoenix's name, and by naming her elevates her from the generic status of "old Negro woman" to an individual, known and therefore already (by the conventional magic of fiction) the object of our sympathy. Undoubtedly the reader unconsciously guessed in the second sentence that the "old Negro woman" would be the protagonist (otherwise why mention her there?), but now that she is named her role is certain. Through an agreement we in this culture make with fiction, we tentatively accord her our sympathy, even in this third sentence of the story, simply because we know she is the protagonist. One of our goals as readers is to find a place to attach our ability to care, and one of the writer's goals is to make that possible; naming helps.

> She was very old and small and she walked slowly in the dark pine shadows, moving a little from side to side in her steps, with the balanced heaviness and lightness of a pendulum in a grandfather clock. She carried a thin, small cane made from an umbrella, and with this she kept tapping the frozen earth in front of her. This made a grave and persistent noise in the still air, that seemed meditative like the chirping of a solitary little bird.

Phoenix is not merely "old"—which the narrator has already told us once—but "very old"; if this repetition is a choice and not a mistake (which criticism must assume as a starting point), then we get a clear sign that being old is a crucial issue, perhaps *the* crucial issue, of this story. Welty reinforces that thought in a way that does not register consciously on first reading by comparing Phoenix to the pendulum of a grandfather clock; the image underscores the notion of time passing, and at the same time the name of the particular *kind* of clock (something Welty could choose at will) reminds us of old age.

For the second time the word "frozen" appears in this opening paragraph. The year is at its nadir—we are not to forget that—and in the immemorial simile, Phoenix is in the December of her life. Yet at the same time, brightness and vitality continues to manifest itself, in the red rag and the steadiness of Phoenix's movement; the sound of her cane tapping the earth is "persistent," and it seems "like the chirping of a solitary little bird"—the sound of something young and assertively alive. She possesses a "balanced heaviness and lightness." In a close reading of this kind one can see how the essential conflict of the story—the question of whether there is enough life in Phoenix to keep her going—becomes an experience in the reader's mind. In an everyday reading none of this is conscious, but it is subliminally present if the story works; and in a reading at normal tempo after having looked this closely, an awareness of all that is happening here registers not intellectually but emotionally, as a more intense experience of the story world itself. To use an analogy created by Alex Gold, reading (criticizing) in this way is like listening to a symphony over and over, each time paying attention to a specific instrument—first the oboe, then the French horn, etc. Having followed the instruments individually, one listens again, allowing all the voices to flood one's attention simultaneously, without trying to discriminate, and finds that the music is richer, more complexly articulated, more moving than it seemed before. In a like manner we must rehearse our reading. The reading of each story is a separate creative act, unlike the reading of others even by the same author; and criticism, when it works, teaches us how that creation happens, by showing with special clarity what the author has done that we are to collaborate with, and what one reader's mind can do with the material we're given.

To skip many interesting turns in "A Worn Path," by the end of the fourth paragraph we are brought, it seems to me, still closer to Phoenix:

> On she went. The woods were deep and still. The sun made the pine needles almost too bright to look at, up where the wind rocked. The cones dropped as light as feathers. Down in the hollow was the mourning dove—it was not too late for him.

In this paragraph, as I read it, we come into Phoenix's consciousness. No longer are we observing her from the outside, an old woman wearing a headrag coming through the woods, but rather we see as she sees: the pine needles are "almost too bright to look at." Once we've heard Phoenix speak, it seems likely that she would say that "the cones dropped as light as feathers." The narrator observes, "Down in the hollow was the mourning dove—it was not too late for him," but at least half of this observation seems to belong to Phoenix; she, who personifies all the forces of nature, would be the one to say "it was not too late for him." This phrase does double duty; it tells us again the time of day—early, because that is when doves sing—and by the way it is said, it makes us ask who or what it *is* too late for. These are, in fact, Phoenix's own concerns; subtly, we have been drawn inside her mind.

The narrator who began by watching from a distance as Phoenix navigated her way through the woods has shown the ability to enter into her awareness of the world; later there is momentarily no distinction between the two when the narrator conveys to us a dream or hallucination Phoenix has, without comment:

> She did not dare to close her eyes, and when a little boy brought her a plate with a slice of marble-cake on it she spoke to him. "That would be acceptable," she said. But when she went to take it there was just her own hand in the air.

No character in this story is close to Phoenix; no one in it shares her subjectivity. Most of the people she meets treat her with condescension or disdain. One subject of the story certainly is the prejudice Phoenix meets with because she is black, poor, and old. But unlike a sociological treatise on this topic, the story, being fiction, has a narrator; and in a world where no character is close to Phoenix, the narrator shares her consciousness, and brings us to share it. So through the artifice of fiction we become the source of the understanding she gets nowhere else, her subjectivity is validated as a way of making sense of the world, and thus in a peculiar way by reading the story, and being drawn into Phoenix's awareness via the narrator, we make the story's affirmation of her life possible.

Exactly to the extent that we, the readers, create a community for Phoenix by reading, we also do the same favor for ourselves. A piece of human experience, not our own, has ceased to be foreign to us, and to that extent our compassion has grown.

I propose that we should criticize with two awarenesses: awareness that one is completing the creation of the story as one reads, and awareness that the writer has made choices that guide the reader's co-creation of the art work. Everyone who loves literature learns early the ability to dream while reading, to enter the world of the art work; if we go far enough in school, we are usually asked to dream while at the same time holding in mind some overarching theory about humanity *en masse* (a good example would be the graduate student asked to do a Marxist reading of canonical works). The undeniable difficulty of this discipline should not mask the fact that it diminishes the art work to an example and one's original passionate motive for reading to a slightly embarrassing enthusiasm. What I'm proposing is the preservation, even the indulgence, of that original passion in a way that I hope no longer sounds paradoxical: study the contrivance, the technique, the artifice of fiction in order to become a better co-creator, better able to enter the world of the dream—to become fully awake, as the writer is, inside the dream. Then that world begins to be alive with its own meaning from beginning to end.

Why bother to do this? Why take time away from science, history, political theory, and yes, even psychology for such an activity? Because fiction crucially includes private experience, which is endangered in our time, and it communicates by being a private experience; it is a kind of knowing that comes into our privacy and seems to make it coextensive with another's privacy, at a moment when community with others is chronically in doubt. It even takes in the parts of subjective experience that the subject himself cannot articulate, and it does that for the reader (in the recognitions it stirs) as well as for its characters. Not only is this a good deal like what we think love is, it may be that literature constantly invents what we think love is and keeps alive an inner inside that can be so reached. The study of how this is done, and how to participate in it by reading, may be more important than critics themselves typically realize, because, in the words of my colleague Eileen Farrell, it may be that "our inner self is in fact a fragile historical artifact, created by writing and reading." Whether or not that rather frightening inference is correct, criticism is certainly the investigation of a technique we human beings have invented for not being alone—for getting both farther into ourselves, and out of the prison of being ourselves (that "painful sense of alienation") into a community of others who share the same condition.

But to speak of investigation or study does not quite say enough, if it seems to suggest explanations or intellectual understandings alone. Our own making of meaning as we read can only fully happen when that inner inside is touched, and can only be fully communicated when critics write artfully enough to make their subjectivity shared (as some have always done). Ideally criticism both studies, and becomes (like fiction itself), the kind of communication that makes community possible and gets us out of lifelong aloneness. In the end it is about saving our lives from isolation and pointlessness by honoring the deepest self—which in the end is all we've got.

Works Cited

Welty, Eudora, "Henry Green: Novelist of the Imagination." In *The Eye of the Story.* Vintage, 1979.

Fred Marchant

🍀 *Widening the Circle*

The problems in teaching students to write essays that explicate poems begin as soon as we try to specify the nature of the practice. We might explain that the word derives from the Latin, *explicare*, meaning "to unfold," and we will note that the central work of the explicator is thus taken to be the unfolding of the meanings within the given poem. We might contrast what we want with the *explication de texte*, as it is practiced in the French school system. There the student is asked to do a mere line-by-line commentary on the poem, but we want something more than that. We want an essay, an argument that uses the detailed analysis of the poem to support an interpretation. We may even be fond, as I am, of Sylvan Barnet's practical, workmanlike description: "Explication. . . . seeks to make explicit the implicit" (11). But as soon as we say these things, student hands begin quickly to rise, and we get peppered with questions. How much of the implicit should the explication make explicit? How much of the meaning needs to be unfolded? Everything? No? How, then, do you know what to include or not? Where do you draw the line? What do you *really* want?

There is a genuine area of ambiguity here, and it would create problems for any writer, student or otherwise. Let me illustrate this by taking a sidelong glance at how a standard textbook, X. J. Kennedy's *Literature*, describes the practice. Kennedy claims that in an explication, the "writer explains the entire poem in detail, unravelling any complexities to be found in it" (1373). Although I have used Kennedy's book many times, only recently did I start to hear in this statement what most students would hear right away: its extraordinary set of absolutes. Explication means, according to Kennedy, that you have to do the *entire* poem, and handle *any* complexities. A student writer might at first think Kennedy must be kidding, but he isn't. He sums up his description by saying that "all the details and suggestions a sensitive and intelligent reader might consider, the writer of an explication tries to unfold" (1373). *All.*

Any student writer, regardless of ability, is likely to hear in that "all" a demand to master the text. No partial understandings allowed, no groping toward meaning, no exploration, no wonder. Instead, the explication essay requires, so it might seem, that the student become omniscient in the small arena of the poem. I should hasten to add that Kennedy is not alone in conveying—no doubt unintentionally—this unreasonable expectation. One can find traces of it in many textbooks. Another one I have used is Abcarian and Klotz's *Literature: The Human Experience.* In this book the editors say that an explication is "essentially a demonstration of your thorough understanding of the whole poem" (1225). I could go on enumerating other instances from other books, but perhaps it would be more useful to trace the phenomenon back to its source, back to the basic ideological thrust of the New Criticism. As many theorists have pointed out in the last few years, a central and sometimes unacknowledged premise of the New Criticism was that the work of art now had to substitute for Scripture, for the word of God. If He was no longer in His heavens, then perhaps the poem—or what the poem *revealed* (a favored word in New Criticism) would be worth believing in. Explication of poems (the predominant New Critical mode of writing) became something resembling contemplative reverence. Or, if that is too passive a role, the explicator seemed a monk illuminating a secular but sacred manuscript; all the while the dark ages descended outside. One can hear echoes of these attitudes in the somewhat unexamined demand that the explication reveal the whole meaning of the whole poem; it is as if salvation somehow depended on the explicator's skill in disclosing the mysteries. Robert Penn Warren, who along with Cleanth Brooks is usually thought of as a founder of New Criticism, has written that "the thing we desire" is "the perfect and immediate grasp of the poem in the totality of its meaning and structure" (qtd. in Feeney, B51).

I think anyone who assigns a student to write an explication essay incurs some of the burden of the form's history. Whether we explicitly ask for the total grasp of the poem or just accidentally imply something like it, we can contribute to all sorts of problems in the student work. We have all seen students struggle sincerely day in and day out, trying their level best to write an explication but coming up with only a limp paraphrase. We have all had students who, after hearing our answer to their question about what we "really" wanted, paraphrase us by saying, "You want us to tear the poem apart, right?" Worse yet, we've all read papers that do just that. It is as if the student has heard the explication assignment as a set of orders for a search-and-destroy operation. This is the sort of "explication" that captures and counts the metaphors, tallies up the ironies, and declares with certitude what the theme is. I am not sure which of these is the more painful to encounter, but I do have the strong suspicion that the (implicit or explicit) imperative for total apprehension, total understanding has a significant, causal role to play in such matters.

There are, however, alternative ways of conceiving explication. In order to make this sort of writing more meaningful for everyone involved, one needs to explore those alternatives. Moreover, the key moments in this exploration invariably occur early on in the writing process, when the student is poring over the poem, both puzzled and elated, convinced that this is the one she wants to write about, but not at all certain of where to begin or what to say. The key moments in this writing process occur, in other words, during the reading and note-taking and conversational beginnings of the paper. How one explicates a text is a direct reflection of the perceptions, values, and desires that inform the reading of the text; and so as a teacher of expository writing, and one who asks students to compose explications, it becomes my responsibility to offer students alternative frameworks for reading poems. What follows in this essay are some of the approaches to poems that have proved useful in my expository writing classes. These classes are not introductions to literature but introductions to writing interpretive essays about literature. What I'll describe is not an introduction to poetry, but some ways of reading poetry that have proved helpful to students who want to write an essay explicating a given poem. My remarks here are somewhat orderly condensations of what is in practice a much more disorderly process of inquiry, of give and take with the students in the classroom, in conference, and sometimes in written response to notebooks, drafts, and papers. Behind all my suggestions is my sense that the explication need not be a tearing-apart of the poem, but rather could be a charting of the student's own exploratory progress in the making of meaning within and with the text.

Octavio Paz has written that "a poem is fully realized in participation: without a reader, it is only half a work" (29). Early in my conversations with students, I would make this idea a touchstone in my approach to poetry. It is an enabling idea, and it asks the reader to contribute to the poem's meaning rather than take something away from it. Paz's idea also sanctions and ratifies a wide variety of reader's response, especially the slightly disreputable kind, ranging from being baffled to wanting to play around with the text. The dogged search for meaning often produces an equally dogged sense of the meaning, and in my opening conversations with students about poetry I assert that in the beginning of this writing process there comes a time where the whole idea is to first experience the poem.

Later, understanding may come, and with it the ideas that will organize an essay. But first one has to let the poem cause any response its words can possibly cause. Whatever that is, there the explication process begins.

Of course, after 12 or more years in school, student writers are not usually patient with such advice. To buttress my point, I also early on introduce into our conversation "What It Is Like," a one-page prose piece by the poet William Stafford. He opens by saying that "poetry is the kind of thing you have to see from the corner of your eye. You can be too-well prepared for poetry. A conscientious interest in it is worse than no interest at all, as I believe Frost used to say" (3). I remember one of my abler expository writing students becoming quite provoked by this remark, thinking that Stafford and/or Frost undervalued his own conscientious interest and serious preparation. In a way the student was right to feel bothered, for Frost, Stafford, and I were all asserting that reading "skills" and knowledge of the technical terms of poetry simply were not enough, that whatever poetry was, it did not yield to the frontal assaults on it by the rational intelligence. It required some other positioning of the reader in relation to it. You had to look at it from the corner of your eye.

To get at what Stafford might mean by this, I would tell the students about the concept of "night vision," something I had learned about when I was in the military. According to the sergeant-based theory of night vision, a soldier could see even in the darkest night by learning how to dilate the pupils slightly and thereby drawing in more of the ambient light. The trick was to look slightly to the side of where you wanted to see, and in so doing, you might very well see the area you wanted. Likewise with poetry, according to Stafford. You had to learn to look at the poem obliquely. "Poetry," he writes, "is like a very faint star; if you look a little to one side, it is there" (3).

A student would be quick to ask what all this meant in actual practice. I would answer that there were many oblique angles I could imagine, but certainly one of the most useful ways of looking at the poem indirectly would be to turn one's gaze inward. Instead of quickly trying to grasp the poem's meaning, one might do better to monitor the effect that the poem had in one's own mind. What did this collection of words make you think, feel, see, sense? Almost like a medical monitoring, one needed to register any fluttering in the brain waves, any palpitations caused by the text. My assumption was that the words did or would have some effect, and I asked the students to share that assumption or move on to a poem that did seem to cause some response. Moreover, I invariably made the recording of these initial responses in the notebook a habitual writing task. These responses were to be conceived of as so free as to be nearly irresponsible, and they were to be so reportorial as to be like the notes one takes when one is conducting a laboratory experiment. I would ask the students to avoid trying to thoroughly analyze the poem, claiming that such work done prematurely would likely analyze the poem away. I would point to

Stafford's "What It Is Like" and read his words out loud: "If you ana-lyze [the poem] away, it would be like boiling a watch to find out what makes it tick" (3). I would ask them to try to look at their own minds and the poem working therein and to report in class the next day whatever it was they saw.

There were no right or wrong answers to the assignment, and situa-tions such as that naturally make students nervous. Moreover, poetry itself—probably more than any other art form—seems to make people in our culture nervous. There are deep, complicated social forces at work in creating these anxieties, and probably the most beneficial aspect of these free-writing, free-associational note-taking exercises was that there was never any penalty for even the most ill-informed or wrong-headed remark. Also, I didn't collect these, but instead would devote ten or so minutes to "first thoughts" about any poem we began to investigate. I would do the writing too, and only volunteers read their first thoughts out loud. The lesson was, if I had to reduce it to a word or two, that one had to begin the explication at the beginning, at the place where the poem and the reader first meet.

This ostensibly carefree writing assignment would often turn up a deep anxiety. In these notebook entries or in the conversations based on them, the single most commonly present metaphor was the frightening sense of being "lost." Often a student would declare himself lost even when he clearly was not, and I came to hear this metaphor as more a protest about the difficulties and worries attendant on the explication task, and not a literal condition. In fact, I began to think of it as a positive sign, that perhaps the student was now starting to sense some of the complexity of the poem, and the poem itself was starting to look like the forest: not-so-lovely, dark, and deep. I would feel the impulse to rush in, rescue the student, and clarify matters, but I had to resist it. I thought that it would be more valuable if the student could find a pathway on his own.

On the other hand, I didn't abandon the students to their notebooks either. Several years ago I discovered a poem by David Wagoner that has proved helpful to me and to many students at precisely the moment when one feels lost.

Lost

Stand still. The trees ahead and the bushes beside you
Are not lost. Wherever you are is called Here,
And you must treat it as a powerful stranger,
Must ask permission to know it and be known.
The forest breathes. Listen. It answers,
I have made this place around you.
If you leave it, you may come back again, saying Here.
No two trees are the same to Raven.

> No two branches are the same to Wren.
> If what a tree or a bush does is lost on you,
> You are surely lost. Stand still. The forest knows
> Where you are. You must let it find you.
>
> (38—9)

This odd, strangely evocative poem has always seemed to be, among many others things, a parable of the writing process itself, especially when one feels in, but is perplexed by, the material one wants to write about. In the case of explications, the poem is the forest, and perplexity with a deadline looming can easily lead to panic. Writers of all sorts and levels of experience know the feeling. One wants to run off to the library and do some "research," or run to the beach, or home, or away, anywhere to rid oneself of the feeling of being lost. This poem proposes the opposite behavior, practically commands it. The writer who is lost is told to let the material find her, to know and be known by it. Consoling as this may sound, what can it actually mean?

In practice, the poem advises that the reader pay attention, careful attention to the immediate surroundings in the text. It implies that the first step in getting "found" is really the finding of oneself *in relation* to the material. In a way, this poem represents in images the idea behind the initial monitoring and recording of the poem's effects in the student's mind. "If what a tree or bush does is lost on you,/ you are surely lost." So when students suggest they are lost, I respond by saying that perhaps they are not as lost as they think, that perhaps they need to go back to that moment of inward gazing, that monitoring of what the poem does in the reader's mind, that glimpse of the poem out of the corner of one's eye.

Some of the most interesting and useful perplexities that emerge as the students work on their explications are concerned less with the technical aspects of verse and more with that creature who inhabits all lyric poetry, "the speaker." The speaker was a shibboleth of the New Criticism. Derived from a reaction against Romanticism's poet heroes, and modeled in part on Eliot's ideas about the impersonality of art, the speaker of the poem for the New Critic was assumed never to be identical with the poet. This fastidious distinction had its uses, and still does, but the emphasis has shifted. We can all agree that we can never know what the author intended, and even if we did, the text itself would be independent of those intentions, for any poem is in part a field where unconscious elements are at play. But the idea of the speaker is useful because every poem is to some extent a dramatic utterance, and there is behind such speeches or musings a fictive self, a character for the reader to understand. The speaker, in an artistic sense, is the real source of the words of the poem, even if the author wrote them. The speaker is the person whose mind and heart motivate the choice of words in the poem, and as with any human being those motivations are often pro-

foundly complicated. One of the most common difficulties of student interpretations of poems is the tendency to forget about the speaker. It is as if the
student views the speaker as a dramatic inconvenience, to be gotten around
so as to get at the real core of authorial meaning in the poem. In so doing,
the student tends to simplify the human complexity of the issues at stake in
the poem. Better to assume that a primary task of the explicator is to come to
some understanding of a relatively complicated human being saying or
thinking the words of the poem. In a sense, the explicator can almost forget
about the author and his intentions and concentrate on what are the givens
in the text.

As with the feeling of being lost, I ask the students to use their
notebooks to work on the problems posed by the speakers of their poems,
and we use these notebook entries to launch the class discussions. Let me
illustrate this with a poem by Gwendolyn Brooks, "The Mother." Students
tend to have widely varied and deeply held responses to this poem. Its
speaker is a woman who has had at least one and probably several abor-
tions. Despite this fact, she claims she loved all those children of hers that
"never were." After reading that poem, some students will come to class
loaded with ammunition against her. They will acknowledge that she is
filled with guilt, but rightly so, since she had killed her own living fetuses.
More feminist-minded students will present passionate defenses of this
woman, arguing that the poem indicates she had little or no choice in the
matter and that the guilt she feels is just part of a larger feeling of genuinely
maternal instincts. The former group will argue that the poem presents a
speaker rationalizing her actions, while the latter will argue that the poem
shows us how much of a mother this speaker actually is. Depending on the
class, the atmosphere may become quite charged and vivid. These students
want to debate each other, but my role in this class is not really to moderate
a debate. Instead it is to show, where possible, that both "sides" were right,
and that there is a way of imagining this speaker as a person who has many
different feelings, some of them quite contradictory and conflictual. My job,
in other words, is to introduce the concept of ambivalence, not so much as a
mediating gesture but as a "meta" conception of the speaker that allows us
to see her in all her complexity.

Conversations of this sort are always a great pleasure. They seem close
to the inclusive spirit of poetry itself. They also are a pleasure because they
reaffirm to the students that in any of us, speakers of poems included, the
inner life need not be starched into some uniform shape. Instead, the rich
and conflictual inner life of a speaker such as the woman in Brooks's poem
gives the explicator *more* to write about. Perhaps some of the pleasure also
comes from the feeling of the community of the classroom itself. It is as if the
15 or 20 people in the room are each parts of a larger mind that has out of its
constituents articulated a complex understanding. Our interchange as a
group nicely models how individual writers, all alone in the middle of the

night before a paper is due, might respond when they themselves feel they are of two minds on a matter concerning the speaker.

Emotional complexity in the speakers of poems is a delight to illustrate in other ways. Think for a moment how our day-to-day vocabulary is impoverished when it comes to describing the emotions, and contrast to that poverty the fact that poetry is always charting contours of feeling. To explicate a poem almost requires that the writer become adept at naming feelings, and I think it is important enough to seize one class to practice it. I ask the students to name as many emotions as they can. I copy what they say on the board. Within a few minutes the board is covered with love and hate and jealousy and lust and so forth. A few more minutes and we are running out of words and board space, and I am squeezing depression in vertically on the margin. When we have no more words, I observe that these emotions are all in us, at least in potential, and I also observe that this listing alone does not exhaust the possible feelings a person can have. For instance there is a feeling that runs the axis of love and hate and is wound around a thread of respect and another one of fear. This is a feeling too complicated for a one-word name, but there are poems such as Roethke's "My Papa's Waltz" that, in effect, try to "name" that feeling, or at least show it and allow a reader to feel it. Poems in general seem to be always trying to "name" the always surprising and seemingly infinite variety of ambivalences and passions our species is prone to. That's why, I conclude, it's crucial to give the speaker of the poem the most careful and imaginatively generous treatment. The explication is always to some extent a portrait of that person, and what he or she discloses by the words chosen, consciously or not. Imagining the speaker is one of the fundamental ways of participating in the making of the poem, in doing the reader's half.

Imagining the speaker is also very valuable to the reader when it comes to interpreting the significance of the technical aspects of the poem. What makes a poem distinct from the ordinary, prosaic use of language is that the poem's language has been shaped into expressive effect. Compression, distortion, tone, rhythm, figures of speech, stanzas, all such devices and strategems exist to increase the language's capacity to mean. But that burden of meaning is not an abstract one. Part of the fictional apparatus of any poem is that we agree to believe that a person is motivated to say these words and shape them. The burden of meaning is the speaker's burden, and although the author surely invented that speaker, the speaker is the fictional creation striving to say what has heretofore gone unsaid. Every poetic element in the poem, in other words, is motivated by that speaker's desire to convey meaning, and the interpretation of those poetic devices needs always to place them in the context of and in relation to the speaker's concerns.

Let me illustrate with an interpretation of some rhyme from "The Mother":

Though why should I whine.
Whine that the crime was other than mine?—
Since anyhow you are dead.
Or rather, or instead.
But that too, I am afraid,
Is faulty: Oh, what shall I say, how is the truth to be said?
(67–8)

What is the meaning of any rhyme? The strict answer has to be that rhyme itself has no meaning, but rhyme can have meaning in relation to its context. In this poem, that context is the complex set of emotions in the speaker. In class conversation with students about this passage, I have heard some very sophisticated analyses of this rhyme-in-context. One student said that maybe this sound is like keening, a mourning song. Another said that this is "clearly" the sound of guilt clanging away in the speaker's conscience. Yet another suggested that these sounds are nursery rhymes that have been aborted. All of these strike me as legitimate readings of these rhymes, and perhaps the truth of the matter is that we as hearers, witnesses, and co-participants in the poem must remain suspended in this webwork of possible meanings. Perhaps that is the meaning in the final sense, for the speaker, the reader, and maybe even the author.

What is true about interpreting rhyme in relation to the speaker is also true of many other aspects of the poem's art. The imagery and figures of a poem do not exist in an abstract environment; they exist within the motivated human environment supplied by the imagined speaker of the poem. They are chosen by this imaginary person, this person made out of words passed through the reader's mind. In Seamus Heaney's "Sunlight," for instance, the speaker of the poem describes (or remembers) a country farmhouse, and a woman (possibly the poet's mother) baking scones in the kitchen.

Now she dusts the board
with a goose's wing,
now sits, broad-lapped,
with whitened nails

and measling shins:
here is a space
again, the scone rising
to the tick of two clocks.

And here is love
like a tinsmith's scoop
sunk past its gleam
in the meal-bin.
(161–2)

The students will wonder why the poet had the speaker choose the word "measling" to talk about the woman's shins. Together we think about the "measles" that are at the root of the word, and how this woman might have got her red, pocked knees, and we can imagine from the word more than the fact this woman has scrubbed her share of kitchen floors. We get also a connotative undertone about this speaker, and his relation to this woman, for the measles are one of those childhood diseases, and one can reasonably speculate that it is the speaker's filial connection with this woman that motivates his choice of "measling."

What about the concluding simile? Why would the speaker see a tinscoop sunk in a meal bin as an image of love? What sort of love is he talking about? The speculation about "measling" gives us something to guide on, for the simile gently conveys the kind of love that nourishes from day to day, that is hard-working and derives its gleam from constant use and service. This kind of love is the real sunlight in the poem, and it does seem to be a portrait of maternal love. Our reading is helped along by the poet's dedication to a "Mary Heaney," probably his mother, but our reading is, in a sense, independent of what the author alone has cued us to think. We've been working with what we can see in our mind's eye of the speaker, and we can imagine the cultural codes and clichés about love these images are intended to counteract. This is not hearts and flowers; this is love seen as housekeeping and all that it implies. As I write this, I am pleased to recall the student who once caught me up and asked how we could be so sure it was a man speaking? Wouldn't it be just as likely, maybe even more so, for a woman to imagine love as something other than the clichés? She was right to weigh in on this matter with this observation, for among other things, it reminded us that we are not dealing with certitudes when we imagine the speaker. We are making reasonable speculations, and not as ends in themselves, but as doorways into a sense of the poem's possible meanings, meanings which we ourselves are helping to create by imagining that speaker in one way or another.

Rhyme, imagery, figures of speech, these are traditional signs by which we know a group of words to be a poem. But what about those poems—modern poems usually—which forgo or violate the conventional poetic devices? To explicate such poems invariably means one ends up asking What is it that qualifies this group of words as a poem? Is it a poem at all? What makes it such? Essays that explicate such poems are haunted by the fact that the poem has placed itself beyond the ordinary critical vocabulary. In response the reader is—sometimes unwillingly—forced to consider and reconsider the nature of poetry itself.

There are, of course, many wonderful poems to illustrate this matter, but one of my favorites is William Carlos Williams's "Proletarian Portrait":

> A big young bareheaded woman
> in an apron
>
> Her hair slicked back standing
> on the street

One stockinged foot toeing
the sidewalk

Her shoe in her hand. Looking
intently into it

She pulls out the paper insole
to find the nail

That has been hurting her
(101)

To begin at the beginning, everyone will note the word "proletarian" in the title and understand that this woman is intended to be representative of her class. Someone quite experienced at picking out religious images or allusions might add that the nail suggests this woman and the class she represents is in small ways being crucified on a daily basis. Someone in a more sociological mood might suggest that the diction of the poem, its spare images, its lack of figures, is threadbare, poverty-stricken like its subject. In the same vein someone else will note that there aren't many musical devices either. Gaining momentum, the conversation might turn toward the question of punctuation. How come there's a period in stanza four, and those words don't even constitute a sentence, but at the end of the poem, where the sentence needs punctuation, there's none? Maybe this too is part of that overall sense of much that is lacking.

On the other hand, another student might observe that there *are* stanzas, and all but the last are quite regular in structure: long line followed by a short. Someone might then point out that the missing last line is in the same category as the missing punctuation and so forth. And a student who may be particularly good with the rhythms of poems might note that the "feel" of each of the second lines is that something is missing when compared to the first lines, and that this rhythmic pattern "climaxes" in the missing whole last line of the last stanza. At this point in the conversation, it is very likely that a student will get impatient and ask what all this amounts to, what it means. It will be a good moment to remember the speaker and wonder why his lines break as they do and why he ends where he does. It will be a good moment for us to note that in reading any poem, a significant amount of the effort is spent in reading the "white spaces" of the poem.

Every poem is to some extent a dramatic utterance, and to that extent every poem is thus a chart of some movement in the speaker's mind. That movement need not always be a relentless progress toward an epiphany, or even a momentary stay against confusion. It could easily be a regression or a swirling eddy of troubling feelings or a deep stillness. The kinds of movements poems may chart are limited only by the kinds of inner life we believe we possess. But every poem does seem to use its white spaces, its "between-the-lines," its absences to help give the reader that sense of shifting thoughts and feelings, of pressures building or slacking, of fractures and jagged edges, of mendings and reconciliations. As in a photographic negative, the white spaces are the necessary contrasts, the empty places that allow meaning to gather around the words uttered inside that emptiness.

In "Proletarian Portrait," the movement in the speaker's mind is akin to that of a zoom lens doing a close-up. The speaker begins by seeing the woman afar, and through each stanza he proceeds in a growing visual intimacy. He can see the insole of her shoe. But, when he says that she is looking "to find the nail//That has been hurting her," something other than good, precise eyesight enters into the poem. At that moment he is imagining what it is that the woman is seeking out. He can't see into her shoe or know how her foot hurts. Instead of knowing, he has to lend himself to an act of sympathetic imagination. He has to walk a little in her shoes. For a split second the distance between observer and observed is bridged, and the observer has become what or whom he has beheld. The poem exists to enact that movement of mind each time a reader reads it. If any reader wonders how this could possibly be poetry, then the coming to this sense of a set of meanings way beyond our expectations should reassure the reader that this collection of words does in its own way the very thing that is the essence of the art.

The basic question raised by the Williams poem seems to be the deepest motive behind any attempt at writing an explication. Every such essay is at bottom an argument claiming that the given group of words is indeed a poem. In *Against Interpretation*, Susan Sontag makes a similar point when she argues that the critic's task is "not to find the maximum amount of content in a work of art," but rather to try to "see the thing at all." Like Stafford, Sontag recognizes that it is not easy to see the work of art for what it is. The real aim of "all commentary on art now," she writes, "should be to make works of art . . . more, rather than less real to us" (23). This is a rather different agenda from that of the New Critics. Instead of asking what eternal truths about human nature are revealed in the poem, the central task of the explicator is to discover and rediscover what in the text makes it a poem at all. This is not a trivial task. Robert Hass has said that "art is an activity of the spirit, and when we lose track of what makes an art an art, we lose track of the spirit" (60). Explications of poems are ways of keeping track of what makes a poem a poem, and in doing that they make some small addition to our self-knowing, our spirit. The poem is not a grail containing the sacred but an *activity* of spirit, and as Paz says, that activity only half exists without the reader.

There also need not be the traditional, hierarchical relations between poet and critic, with poet as genius and critic as acolyte. Explication in the best sense of the word can be an unfolding conversation between text and reader, reader and text, each participant of equal significance to the other. As a poet and critic myself, I realize I have a vested interest in arguing for more democratic relations between the parts of my own self. At the same time, however, the idea of equality between poet and critic, and between their writings, allows us to see them as different modes, twinned faces of the same fundamental processes.

This equality of modes makes good sense in another way. If we shift our view out of the sacred circle of the classroom, and widen it to include the larger arenas of our culture, we can see that the close reading and interpreting of texts is a central intellectual activity in our time. If the semiotically based upheaval in literary theory of the past few years had to be reduced to one enduring legacy, I would bet that it would be the notion that all cultural artifacts can be read as texts written in the "language" of a given culture. Our self-understanding—our sense of the spirit, if you will—depends on how well we both make and explicate the texts of our moment in history, our place on the planet. Even if most of my students are neither poets nor critics, they will—as with any of us—need practice explicating the complex cultural signs that surround them. Lyric poems are always good places for that practice to begin.

Works Cited

Abcarian, Richard, and Marvin Klotz. *Literature: The Human Experience.* New York: St. Martin's Press, 1982.

Barnet, Sylvan. *A Short Guide to Writing About Literature.* 3rd ed. Boston: Little, Brown, 1975.

Brooks, Gwendolyn. "The Mother." In *Contemporary American Poetry,* 3rd ed. Ed. A. Poulin. Boston: Houghton Mifflin, 1980.

Feeney, Mark. "The Message of Mr. Warren's Profession." Rev. of *New and Selected Essays,* by Robert Penn Warren. *The Boston Globe.* 16 April 1989:B51.

Hass, Robert. "One Body: Some Notes on Form." In *Twentieth Century Pleasures.* New York: Ecco Press, 1984.

Heaney, Seamus. *Poems 1965–1975.* New York: Farrar, Strauss, and Giroux, 1980.

Kennedy, X. J. *Literature.* 4th ed. Boston: Little, Brown, 1987.

Pax, Octavio. *The Bow and the Lyre.* New York: McGraw-Hill, 1973.

Sontag, Susan. *Against Interpretation.* New York: Dell, 1964.

Stafford, William. "What It Is Like." In *Writing the Australian Crawl.* Ann Arbor: U. of Michigan P., 1978.

Wagoner, David. "Lost." In *A Geography of Poets.* Ed. E. Field. New York: Bantam, 1979.

Williams, William Carlos. *Collected Earlier Poems.* New York: New Directions, 1966.

Victor Kantor Burg

✌ *Sentenced: Writing About Plays*

I learn, reliably, from unexpected sources. From an article on teaching English as a foreign language, I discover that different kinds of cultures approach solving problems in ways that can be illustrated as follows:

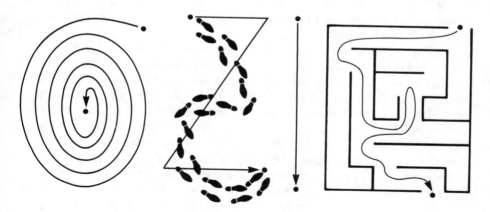

However, from an Indian economics instructor, I learn that using simple drawings to portray any culture's mind is at least condescending and at best largely inaccurate—but that the pictures could reasonably reproduce the minds of any novice struggling to understand, say, cost-benefit analysis. In discussing these approaches with mathematics teachers, I find that contrary to my math-depleted assumptions, students learning that elegant and precise language also wander through many such squiggles before they arrive at the straits of comprehension. From my own experience I know that my writing mind, like that of my students, often duplicates all these pictures, depending on which stage of the writing process one wishes to illustrate.

One thing plays do is to spotlight—dramatically—the working of the human mind, and this, I would suggest, is one reason to read dramatic literature, closely, with apprentice writers. Studying dramatic language, writing scripts and essays, teaching the writing and reading of these forms has shown me an apparent paradox of value for my students and colleagues: namely, that the mind of a writer, student or otherwise, will and *should* whirl in a vortex or meander through an alley in just the same way that the mind of a well-created character does, whether that character be an aristocrat of Chekhov's, a mad monarch from Shakespeare, a David Mamet tough or a Samuel Beckett exile.

Of course an essay must impose some kind of order on the whirl or the meander of the mind. The voice of the completed essay must be reasoned, which the voice of the dramatic character most often—by definition—isn't. But in order for the writer to gain and hold that reasoned voice, she must (like the actor who will make Lear come alive for us) spin, wander and daydream first. She must note, write, rewrite: rehearse, rehearse, rethink, run through it still another time. Thus, theater offers the writing instructor two useful parallels: the mind's whirl as it is articulated by a character suggests the writer's mind at work; and the actor's process of getting inside that mind by rehearsing suggests the writer's process of getting inside her own mind by revising.

If our writing students can be made to see the balance that lies behind—but is refused by—the character's illogic, this may help them to alter the illogic of their own work-in-progress. As dispassionate readers, our students can ferret out the clear rhetoric that a character's passion contradicts. They can parse the argument his anger clouds. We can observe and admire with them the "bad" writing—the illogical, fragmented, elliptical, incorrect language—that plays demand. We can make an equation between this and our students' weaker writing. And we can then go on to use our observations to improve their prose. We can in effect regard the sentences and paragraphs of dramatic language as if they were intended to be clear expository writing, which they are not, and compare them to the successive drafts of student papers. By so doing, we can find a way of looking at the human mind, the human heart, and the human "essay" in progress.

Certainly, analyzing or interpreting the characters in a play can provide the subject for student essays. But my purpose here is to demonstrate the value of scrutinizing the very language with which characters construct themselves on the page (as on stage): their rhetoric, their syntax, their sentences. I'd like to examine sentence fragments, weak or overly modified phrasing, a series of ideas without transitions, a jumble in search of its own logic. I'd like to view a few instances in which half-rhetoric makes the language of excellent drama and offers the expository writing instructor instant exercises in revision and rethinking.

Theatrical language supports this kind of exercise better than its counterparts in fiction and movies, for although any written dialogue is meant to represent the sound, rhythm, and configuration of human voices, dramatic speech is (for the most part) unmediated. Plays are constructed entirely of talking, of human voices in conflict and in love with one another. Rarely do plays have any narrator. As a result, when we read a play in the classroom we must "create" the voice of the individual character, the shape of his soliloquy, the pattern of the scene—all of which the fiction writer stages for her reader. Even more than the novel or short story, the written text of a play demands active collaboration on the part of the reader.

Sentences in plays—and the "logic" that they create or combat—do more closely resemble the dialogue in movies than their cousins in fiction. However, in screenplays an important difference obtains: it is virtually impossible to read a published movie script and consider it to have any other rendition than the already produced version (read *Casablanca* and hear "You played it for her, now play it for me" in any other melody than Bogart's). And it is precisely finding the rendition, picturing the scene— exactly that kind of consideration—that constitutes the first step toward opening a play's heart and mind and the first step toward making our model palpable. Understanding the mind of a character in distress is like understanding the mind of a writer in distress.

Let us begin with Shakespeare. Assuredly, other playwrights employ "bad" grammar, and they can be used equally well. I have chosen Shakespeare because his language is so often the measure of excellence in theatrical speech, in great and "bad" rhetoric. Let us consider a splendid fragment from the character who is bigger than any single whole: Sir John Falstaff.

Our first glance at his syntax will occur as he waits for the arrival of the newly coronated King Henry the Fifth, formerly Prince Hal, Falstaff's "sweet boy," his tutee in boyish misbehavior, in witty indolence. We see Falstaff with his underworld cronies, see him knowing, as we know, that he has not behaved well lately, has behaved wickedly as always, that Hal's father has deservedly willed his son the throne, that Hal has not contacted Falstaff since that time and has not seen him for nearly the full latter half of this play, *Henry IV, 2*. During this time we have seen Hal visibly mature, palpably begin to embody the sovereignty his nation will have rightly conferred upon him. We cannot help but understand, and Falstaff will not be able to help himself from seeing, that things have changed between himself, once a father-surrogate, a tutor in the ways of mischief and careless intoxication, and the youth that Hal once robustly was.

And suddenly this former pal is about to arrive, and as abruptly, everything looks wrong to Falstaff—everything about him feels and then looks shabby, tatty, threadbare in the light of this new day. A severe dryness in his mouth which no quantity of "old sack" will quench, Falstaff fears that how he looks will not look right to this new Henry, and that who he is will not sit right either. Nervously, he seeks his retinue: "Come here, Pistol," he insists, but then recommends, "stand behind me." He wants someone near, but who, and how? "O!" he cries, perhaps seeing too much of his clothing reflected in the ragamuffin Pistol. "O! If I had had time to have made new liveries . . ." With this he begins a theatrical paragraph wonderful for its drama and illuminating as to the nature of sentencing. In order that the reader may better follow my points, I have linked together Falstaff's thoughts and have omitted the responses to them. It is Falstaff's mind at work that matters here:

> Come here, Pistol; stand behind me. O! if I had had time to have made new liveries, I would have bestowed the thousand pound I borrowed of you. But 'tis no matter; this poor show doth better: this doth infer the zeal I had to see him.
> It shows my earnestness of affection.
> My devotion.
> As it were, to ride day and night; and not to deliberate, not to remember, not to have patience to shift me.
> But to stand, stained with travel, and sweating with desire to see him; thinking of nothing else; putting all affairs else in oblivion, as if there were nothing to be done but to see him.

These are the words. This is the "essay." But what is there to say about it that will instruct the apprentice writer of expositions and arguments? We can work backwards and forwards, stretching the muscles of the play's mind and of our own, generally the best way to read a play or work an argument. We can, in effect, rehearse.

But let me explain what I mean by rehearsing. The word itself gives clues. Its source is a noun, the *harrow*, a tool of the field, a sort of small spade used for working the earth, for pulverizing and smoothing soil. Containing spikes, spring teeth, discs, a harrow sounds to be a rugged instrument ready to deal with poor soil, and while farming is hardly what one first thinks of in connection with rehearsal, the source is apt. Rehearsing is painstaking, slow, repetitious, inefficient. Harrowing. To rehearse is to go over and over the lines, digging; to look and re-look, try and step, trip and stand, relook and look again. In rehearsal, an hour may easily be spent on the moment Falstaff first recognizes his shabbiness.

The students I know best have rarely experienced how much redoing is necessary to produce excellence, in any domain, unless they have worked in the theater, in a rehearsal setting, or in music. Or in athletics. A good high-school basketball player will be told to practice jump shots three or four hundred times a day. A serious middle-school piano student will be told to practice scales for an hour a day. What student writer will be required or encouraged to do comparable work at a task at least as difficult, and as rewarding? The reading I am about to propose—of Falstaff's "essay," and of other passages—comes from that sort of repetition, comes from it and, I hope, makes a system by which others may do this rehearsing and digging, harrowing though it can be.

To begin with, let's look at what sounds like an odd transition: "Come here, Pistol; stand behind me." Why "stand behind me"? And if Pistol is standing behind him, then to whom is the next exclamation made? To Pistol? Could Pistol have lent Falstaff a thousand pounds? If you thought Falstaff was dressed badly, take a look at Pistol. Or is it a statement in rehearsal for Henry-yet-to-come? A debt, a deficit surely confronts Falstaff, but one he wants behind him. When Pistol comes to him, much of what Falstaff sees is what he least wants to see; most of what he sees he wants out of his sight. Thus: "Come here Pistol; stand behind me." What a student can do after scrutinizing this awkward transition is to look at transitions, in general, in his own work.

For example:

> Hamlet loves his mother. She married her brother-in-law suddenly. Hamlet's uncle is angry at him for sulking. Hamlet talks to himself to psych himself up. His mother doesn't understand.

Just as one may ask why Pistol must stand behind Falstaff, one may ask the student writer what Gertrude's love of Hamlet has to do with her hasty marriage. Or one may ask what Hamlet's mother doesn't understand, or what it might mean to speak to oneself. An unruly group of sentences to be sure, this is also one that can be made to touch on serious questions in Hamlet. If a student supplies what's missing, and only what's missing, this weak writing can at least move in the direction of coherence:

> Hamlet loves his mother but she neglects his feelings. Her love for Hamlet's uncle is strong but Gertrude cannot convince Claudius and as a result he fears Hamlet will undermine his power. Sensing Claudius's fear, Hamlet avoids him, which Claudius takes to be intentional. However, Hamlet, ignored by Gertrude, delves deeper into himself for answers. Gertrude takes his privacy, his musing, to be anger at her.

But why confine our examples to students? Student writing is shaky because so much of what students read and hear is scarcely intelligible. Here is a text articulated by Kansas Senator Robert Dole on the subject of the

Supreme Court's decision that burning the American flag is not unconsti-
tutional:

> Maybe those who sit in ivory towers agree with the Supreme Court. Maybe.
> As the man who burned the flag, millions of people hate America. Hate the
> flag. If they do, they ought to leave the country. If they do not like America,
> that's fine. Go find something you do like. If they don't like our flag, go find
> one you do like. (qtd. in *The New Republic*, July 17 & 24, 1989, p. 4).

What unspoken, unwritten words might join these phrases, one may
ask. What links might one find to bind the court, the towers, the man, the
flag? What does the word "like" mean in this opinion? What happens if you
simply complete the sentences? How much more does the speaker know
than what he has articulated? How might a student writer fill in this rough
draft, how might it be used to teach him that a poor final draft may be the
very best rough version possible? How to rehearse and redo this prose and
argue it into a text Dole might want included in his collected papers?

Comparably, consider that Falstaff can either be speaking to Pistol
about the thousand ("O! if I had had time to have made new liveries, I
would have bestowed the thousand pound I borrowed from you") or preparing his greeting to Henry. Both tacks require that we see what he doesn't
want to see and both insist that the semicolon separating Falstaff's commandments needs a closer look: "Come here, Pistol; stand behind me." A
well-written sentence would put words in the place of that semicolon.
What, we may ask ourselves and our students, could those words be? Come
here, Pistol. Oh God, look at you. Go away. No, stand behind me. Or:
Come here, Pistol. (He scrutinizes Pistol.) No, I can't have Henry seeing
you first. Stand behind me.

In such detail can one wander back and forth through a line, a sentence. And we can also apply this technique fruitfully to the longer passage,
the theatrical paragraph. Having completed his line about borrowing and
clothes, Falstaff continues:

> But 'tis no matter; this poor show doth better: this doth infer the zeal I had to
> see him.
>   It shows my earnestness of affection.
>   My devotion.
>   As it were, to ride day and night; and not to deliberate, not to remember,
> not to have patience to shift me.
>   But to stand, stained with travel, and sweating with desire to see him;
> thinking of nothing else; putting all affairs else in oblivion, as if there were
> nothing to be done but to see him.

One can look to unearth the possible completeness in this final bumpy
fragment. One can see that "nothing else to be done but to see him"
contains the goal, the moment toward which this piece of rhetoric lurches.
And briefly let us consider what occurs immediately after it, for retrospec-
tive light can further illuminate our reading.

In the moment after Falstaff finishes his fragmentary speech, he is informed that Hal-now-king has arrested Falstaff's Doll Tearsheet, the "Helen of [his] noble thoughts." Arrested she is, although "the laws of England"—Falstaff had informed all, learning of Hal's ascendancy—"are at my commandment." But the laws of England have now leaned from the nighttime to the day. In *Henry IV, 1*, in an era when Falstaff could tell the difference between a proper monarch-to-be and his rascal-prince Hal, he had lightly told that boy: "Sweet wag, when thou art king let not us that are squires of the night's body be called thieves of the day's beauty . . . let men say we be men of good government, being governed as the sea is, by our noble and chaste mistress the moon, under whose countenance we steal."

To this sly and charming constitutional principle Hal had cheerfully assented, at that time—himself stealing around his England in the dark. But by now, now that he is the king, Hal has learned what it means to be the son of the man who wears the crown, has learned what is required to literally embody his nation. Hal now is becoming a monarch, and a good and brave one, as the final play in this quartet, *Henry V*, will demonstrate. King Henry the Fifth has witnessed King Henry the Fourth's passing away, has placed the crown, however uneasily, upon his own head, has calmed waters his own misbehavior had roiled. And has taken a first step, in the arrest of Falstaff's Doll, toward assuring his ministers and his parliament of his seriousness. This Falstaff finds out instants before Henry's arrival. This is the man whom he will greet in his tired, debtor's clothing, this sober ruler with whom he had once drunk and played at misrule. Out of time and chances, a desperate heat fires Falstaff's rhetoric, blasting it far from the grace and wit of which he is capable (as witness his speech regarding nocturnal governance).

And what this has to do with student writing is that by reading backward—another way of rehearsing—through the paragraph at the center of our concern, we can begin to find out what creates its fragments and how a whole might be made. For if the "essay" in question here ends with "nothing to be done but to see him," then the material following it (namely, the news of Doll Tearsheet's arrest) helps us, as it plays back through his aria, to read the passage properly. We see that the growing uneasiness at work here will prove fully justified. We understand why the prose gets more and more unruly, until it ends with a stumpy fragment, lacking both subject and conjugated verb.

Earlier in his remarks, Falstaff is able to say of his own raggedness: "this doth infer the zeal I had to see him." He is able to claim "earnestness of affection," "devotion," the need to "ride day and night." These are explanations that in effect he is trying out, rehearsing; he is preparing to offer these explanations to his wag, his Hal, and they seem to answer the question why he has not had time to get new liveries. But as he improvises, Falstaff begins to realize that his liveries are not the problem: he is. And how will he explain himself away? How can he possibly compose the essay he is trying to compose? He hears how his draft is failing, he feels how weak his "writing" is. It isn't working. Therefore, the further he goes into this text, the deeper the hole he digs.

Until he gets to his final sentence, which is not a sentence: "But to stand stained with travel, and sweating with desire to see him . . ." We can find a real beginning to this thought only by going as far back as "It shows my earnestness." Put all his lines together, change the punctuation, and there is a genuine if overly extended sentence to be found in this speech, a coherent thought. But it is buried, as coherent thoughts so often are in early drafts. Let us point this out to our students and, by reading Falstaff in this manner, let us model for them a way to read their own emergent essays.

The writer of any unwitting fragment is likely to be wandering, as is Falstaff, looking forward for a way to end, desperately seeking to find a resting place, a point, and losing sight, in the process, of both the beginning of the thought and its closure. However, studying the fragments scattered across this Shakespearean page can suggest to both teacher and student the virtue hidden in the fragment, the shapable rough material.

What student's mind—what writer's mind—has not begun to write without knowing really where it will go, only to learn at the end where it meant to start? "The state of Denmark," I have read, "is troubled. People fear shadows. They are hoping things are okay. No one knows who says the truth. Hamlet is like a detective." Simply beginning with "Hamlet is like a detective" gives some shape to this disconnected group of sentences. Had Falstaff wished to make an essay, he might wisely have begun by acknowledging that "nothing else to be done but to see him" was his most important thought.

But beyond his lack of organization, even Falstaff's choice of individual words reflects the despair beneath the rhetoric. Compare his clumsy repetitions of the terms "else" and "see him" in this desperate fragment ("sweating with desire *to see him;* thinking of nothing *else;* putting all affairs *else* in oblivion, as if there were nothing to be done but *to see him*" [my emphasis]) with his graceful lines from the earlier play: "Let men say we be men of good government, being governed as the sea is, by our noble and chaste mistress the moon, under whose countenance we steal . . ." His verbal clumsiness at the approach of Henry, the fact that his language falls apart here, is remarkable theater. This "bad writing" represents the end of a thought that began with his wishing for more time. But he is out of time now and, up against the consequences of that wall, his rhetoric fails him, his eloquence is long gone.

For our students, an exercise that rewrites Falstaff's entire paragraph or that begins with "O! if I had had time to have made new liveries" or that discusses rationalization—any of these is a way to enter sentences, character, and the speaker's desperate mind. Or we might have students focus on the nouns in this passage, along with the crucial pronoun "him": time, new liveries, thousand pound, poor show, zeal, him, earnestness, affection, devotion, day and night, patience, travel, desire, him, nothing else, affairs, oblivion, him. Which are the concrete nouns, which the abstract, and how do they connect? Why does the pronoun "him" recur so often, and in connection with which nouns? What is the effect of the whole passage ending with "him"?

What we begin to understand from such a rehearsal, such a rereading, is that Falstaff had a potential thesis for this paragraph in his very first line about new liveries but that had he followed his premise there (as the writer of a polished essay might), he would have risked arriving at the logical end of his thought, would have risked confronting the dire predicament he is truly in. He would have risked realizing that Henry must banish him. But Falstaff is not the author of an essay, he is a character in a deep quandary. We the readers and writers about him can take the powerfully fertile draft his scampering, scuttling mind has produced and see in it all that is hidden, all that is incomplete, all that is there to be unearthed. And we can contrast this draft (this rehearsal) with what the final essay (the finished performance) might be.

As we can ferret out what might lie beneath the wandering and hunting of this character's mind, so we can view student writing and ask students to view it. As one can parse Falstaff's furtive rhetoric, so one can ask a student to unravel hers. Look then to prior fragments, to earlier sentences, and to succeeding ones, too. Read not only between the lines but between the words and the phrases. Regard any piece of human discourse as being, at least potentially, a rough draft that, rehearsed, reseen, rewritten, might contain that clear poised voice we seek.

In this light, let us consider the following text, spoken by five-year-old Jennifer Royal, as transcribed by *Life* magazine reporter Valerie Gladstone (October 1989, pp. 16–17):

In the morning I ate breakfast and brushed my teeth. We was playing outside. Peaches and me play ring-around-the-rosy. Little boys was fighting about a dollar in front of the house, and it scared me. Then I see Michael Ward—I didn't know his name then—and he say, "Anybody move, I shoot," and he shot me. It scared me.

When the bullet got me, it felt like a firecracker. My head hit against the door. I had a long scratch on my head. Peaches almost made it. Then I knew Peaches was dead. Mama was froze. The policeman held me. He was crying. It was hard for me to talk. I swallowed my throw-up. Then the doctors put me on a board to go to the hospital with my mama and my auntie. The bullet fell right out of my back. I told them, "I'm not going to die. God's not ready for me yet." But there was blood coming out of me. Michael Ward. He shouldn't have did that to me.

The voice of this narrative is as striking as Falstaff's, and it too can be read as "bad writing" of daunting strength. It too can serve as an exercise in close reading in the context of a writing class. Let us admire the effortless power of the narrative first, its ellipsis ("Peaches almost made it"), its vivid concision ("When the bullet got me, it felt like a firecracker"), its moving simplicity ("he shot me. It scared me").

Then let us allow ourselves questions about what this soliloquy tells the reader to see, what it keeps from his view, and what senses it calls on to contribute to his experience of the whole. If we think of Robert Dole's paragraph as persuasive prose, then Jennifer Royal's is personal, but not without its final lesson. Working back and forth through her sentences, as we did through Falstaff's, we find that "He shouldn't have did that to me" is the final point, the idea toward which the whole passage moves. This is not, then, simply a personal narrative, but also a lesson—an argument—illustrated by incident.

And what we see is breakfast, brushed teeth, ring-around-the-rosy, boys fighting, Michael Ward, a gun. We see a firecracker, the narrator's head and the door, a scratch, Peaches' death, Mama, the policeman crying, doctors and a board, mama and auntie, the bullet, blood, a memory of Michael Ward shooting. We also sense particulars: fear, a man she didn't know, fear, Peaches' struggle, Mama paralyzed, an inability to speak, courage, judgment. As brief as the actual narrative is when quoted fully, we get a sense of this crime even more quickly when we outline (as I have just done) its actions and its feelings. And listed, as any writer's words can be listed, at any stage of writing, these words themselves invite decisions. Is there more to say about breakfast? Was there a fear before her fear about the boys fighting? What did this game of ring-around-the-rosy look like? What did Peaches look like? How common was it that strangers visited this neighborhood early in the morning? What time of day, what season was it?

In fact I would not want to change a word of this remarkable narrative, this haiku of an eyewitness account. But looked at for a moment, for the purposes of pedagogy, as akin to all the rough drafts students submit to us in the guise of final drafts, this passage offers an opportunity—as does even Robert Dole's jumbled exhortation—to consciously craft a paragraph that might draw the reader even deeper in. As we know and our students need to learn, the difference between a rough draft and a reworked version of it is usually that the former speaks primarily to its author, while the latter turns outward to address its audience. Thus, here, were the narrator to amplify her images and actions, her audience would even more vividly see that porch, that game, that shot.

By the same token, the narrator's final judgment—"He shouldn't have did that to me"—might be rendered even more powerful, were we given a fuller picture of Michael Ward. What does he look like when he says, "Anybody move, I shoot"? Is Jennifer's mother present in that instant, does she hear this threat? Where is Peaches' mother, where does Peaches live? From how many points of view can the narrative be told? Which is the best way to tell it and how does one's angle of vision, or any other, color what we will see, think, feel, decide?

These are the questions I would ask my students of this text, these are the questions that often need asking of their own work. In sum, what is the difference between what you know and what you have told me?

Questions elicited by Jennifer Royal's text suggest more questions about Falstaff's troubles, which were far from over when we left him. For no sooner has he realized that his Doll has been arrested—which news he greets with the assurance "I will deliver her"—no sooner has this occurred than Henry enters, magisterially, the new king. Falstaff calls desperately, "God save thy grace, King Hal! my royal Hal!" and "God save thee, my sweet boy!" These indiscretions then put the burden on Henry's rhetoric, which is as follows:

> I know thee not, old man: fall to thy prayers;
> How ill white hairs become a fool and jester!
> I have long dream'd of such a kind of man,
> So surfeit-swell'd, so old, and so profane;
> But being awak'd, I do despise my dream.
> Make less thy body hence, and more thy grace;
> Leave gormandising; know the grave doth gape
> For thee thrice wider than for other men.
> Reply not to me with a fool-born jest:
> Presume not that I am the thing I was;
> For God doth know, so shall the world perceive,
> That I have turn'd away my former self;
> So will I those that kept me company.
> When thou dost hear I am as I have been,
> Approach me, and thou shalt be as thou wast,
> The tutor and the feeder of my riots:
> Till then, I banish thee, on pain of death,
> As I have done the rest of my misleaders,
> Not to come near our person by ten mile.
> For competence of life I will allow you,
> That lack of means enforce you not to evil:
> And, as we hear you do reform yourselves,
> We will, according to your strength and qualities,
> Give you advancement. (To the Chief Justice) Be it your charge, my lord,
> To see perform'd the tenour of our word.
> Set on.

Henry's first response is to avoid Falstaff altogether and to command the chief justice to "speak to that vain man." Falstaff's response to the justice's rebuke is of course to ignore him and speak directly to Hal: "I speak to thee, my heart!"—as complete a sentence as it could possibly be. But "I know thee not, old man," Henry says, for the second time failing to address him: "Fall to thy prayers; How ill white hairs become a fool and jester!"

The sermon and judgment to come is one of the most poignant in the work of a writer profoundly capable of finding and showing poignancy. It pictures Henry's renunciation of Falstaff, a banishment on political grounds, an exiling due to considerations of state, not heart—a public statement of a private relationship's demise. As a speech, an open letter, a sermon on self-improvement, it is intended to inform Falstaff of the way things stand and simultaneously to inform Henry's court and the courts of other nations exactly who this new leader is. It is a cautionary memorandum, the answer to Falstaff's remarks about being a man "of good government, being governed as the sea is, by . . . the moon."

But if its thesis is straightforward, our understanding of it as an "essay" is forged by the disparity between Falstaff's audience—Hal, Falstaff's heart, the most intimate of listeners—and Henry's audience(s): the world, the nation, his soon-to-be-former friend, and his own "former self." Henry has not made such declarations before. Their articulation, we must steadily hear, is new. He both knows what he wants to say and makes this up as he goes along—an excellent way to capture character, and to write first drafts. But not (as students are wont to think) coherent final drafts. Henry's "essay," then, will have its rhetorical problems. And these will be considerably complicated by his awareness of the different audiences he must speak to simultaneously.

Just as Falstaff and the king have audiences to address or to ignore, Shakespeare has us. And in this scene he makes great demands on our minds and sympathies, demands that directly touch how we perceive the scene's language. We must be made to sympathize equally with both men. We cannot simply find a newborn politician casting off old friends who dress badly or speak with the wrong accent, we need to see the wisdom in Henry's decision. We cannot simply see the fondest of old rogues, we need to see Falstaff's unappealing sagging flesh. We must see that he does represent a riot, an anarchy that, however charming its personification, must be legislated against. We must see that Henry could not have found a way to have made an exception for Falstaff. In short, we must perceive and feel as many ambiguities as possible—both to sense the fullness of the scene and to understand its turns of speech.

In *The Poetics,* Aristotle asks "what sorts of occurrences arouse dread or compassion in us," and responds that it is "when sufferings happen within friendly relationships" that this occurs. Just this kind of exquisite occasion is the ground upon which Henry composes his treatise.

And holding in mind as much of this pained balance as possible enables an audience to make sense, initially, of Henry's unwillingness to speak to Falstaff, and later to make sense of his shift from the first to the third person—bad writing even in the best of kingdoms. So allowing potent ambiguities in Henry's mind and heart permits us to understand that for him to let any of Falstaff's charm and appeal affect his argument would be to let all of him in, and to undermine the case altogether. For Henry to be Henry, Falstaff must be an abstraction, not a person. Whence the elliptical nature of his sentences, sentences that, though literally complete in themselves, fail to express all the writer knows. The writer knows what he means, he just doesn't include that knowledge on the page. The writer knows whom he is speaking to, he just doesn't give us a transition as he turns from one to another. He prevents us, intentionally, from knowing and from entering.

Falstaff represents a riot in the play and a riotous echo within Henry. He also embodies a happy part of Henry's youth. If Falstaff gains full entry, Henry becomes a Hal. In order to be a Henry, he must do without a Falstaff. "When thou dost hear I am as I have been," he says, "approach me, and thou shalt be as thou wast, the tutor and the feeder of my riots." But: "Till then, I banish thee."

This is the turning point of the speech, an explicit recognition on the king's part of what has been, but an acknowledgment in the shadow of "Presume not that I am the thing I was," which is the premise of the speech and which gave rise to Henry's unwillingness at first to speak to Falstaff. Assuredly, Henry has known before this moment that he will need literally and figuratively to rid himself of Falstaff, but now he is doing it, wrenchingly. So he alternates in his speech between a dream "of such a kind of man . . . so old, and so profane" to being awakened and despising the dream, to advising Falstaff on how to change himself. The transitions are not obviously weak, they are not the ravings of a sleepwalking Lady Macbeth, but they do suggest the difficulty Hal is having in moving toward that portion of the aria where he will banish his old friend—the struggle of the essayist who does not yet know where one sentence ends and where another should begin.

In his weakest sentence, Henry says, "Till then, I banish thee, on pain of death, as I have done the rest of my misleaders, not to come near our person by ten mile." This sentence fails (as students' sentences often do) because of the shift in person, a shift that derives from Henry's own movement away from his former self. He can make the change from singular to royal because he has moved from being Falstaff's heart to being Falstaff's monarch, because he is no longer his former self. A Hal could not take this action, this Henry must. A lesson in dramatic syntax, an example of bad work and its sources, this transformation has something to teach all students of writing.

The first student of this lesson is Falstaff, who soon after Henry has exited, emptily assures his cronies, "I shall be sent for in private to him . . . I shall be sent for soon at night." Who will send for Falstaff? Hal? Why does Falstaff not name him? Because he isn't sure it's true. Because he doubts it's true. Because he believes it won't happen. Because only with the last shred of his vanity and spirit can he speak words that include the possibility that it might be true. Because he doesn't know what to call him who will send. He had just called him "King Hal" and that name spoiled in the air. That name, he has been informed, is not anyone. It isn't who Hal used to be and it isn't who Henry now is. Falstaff drank and caroused with Hal, a ne'er-do-well of a prince who became a king by dint of natural talent and considerable effort and the recognition of whose child he was. And so who would be the subject of the sentence, were it to be spoken in the active voice, must be unclear. Falstaff doesn't know it, has never known it, and cannot recognize it now it comes before him. What a passive this is—and how it illuminates what the passive voice in its ordinary flat way can be. For with these words Shakespeare offers us a moment in a character's life when syntax and loss concur. This character cannot speak this sentence any other way. And speak he must, snubbed before his own court as he has been—and find an answer he must, as earlier he had tried to find a way to dress up his ragged clothing. He has to let these people know that this monarch is who Falstaff had told them he was, because unless Falstaff will be sent for, he himself cannot be who he must be, in order to continue. At so desperate a pass is he. At such a point. In that sense this passive is exactly what a passive should be: vague because agentless, and wholly necessary. (Ronald Reagan had a comparable problem in the first weeks after disclosures about the Iran-Contra affair, and his response was often to allow that "mistakes have been made," never creating a subject for a sentence for which he could not have created a subject and still remained president.)

The whirl and the meander of the mind at work, composing, scrutinizing, denying, blaming, confronting—this and more we experience in the pages of our essays when we write, and this we recognize in the dramatic characters set forth for us on stage, for whom we so willingly suspend our disbelief. If students are instructed to see an individual mind within a play of Shakespeare's (or any other playwright's) as, in its turmoil, resembling a turmoil they may know—as they write, as they read—and if they are helped to interpret that turmoil, to read it as an early draft that carries within it the germ of a fully formed essay, then perhaps it will be easier for them to grapple with the early drafts of their own compositions.

Our students deserve the chance to have worked very hard at reading and at writing, harder than they think they can work. They deserve to experience the illumination that a real rehearsal—a real revision—offers. So look again at a dialogue you love and see if there aren't rough drafts in it, to be explicated, harrowed, reseen. Take a look at an essay you love and open up its drama. Play it back and forth, as you do when you write, or read. Let plays—rough drafts in the best sense of those words—instruct our reading of all pages.

Pat C. Hoy II

🐦 *Shaping Experience, Creating Essays**

Annie Dillard says that the "writer of any work, and particularly any nonfiction work, must decide two crucial points: what to put in and what to leave out" (*Inventing*, 55). Dillard is right, but there is another problem, perhaps a more complex problem for student writers: how to shape the experiences that go into the text, how to turn the raw material of everyday life into useful evidence. Dillard calls the whole process fashioning a text. My mother might have called it lying. I'm going to call it fictional truth-telling and investigate its nature. It's all a matter of learning to tell truth, I think, a matter of learning that personal (familiar, exploratory) essays depend on the imaginative reconstruction of experience to make their *ideas* come to life. Such reconstruction turns *images of experience* into the impersonal stuff from which good essays are made.

Telling my version of the truth to my mother never seemed very complicated. Challenged about staying out too late or driving the car too fast, I could always tell a fairly good story about what had happened. I did it quite naturally, prepared my defense in my head even as I talked (I had, of course, mulled my case over before coming through the sleeping porch door), yet I never thought once about rhetorical strategies, or beginnings, middles, and endings, or any of those other notions my high school English teacher might have been trying to drum into my head. I told a pretty good

---

* Some of the material contained herein will be included in a forthcoming book entitled *Reading and Writing Essays* to be published by McGraw-Hill.

story to my Mom because I knew I had to make sense; someone who cared was listening, and I had to keep straight in my head, as I went along, what I wanted her to understand.

I know now that I was recreating experience every time I told one of those stories. I know now that I shaped experience: I didn't tell her everything that had happened on the night I was late, and I didn't fabricate events (I was, after all, involved in truth-telling). I certainly didn't render a step-by-step, minute-by-minute account of a fair summer evening. I was not a reporter. I was a walking, talking essayist. I told her enough to make my case for lateness reasonable, interesting, and persuasive. I wanted to get past her sleeping porch into my own bedroom; I had music to listen to, a phone call to make, a letter to write. I didn't want to spend any more time than necessary shifting from foot to foot as I led her to see things my way.

Telling those stories while I was growing up, I learned something about artful persuasion. I learned that telling too much of the story could lead me astray, even get me in hot water. I learned that my mom was impatient with too much detail that delayed my getting to the point of my story, to the explanation for my lateness. In short, I learned not so much what would sell but how to sell it.

Thinking back on those occasions when I was recreating my own experiences for my mom's edification and for my defense, I think about how difficult it is to get students in a composition classroom to recreate their experiences and put them to good use. Students today are certainly no less adept at story telling than I was, but when I ask them to write an essay about something they believe in, I ask them to become *conscious* of a process that's as old as language itself; I ask them to step outside their experience and make sense of it . . . in writing. I ask them to become conscious. Becoming conscious, they begin to look for something complicated, fretting and straining for the grandiose and hyperbolic, forgetting that the language of everyday can satisfy whatever requirement I devise. They forget that telling the truth in an interesting and persuasive way can be no more complicated, in the long run, than telling a good story.

Joan Didion begins her essay "The White Album" with these words: "We tell ourselves stories in order to live." She ends her opening paragraph with a clarification that links storytelling, writing, and living: "We live entirely, if we are writers, by the imposition of a narrative line upon disparate images, by the 'ideas' with which we have learned to freeze the shifting phantasmagoria which is our actual experience" (11). When Didion writes about imposing "a narrative line upon disparate images," when she writes about freezing "the shifting phantasmagoria which is our actual experience," she suggests that life appears to us as a disordered array of images; meaning does not spring into our lives ready made. Things happen in seemingly random fashion; we remember—store in memory—certain of these events. We store them as images or pictures. When we try to make sense of our lives by writing, we impose order on the pictures, arrange them for a particular rhetorical purpose. We stop the moving picture show—the shifting phantasmagoria—to make meaning.

But writing even the simplest narrative involves more than freezing images. First there is selection, then reconstruction. Both processes involve memory, the recovery of something already experienced. We can't always recover experience in a way that would satisfy the logician or the scientific investigator. But we need not. Familiar essayists work under more flexible laws than logicians; they have more latitude. Didion tells us that in her notebook, where she tries to keep track of some of the things that happen to her or around her, she doesn't "try to have an actual factual record of what she's been doing or thinking" (*Slouching*, 133). Instead, she records *"how it felt to me."* Other accounts of the same event may differ from Didion's; other observers may remember in an entirely different way. So be it.

When I ask my students to "freeze the shifting phantasmagoria" of their actual experience and impose order on it, find an idea in it, they discover very quickly that they cannot tell everything. They face every writer's problem: what to put in, what to leave out. How to fashion a written text. How to order experience, how to shape it, how to describe it, how to narrate, how to tell the story, how to present the idea. Inevitably students learn that a mere record of facts will not suffice. Readers expect illuminated moments, moments remembered, reconstructed, made interesting. They expect something coherent.

——— *Counterpoint* ———

The complexity involved in the ordering of experience belies the claim of those composition theorists who dismiss personal essays because they are merely *expressive*. Every time students write essays of any kind, they have to deal with personal feelings, their honest, spontaneous response to an idea (expressive), just as they have to deal with the recursive, never-ending, mindful reflection about those feelings and their experiences (cognitive), and with the classroom audience—or any other audience—who represent a fairly complex discourse community (social). We teachers-turned-theorists have become, perhaps, unnecessarily Aristotelian, so bent on classification and distinction that we are no longer able to comprehend the whole complex writing process because we have created so many fragmented ways of looking at it.

Reactions against the personal essay are often very personal. I had the frustrating pleasure of participating in an unusual conference where a colleague objected loudly and often about the so-called personal essay. He kept associating such essays, whether they were written by Montaigne or Joan Didion, with what he called a "cult of sensibility." He objected to such essays in a college composition course because, in his view, they do little to prepare students for the kind of academic writing required within a university.

The discussion leader had been tracing the evolution of the personal essay, showing how philosophy and rhetoric, exploration and persuasion had manifested themselves in Montaigne's imagination and in his essays. The speaker had begun to move past Montaigne, considering later essayists—Addison, Steele, Lamb, Arnold, Pater, White—but the interruptions from my disgruntled colleague occurred so frequently he could not finish his presentation. Those of us interested in the personal essay, those of us willing to defend it, were generally ineffectual in that charged environment.

As the meeting began to break up, I tried one last time to make my colleague see how such an essay might teach students a few of the most important aspects of a liberal education. I had in mind Discourse VII from *The Idea of a University*, where Cardinal Newman argues that "it is not mere application, however exemplary, which introduces the mind to truth, nor the reading many books, nor the getting up many subjects, nor the witnessing many experiments, nor the attending many lectures. All this is short of enough; a man may have done it all, yet be lingering in the vestibule of knowledge:—he may not realize what his mouth utters; he may not see with his mental eye what confronts him; he may have no grasp of things as they are . . . no power of discriminating between truth and falsehood, of sifting out the grains of truth from the mass, of arranging things according to their real value, and, if I may use the phrase, of building up ideas" (134). I wished I had been able that afternoon to quote Newman to strengthen my case for the personal essay. But alas, I had not.

"You had better be careful when you try to teach students to think," my colleague said as I concluded my plea for making the personal essay an important first step in a freshman composition course. "You had better be careful," he continued, "because when you try to teach students to think, *you* are probably trying to teach them how to feel."

Close, I thought, as I walked away, but not close enough. Teaching students to feel is beyond my purview; teaching them to consider their feelings and their experiences, a most important part of my charter. I want them to recognize how feelings point toward values, toward judgment.

I wished that I had summoned Pater during that exchange about the essay, wished that I had been able to cite the crucial passage from the Preface to *The Renaissance* where Pater corrects Arnold: "the first step towards seeing one's object as it really is, is to know one's own impression as it really is, to discriminate it, to realise it distinctly. . . . Our education becomes complete in proportion as our susceptibility to these impressions increases in depth and variety. And the function of the aesthetic critic is to distinguish, to analyse, and separate from its adjuncts, the virtue by which a picture, a landscape, a fair personality in life or in a book, produces this special impression of beauty or pleasure, to indicate what the source of that impression is, and under what conditions it is experienced. [The critic's] end is reached when he has disengaged that virtue, and noted it, as a chemist notes some natural element, for himself and others" (xix-xxi). I had said none of these things, and it was just as well, I suppose. For what I wanted to say was much more to the point and less theoretical. I wanted to make a case for beginning my composition course with a personal essay.

I wanted to enlarge my antagonist's sense of the personal essay, wanted to show him that the merely personal in the hands of a good writer transcends the bounds of a single life. I wanted to make him see that teaching students to transform experience into evidence and evidence into essay, we teach them the basis for all coherent writing whatever its purpose.

––––––––– *Practical, Theoretical Musings* –––––––––

Students usually come to my courses without a fundamental sense of their own values, without a clear understanding that all essays require personal judgments. They come confused about how ideas take shape out of experience. What they do not usually know how to do is *reflect*. They do not know how to "sift out the grains of truth from the mass"; they do not know how "to distinguish, to analyse, and separate from its adjuncts" their reaction to an object, whether that object be a book, a painting, a person, or their own experience. I find that if I can get them to separate themselves from their own experiences—to reflect on themselves, to create an "I" in their texts who is different from the writer creating the texts—if I can do that at the beginning of a composition sequence, everything else falls into place, more or less naturally. Students will never again be so naive as to believe that they have disappeared from even their most objective texts or that the "I" in their most personal essay actually accounts for the many other "I's" they could have created but didn't.

We begin always with *images of experience* so students can see that their lives provide rich sources of evidence they can shape and use to capture their readers' attention. Learning to use their own lives as evidence, they also learn how experience shapes ideas and influences judgment. As they modify their views through reading and research, students begin to understand how their own education influences their writing—what they say, how they say it, how they select appropriate forms to express what they know.

The most intriguing thing about the exploratory essay is its deceptive simplicity; students sense right away that they can write one, and they enter into the act of writing unaware of that particular essay's inherent complexity. They begin writing without being inhibited by the formality of argument. Because they produce texts they care about, texts they want to improve, they listen more attentively to suggestions for improvement. Those suggestions and their own subsequent revisions expose them to the limitless ways in which their work can be improved, the limitless ways in which writers make their essays cohere. They learn willingly about form.

Over time they learn about the exploratory essay's inherent complexity. They learn through experiment how to write scenes, how to write dialogue, how to create stunning images, how to create a persona—but they learn much more. They learn to turn those literary techniques to the end of persuasion. Through reading, through collaborative sessions, through experimentation, they learn the craft of writing.

As students move from the apparent informality of exploration to tighter, more formal analytical and argumentative essays, they move with a better sense of possibilities, with a surer sense of their ability to use language on their own terms and with a better sense of their minds' ability to shape evidence, draw conclusions, and persuade an audience. They move too with a better sense of their own values, and they begin to see how value judgments form the basis of all that they write. Those judgments lead to ideas; ideas make essays cohere. The personal, exploratory essay provides a natural beginning, one that leads students away from solipsism and the cult of personality as energetically as it leads them away from the cult of objectivity. It leads to discovery.

Informing this whole notion of composition is the lesson it took T. S. Eliot 40 years to learn. In 1919 when he called for the "extinction of personality," Eliot saw the writer as a "medium and not a personality," his mind a "shred of platinum," a catalyst separate from the "man who suffers" (*Prose*, 40–42). Two decades later he enlarged this flawed view. When he wrote about Yeats in 1940, he began to see more clearly a quality that distinguishes all good writing. Reading Yeats, Eliot discovered "a unique personality which makes one sit up in excitement and eagerness to learn more about the author's mind and feelings." And in the face of that evidence, he tried to 'uncontradict' himself: "There are two forms of impersonality . . . The second impersonality is that of the poet who, out of intense and personal experience, is able to express a general truth; retaining all the particularity of his experience, to make of it a general symbol" (251). Eliot finally acknowledged that the great poet is indeed present in his poem. So is the essayist always present in the essay, no matter what its form.

Scott Sanders, a fine essayist and a teacher of composition, puts it this way: "I choose to write about my experience not because it is mine, but because it seems to me a door through which others might pass" (*Sewanee*, 667). Sanders sees the personal essay as a "weighing out, an inquiry into value, meaning, and the true nature of experience; it is a private experiment carried out in public" (665). He also issues a warning about the essayist's responsibility: "You cannot stand back from the action, as Joyce instructed us to do, and pare your fingernails. You cannot palm off your cockamamy notions on some hapless character. If the words you put down are foolish, everyone knows precisely who the fool is" (661). In short, Eliot and Sanders remind us that our relationships to the texts we create are complex, that we can be in the text and out of it at the same time, that appearance is followed by disappearance and disappearance by appearance. It's all mighty complex business, and we need not—in fact we ought not—clutter our students' minds with these theoretical notions that give us courage to walk into our classrooms and experiment with *their* minds. But we should be pretty clear in our own minds what we're up to and why. We need to know that when we teach students to write personal essays, we're not teaching them to write unreflective, expressive accounts of experience.

Because students have all had such marvelous experiences before they come to college, because they have traces of those experiences stored in their memories, because they do not have to go to the library to retrieve those experiences, and because those experiences (if we can get them to the right ones) usually lead students to claim ownership of the texts they create out of them, I challenge students on the first day of class to begin to see themselves more clearly. I ask that they get inside their memory and try to get down on paper an *image of experience,* some picture of an event that was for them profound, something powerful enough to have lasted, something lingering there in memory waiting to be reconstructed.

What I get, of course, are usually simple but interesting narratives, and because as one of my friends says, "We come into the world coded for story telling," I get narratives that are relatively clean and free of garbled syntax. If they are not, I know that I have a serious problem on my hands. Students know, people know, how to tell stories without our telling them how. We come coded with an inherent sense of order. And we learn through experience, as I learned with my Mom, to improve our story telling. Our stories have beginnings, middles, and ends whether or not someone prescribes them. But when students try to turn experience to the service of the essay—when they begin to have to reshape those stories and reflect on them—they cry out for help. Naive as they are about the writer's "I," students need help discovering that their story, their image of experience, is full of ideas. Discovering within the image an idea worthy of an essay, discovering how to reshape their original account of experience and put it to the service of the idea, discovering that other stories, other images will cluster naturally around the selected idea, and that those other stories can be brought together to create an essay—those are tasks that demand collaboration. Those are the tasks we teachers ought to be good at. Over time, with our help and then with the help of peers, students learn that personal narratives shaped and woven together turn into essays . . . essays that transcend the merely personal.

——— *Other Essayists, Our Fellow-Collaborators* ———

Much of what we need to know to help our students we can learn from professional essayists. We can learn directly when those writers actually write about writing, as we have already learned in this discussion from

Didion and Sanders. And we can learn indirectly from studying their other essays, mining those essays for techniques that help all writers turn raw experience into persuasive evidence.

Russell Baker tells us that after writing his autobiography, *Growing Up*, he waited for more than a month for his editor to call and shower him with praise. "Eventually," Baker says, "I began to sense that there was something wrong, and one night I took [the book] out of the drawer and sat down in my office and started to read. I nodded off on about page 20." With the help of his editor, Baker got to the heart of the problem:

> I had given Tom this manuscript of faithfully reported history of what people remembered of the '20s and '30s, and in it I had written what I thought was a good chapter about my Uncle Harold. It's the one that begins: "Uncle Harold was famous for lying." And I knew that was a good chapter because I "got" Uncle Harold—I turned him into a character. I hadn't reported him; I made him the man whose memory lived inside me. At some point in the book I made a conclusion about him: I said that Uncle Harold, an uneducated and an unread man, was famous for being a great liar. But he wasn't really a liar; he just wanted life to be more interesting than it was . . . I said that in his primitive way Uncle Harold had perceived that the possibilities of achieving art lie not in reporting, but in fiction. And Tom Congdon sent that page back to me underlined in red, and he wrote on it, "I honor Uncle Harold." (*Inventing*, 44)

The possibilities of achieving art lie not in reporting but in fiction. That seems like a lesson worth learning. Baker is not encouraging us to lie; he is simply instructing us about the nature of artful writing. When asked how much of his book was truthful, Baker replied, "Well, all of the incidents are truthful. A book like that has certain things in common with fiction. . . . but the incidents that *are* in the book, of course they happened" (49). In other words, we must "fashion" the texts we create; they do not spring out of our heads or out of experience readymade.

I want to examine a scene from an essay of mine so that I can discuss the experience of writing that scene and highlight some of the decisions I had to make about what to put in, what to leave out of it. The scene is from an essay called "Mosaics of Southern Masculinity," an essay in which I try to come to terms with my own masculinity and with my father, who was essentially absent from my life. Writing this essay at age 49, I wanted to try to figure out some of the ways in which my father had been influential even though he was never around to influence me. He left home when I was five. Right before this crucial scene, I've been having fun in the essay tracing in my life genetic remnants I inherited from my father—the way I make my 5s starting from the bottom up and the way I like driving fast cars.

When I began to write this particular scene, I wanted to show my readers how my father appeared in my imagination one night as I walked into a honky-tonk outside Fort Leonard Wood, Missouri. I had never been in a place like that in my life, but when I went there with two fellow Army officers, I knew almost immediately that I was under my father's spell, that I was in his world. My task then was to recreate the scene more than a year after I experienced it and to recreate it so that it would serve my rhetorical purposes in the essay. I had nothing to go on but my memory. I remembered only how it felt to me at the time. Here is the scene itself, as I recreated it:

> The club across the street from the restaurant was small and close, but it felt friendly when we walked in in our khakis, polo shirts, and docksiders. The Missouri cowboys paid no attention, but the waitress seemed amused when she brought the beers. A Willie Nelson number drew couples out into the hazy space of the dance floor where refracting lights played softly around cowboy hats and occasionally found a patch of sequined hair. A strapping, lithe woman and her little man caught my eye. They were feeling their way around the floor, lost in the rhythms of those "lonely, lonely times."
>
> Before I knew it, one of my buddies was on the floor, cutting in. The little man went back to his table, sat down, and tilted his hat forward just a bit. He sat with his back to us, but I could see him hook the heels of his boots over the bottom rung of the chair, slightly defiant.
>
> The woman seemed unaware that she had changed partners. When she went back to the table, her man continued to stare at the door.
>
> The vocalist didn't sound much like Anne Murray, but when she launched into "Son of a Rotten Gambler," I knew I couldn't sit there drinking beer any longer. I walked over to the strapping woman and asked her if she'd like to dance.
>
> Reaching for my hand, she said, "I'd really like to, but I can't."
>
> I asked her why not.
>
> "He doesn't want me to dance with anyone else."
>
> I looked over at him, sitting there immobilized, still staring at the front door. He might not have moved for three songs. They hadn't danced again. So I moved between them.
>
> "Would you mind if I danced with your friend?" I asked, feeling my way into the protocol.
>
> He didn't move his eyes.
>
> "Look," I said pulling up a stool from the table behind us, "I'm not after your woman. I just want to dance this song with her."
>
> He cleared his throat but kept up his business with the door.
>
> She reached up and put her hand on my arm, pulling me down in her direction as she said, "I'm sorry. I really would like to dance, but I can't do it tonight."
>
> I made it back to our table as the singer slid into the last stanza. "He'd be the son of his father, / His father the teacher." But the teacher wasn't there to ask. I wondered what he would have done, wondered what the honky-tonk rules called for?

What to put in. As I began to create this scene, I realized that I wanted to do no more than hint about my father. I did not want to declare straight out what was going on in my head when I walked in the honky-tonk. I wanted to draw the reader into the scene. I also wanted my own uneasiness to show, my ignorance about the unwritten protocol of the place. I wanted to suggest that we three army officers were a little out of place.

What to leave out. I chose to leave out conversations that I had with my friends, a conversation that one of my friends had with the waitress, our frequent trips to the bathroom after several beers, how we were isolated even in the middle of a very small place. I was not obligated to report everything that had happened. I needed to use only what would serve my purpose in the essay.

What to create. When I sat down to write, I could not remember the music that was playing while I was in the honky-tonk, but I could remember songs that I had been listening to for years that reminded me of the honky-tonk itself and also reminded me of what I imagined my father might have been like. I decided to use Willy Nelson's "Always On My Mind," without naming it. The knowing reader would have an added bonus, recognizing "lonely, lonely times." Willy Nelson would be the right singer for the place, and I didn't want to clutter the scene with the title of two songs. So I used Nelson for ambience, for authenticity. The title of the second song was much more important ("Son of a Rotten Gambler"); I wanted to use it to hint at a relationship between me and my Dad. The words were even more important for what I was trying to make the scene say for me: "He'd be the son of his father, / His father the teacher." The point was, of course, that my father had not been the teacher, yet I felt his presence in that place. He came back to me, and I wondered what he would have been doing. I selected those songs out of a different place and time, but I used them for very specific rhetorical purposes. They were right for the scene. I engaged in a bit of fictive truth-telling.

Beyond those immediate concerns that I have already expressed about the scene, I wanted to begin to enlarge my readers' notions about masculinity. To that end, I decided to frame this scene, attaching material to the beginning and to the end to make my presentation a bit richer. Following a paragraph that explained how I happened to be in Missouri with two friends, I added a paragraph about the *anima*, the woman, according to Carl Jung, that every man has in his head. What I say in that paragraph actually happened during the summer when I was traveling with my fellow officers. At the end of the scene I added another short clip from my memory bank that goes back to Jung's *anima*, reinforcing an idea that I touch on throughout the essay. Here is the entire section minus the first descriptive paragraph about coming to Missouri:

> Our favorite pastime during the previous summer had been a Jungian game. We tried to second-guess each other's taste in women, tried to guess the nature of the woman in the other man's head. It was a game of images. We tried to predict "grid overlap," guessing when the woman in the classroom or the airport or on the plane would match the imagined woman in one of our buddy's heads. We joked about "anima seizures": spellbinding image overlap. The game was an older man's contribution to the summer fun.
>
> The club across the street from the restaurant was small and close, but it felt friendly when we walked in in our khakis, polo shirts, and docksiders. The

Missouri cowboys paid no attention, but the waitress seemed amused when she brought the beers. A Willie Nelson number drew couples out into the hazy space of the dance floor where refracting lights played softly around cowboy hats and occasionally found a patch of sequined hair. A strapping, lithe woman and her little man caught my eye. They were feeling their way around the floor, lost in the rhythms of those "lonely, lonely times."

Before I knew it, one of my buddies was on the floor, cutting in. The little man went back to his table, sat down, and tilted his hat forward just a bit. He sat with his back to us, but I could see him hook the heels of his boots over the bottom rung of the chair, slightly defiant.

The woman seemed unaware that she had changed partners. When she went back to the table, her man continued to stare at the door.

The vocalist didn't sound much like Anne Murray, but when she launched into "Son of a Rotten Gambler," I knew I couldn't sit there drinking beer any longer. I walked over to the strapping woman and asked her if she'd like to dance.

Reaching for my hand, she said, "I'd really like to, but I can't."

I asked her why not.

"He doesn't want me to dance with anyone else."

I looked over at him, sitting there immobilized, still staring at the front door. He might not have moved for three songs. They hadn't danced again. So I moved between them.

"Would you mind if I danced with your friend?" I asked, feeling my way into the protocol.

He didn't move his eyes.

"Look," I said pulling up a stool from the table behind us, "I'm not after your woman. I just want to dance this song with her."

He cleared his throat but kept up his business with the door.

She reached up and put her hand on my arm, pulling me down in her direction as she said, "I'm sorry. I really would like to dance, but I can't do it tonight."

I made it back to our table as the singer slid into the last stanza. "He'd be the son of his father, / His father the teacher." But the teacher wasn't there to ask. I wondered what he would have done, wondered what the honky-tonk rules called for?

I remember his stopping by our house late one afternoon when I was about 13; he was on the way out of town, on the move as usual. I could smell vodka over Dentyne. Mom asked him where he was headed.

"Juking."

"Where to?"

"Chula."

I didn't know where Chula was, but I guessed it was the Howdy Club in El Dorado, miles away over the dump, a long stretch of suspended roadway surrounded on both sides by the Ouachita River. I expected him to die there. But in those days, his life seemed charmed. Chula, I now suspect was Xanadu. It was there he had built his "dome of pleasure," there he had "drunk the milk of Paradise." And perhaps, like me, as he listened to the "woman wailing," he "heard from far / Ancestral voices." I felt close to him that night in Missouri, very close, felt him in my bones again. And I felt too a painful advantage. He didn't have the wherewithal to distinguish the woman in his head from the one outside. Seizures carried him through life, and when the charms wore out, his liver couldn't carry the load.

The next morning at the post exchange, I saw the strapping woman. The image had dissipated; it couldn't hold up under the light of day. But she held up quite well. She apologized again, said her man had had a hard day, said he wasn't usually like that, said he was a good man. She thanked me for letting them be the night before. I liked her, liked my Dad. I think he would have left the cowboy alone too. He was good at that, leaving people alone. Until that morning, it had never seemed a virtue.

The selecting, shaping, and fictive truth-telling I did to create that section of my essay is typical of what every essayist must do to "fashion" a scene or tell a story that is to serve some rhetorical purpose. Often the task is more complicated and the technique more complex. But the basic writing tasks are always the same: what to put in; what to leave out; what to create; how to weave it all together to serve the essay's ideas.

──────── *The Classroom: Images and Embedded Possibilities* ────────

How then to proceed in the classroom, how to help students learn to fashion their texts? Confident that we are trying to teach students to shape experience even as they fashion their texts, we need also to be mindful of the immense potential of those *images of experience* that we ask them to recreate in words. Asking for *images*, we ask for something different from first-person accounts of a particular experience: the summer trip, the first day of school or camp, a visit to a museum or art gallery. Asking for something that differs from a report of what happened, we actually free students from the traditional task of writing first-person, linear narratives (that usually remain lifeless), and ask instead that they create an image of experience, ask for a rendering of some powerful moment from their past. The student's initial task is to recreate the moment in such a way that readers can experience its power. The traditional task restricts; the imaginal task liberates.

In an essay called "Why I Write," Joan Didion theorizies about images that "shimmer." In that particular essay, she's writing about fiction, but the same principles apply to nonfiction. Shimmering images are the good ones, the ones worth writing about. They have life in them; they have energy. She even claims that they contain a "grammar" of their own, an inherent form that helps the writer record the story contained in the image (2, 98). Like Didion, Loren Eiseley insists that the writer does not have to impose a story on these pictures; the story is in the picture, waiting for the writer to discover it, to turn it into words; the "story already lies there" waiting to be retrieved (*Strange Hours*, 155).

Toni Morrison says that when she begins to think about certain people, "the images that float around them . . . surface so vividly and so compellingly that [she acknowledges] them as [her] route to a reconstruction of a world, to an exploration of an interior life that was not written and to the revelation of a kind of truth." These images may be as "ineffable and as flexible as a dimly recalled figure, the corner of a room, a voice." In her own writing, Morrison says that she moves "from picture to meaning to text" (*Inventing*, 115–17); essayists do the same thing; they move imaginatively from experience to essay.

Didion's pictorial grammar, Eiseley's pictures, and Morrison's floating images are of a psychological piece, and they point to a psychological truism: image and idea are one. James Hillman, the archetypal psychologist, agrees with Jung that "nothing can be known unless it first appears as a psychic image." Becoming conscious means becoming aware of images, becoming aware of their inherent poetic possibilities. Consciousness, Hillman argues, "refers to a process more to do with images than with will, with reflection rather than control, with reflective insight into, rather than manipulation of, 'objective reality' " (*Anima*, 93–94). In other words, we perceive the world through images, but we do not create the images; they create us. They have a life of their own. They operate like the "original meaning of idea (from Greek *eidos* and *eidolon*): not only 'that which' one sees but that 'by means of which' one sees" (*Archetypal*, 12). As Didion and Eiseley suggest, what we are looking for is in the image, in the picture, already. Our task as writers is to discover it, to let our imaginations work on the image. Images come to us encoded, and we have to get to know them imaginatively. Moving through image to idea, we move beyond the merely personal to a text that is both personal and universal at the same time, something like Eliot discovered in Yeats.

Let me reiterate the basic notion: images contain ideas; images are ideas. Hillman makes it quite clear that "image-work restores the original poetic sense to images, freeing them from serving a narrational context, having to tell a story with its linear, sequential, and causal implications that foster first-person reports" (*Archetypal*, 15). What Hillman's claim leads to is a new, fresh approach to writing, if we are writers, and to a new, fresh approach to teaching composition, if we are teachers.

Keeping Morrison's process and Hillman's notions in mind, let's see just how we might move from picture to meaning to text in our classrooms. The student writers we will consider knew about Didion, Eiseley, and Morrison. They had talked briefly in class about images and the reconstruction of experience. The first student was asked to recall two moments from past experience: his earliest and his most profound. Here are his two short responses:

> Standing in a classroom learning to skip is as far as my memory reaches. The room was oddly shaped not resembling the typical rectangular shape of most classrooms. A large white circle took up a major portion of the room. I stood with my classmates around this circle and learned how to skip. We went around and around this circle many times. I skipped home because I was so proud of myself for learning this new mode of travel.
>
> My sister and I walked to school together very often at my early age of 7.

This one day she must have learned the art of getting dizzy and decided to test this newly learned trick on me. She started to twirl me around and around in front of the neighbors house. I began to laugh and told her to stop, but her desire to see what would happen over came her. She laughed then lost control of me, and I had lost control of me long before she did. I fell and hit my head on the curb which didn't take half the damage I did. I didn't get stitches but I did get a headache.

After this student read these pieces in class, he saw no relationship between them, saw no poetic possibilities, saw no way to connect them. His task was to try to discover the ideas embedded in the images. As it turned out, he was comfortable reporting his experience—telling his story—but uncomfortable thinking about ideas. But after interesting discussions about his pieces and others among members of the class, he wrote a coherent essay, exploring the idea that "practice is the most important part of learning." That essay developed out of his two fragments of memory, but he made direct use of neither as evidence; here is a revealing paragraph from his essay:

The hardest part of learning is practicing. I am a kayaker, and one of the most [pleasant]—and most dangerous—things about kayaking is the eskimo roll. The eskimo roll is an exercise where you flip upside down under water and then roll back up while in your kayak. The first time I did this roll, I saw my life flash before my eyes as water filled my nostrils. Even though I was scared to do it, I practiced more and more until I mastered the eskimo roll. My cousin knew this and took me to a whitewater river where we dedicated a whole day to whitewater kayaking. I flipped over once and easily flipped back up because I had practiced so much.

This paragraph about kayaking was the final one in the middle of an essay that focused on the relationship between practice and learning. The writing exercise showed him that his early image-work could lead to an idea and to other moments in his personal life that he could bring out of memory into his essay. The circular images—the skipping and the spinning—led him to the eskimo roll, that other, related experience. Retrieving that incident, he began to use his imagination to explore and order experience. He also began to have fun with ideas and to discover their sources.

This student taught me a valuable lesson about restraint. When he read his two pieces in the classroom, my imagination began to play with the notion of disorientation and recovery. Twice this student had gotten excited about being disoriented, and his images made me think about how pleased I am on occasion when I find my way out of chaotic situations. I began to rummage around in my "attic" full of experiences. My mind turned naturally to writing, to the experience of sitting before a blank page of paper, all my experiences whirling in my head and no sense of order; my mind turned too to Vietnam where I had spent a year of my life; I remembered moving a small artillery unit, the disorientating chaos of helicopters coming in to pick up loads of equipment that men had prepared; I remembered the turbulence of one of those days when we kept loading supplies in nets and the helicopters kept coming until finally we were all on the ground somewhere else, organized, dug in, and safe; my mind turned too to my own office, which at that moment was a chaotic mess—a room full of books, stacks of papers grouped according to various projects I was working on, an over-flowing trash can, my haphazardly arranged bulletin board: all of it a picture of delirium to an outsider but a sanctuary to me, a place where I like to discover order in the midst of chaos. I had fun thinking about these images and the idea of pleasurable disorientation, and I know even now that it would be fun to explore that notion in a essay of my own. But had I tried to impose that notion on my student, he would have made no discoveries of his own; he would never have exercised his imagination. And he would have come to me repeatedly to find out what I wanted him to say.

On the other hand, I have found that students who reconstruct won-derful moments from memory (and initially see no ideas embedded in them) often benefit from hearing other students react to those reconstructed moments. Listening to others reflect about their images, they begin to see what was at first hidden, begin to understand their own experiences, even begin to see how such moments might be reshaped to clarify an embedded idea. The sequence for turning images of experience into essays is fairly complex: first the writer recalls the moment and reconstructs it, then the reconstructed moment yields an idea, then the account must be reshaped and put to the service of the discovered idea. The process is recursive as well as linear, and too often we encourage expressive narratives but do not go on to encourage reflection and reconstruction. We do not go on to teach students how to turn those early texts into essays—how to discover, formu-late, and defend ideas.

An idea differs from a thesis in important ways. A thesis suits the argumentative essay: "Water pollution in Albany must be brought under control" or "Final examinations should be abolished" or "Abortion laws in New York state are unfair." There is something about these judgments that calls for "proof"; they demand something akin to a hearing in court, some-thing reasonable, direct, and persuasive; they lean in the direction of scien-tific certitude.

An idea, on the other hand, is more akin to exploration, to inquiry. An idea is more supple, more seductive than a thesis; it cannot so easily be reduced to a single declarative assertion that begs for logical proof. Ideas are at the very heart of the personal, exploratory essay. It goes against the very nature of one of these essays to reduce its gist to a single sentence. Ideas in the hands of a skillful essayist gain appeal and power through piecemeal and accumulation.

These opening and closing paragraphs from a student essay called "Lucky Icarus" give us a sense of the suppleness of a good idea; the body of this essay consists of an artful presentation of what happened to young

Icarus when he momentarily threw caution to the wind and soared beyond his ability to control his destiny; these two paragraphs frame the story of Jadran Lee's exploits:

> The snow had been growing wet and heavy in the warm sunshine of the past week. From the ascending cable car I saw that at lower altitudes the melt had exposed patches of damp earth and strawlike grass. Spring was climbing out of the valley. All week I had taken no risks, always skiing or surfing with at least one friend, but today I was alone. I felt that winter's end called for memorable bravado. Although I could not ride a snowboard exceptionally well, I was helplessly addicted to the sensate rush one feels when tearing down a powdery slope on this modern relative of the ski.

> ————————

> Surfing into the valley was easy enough after that. Rather more difficult was the task of coming to grips with my experience. I ordered a beer at a café and sat down to think. Would my little tryst with fear mean that I would never again be afraid of dying? Clearly not, for I was shivering. I could no more rationalize away the innate dread of death than I could become blind to the redness which affrights in the blood. Perhaps people who face danger daily, like soldiers, completely lose their fear of death, as paramedics learn to master their inborn aversion to gore; but I had not seen nearly enough to count myself so brave. Yet I was less afraid of death now than I had ever been. Some of the awful mystery of dying was gone: I now had an inkling of what it must be like to face imminent death; I now had some reason to hope that I might greet my passing with dignity. I was frightened, but my fear was the quieter and more reasoned fear of one who has come to know himself better.

We cannot find in these two fine paragraphs anything that resembles a thesis; there is no declaration of truth. Nevertheless, the paragraphs are enticing; they make us want to read the entire essay. We want to know what happened to young Icarus; we want to know what made him so meditative about his brush with death. We want to know what actually happened, how he handled the catastrophe, whatever it may have been.

It is clear from these two paragraphs that he has had an experience that has shaken him to his foundations; he knows now what it's like to reckon with death, what it's like to face it and move past it. And while our young hero has moved past it, he has moved respectfully, learning something in the process about himself. He adds depth to his story with these two sentences, near the middle of his account: "I was a lucky Icarus. A clear pocket in the cloud enabled me to see the three-meter dropoff just as I came upon it." That allusion to Icarus puts his story in the context of an older story, suggests a mythic dimension that makes his story our story. We're all prone to get our egos inflated on occasion and try to fly too high. This is the old story of derring-do. Yet this is not any Icarus we're reading about; this is a "lucky Icarus," lucky because he came to his senses there in the face of death. We had a choice and in making that choice learned something about fear and recovery. He became conscious in the face of death.

Jadran begins his essay by mere suggestion, by setting us up for a bit of "memorable bravado," by letting us into his frame of mind as he rides the cable car to the top of the mountain for an excursion on his snowboard. As he develops his essay, we watch the bravado turn to fear, and then resolve; we watch him respond to his luck, watch him move crablike down the mountain to recover his snowboard from a crevasse, watch him survive. But we also watch his meditative, reflecting mind play over the experience even as he recreates it for our edification.

By the time we consider his ending, that final meditation (second paragraph, above), we can see that there is *distance* between Jadran Lee the writer of the essay, and that young Icarus (a more daring, a more naive Jadran) who is the essay's focal point. In the time interval between the experience and the writing—or more precisely, between his initial reconstruction of that image of experience and the revision that created an essay, an idea evolved. The older Jadran began to reflect on the younger Jadran; that reflection let the older writer make sense of an experience. Jadran makes his idea more enticing and seductive by the way he explores his own reaction to his younger self. The idea—Jadran's judgment about death—doesn't call for proof; it asks instead for that hearing on the front porch in a rocking chair. The idea wants only a receptive mind, an unhurried reader (listener) who has time to let the idea evolve by piecemeal and accumulation at a fairly leisurely pace.

Jadran Lee's essay develops around a single experience; at it's core is a single, central image of experience. The idea Jadran found in that image was about death, about facing it, learning to respect it, moving past it, respectfully. The idea is bound to a reflective self that is recollecting experience, thinking about that experience, creating meaning out of it.

Personal essays, of course, need not be limited to a single recollected event. I want to turn now to a more complex essay, one that works in a different way. We will consider this essay in its entirety and look at its evolution from start to finish. We will trace it "from picture to meaning to text"—from images of experience to essay.

The initial requirement asked students to retrieve "an embedded moment from memory." China Forbes wrote a short narrative about her sister's going to school while she had to stay at home. Here is the beginning of her narrative account:

Bus Stop

In the summer I was naked, stumbling over cold flat stones, and cool, dew-laced grass until I tumbled giggling into my mother's arms. On the patio, she sat with a book, sheltered by the weave of wisteria that perfumed the air. With the book left open, face down on the flat white table that wobbled with the burden of summer drinks, my mother looked down to me with violet eyes and straight black eyelashes and smiled. We would chat a while, and I needed to stand on my favorite rock while I talked. My rock came right up out of the patio floor, and it had an iron pole beside it, holding it in place. And when I stood on my rock, I held the pole tightly with one hand, one outstretched arm, a locked elbow, and my other hand fell on my waist in such a way that with hip cocked to the side, I became Marilyn Monroe until I tired of it. Usually when I assumed that position, I was bathing suit clad, but not always. For in the summer, I was mostly freely, happily, obliviously naked.

This opening is followed by account of how China left the quiet security of the pool-side and the house and followed her sister one morning to the bus stop, where children on the bus laughed at her because she was naked. She read "Bus Stop" in class, so when she came to her conference she had thought about the comments I had written within the narrative and about the comments her fellow students had made in class. My comments had to do with style; the comments in class came mostly in the form of laughter or sighs when she read about nakedness within the frame of her narrative.

By the time she arrived at the conference, she had decided to write about nakedness. She had a *subject* for her essay, but she did not have an *idea*. Nevertheless, her judgment about nakedness was already implicit in "Bus Stop"; that judgment would lead her to an idea. She was concerned about what happens when we walk out from behind barriers. She had a notion about the way society looks upon nakedness, and she wanted to explore that notion.

Before the conference, she had also thought about other scenes from her life that had to do with her subject, so she had a cluster of images to work with. She decided to retain the patio scene and the bus scene and to reshape them, but she wanted to create additional scenes based on an encounter with a boyfriend and an encounter with her roommate. In her final essay, she uses what Tom Wolfe calls "scene-by-scene construction." The scenes move the reader along through a time sequence, commenting on each other. Very little explanation is required if the writer constructs these scenes effectively. They speak for themselves, dramatically. Here is her entire essay, consisting of a beginning (a single, two-sentence paragraph), a middle (four scenes), and an ending (one meditative paragraph):

Naked

1   In the spring I was born naked. I was stuffed into a chamois cloth and presented to my mother.
2   In the summer I was naked, stumbling over cold flat stones and cool, dew-laced grass until I tumbled giggling into my mother's arms. On the patio she sat with a book, sheltered by the weave of wisteria that perfumed the air. Leaving the book open, face down on the white table that wobbled with the burden of lemonades, my mother looked down to me with violet eyes and smiled. We would chat while I stood on my favorite rock that came right up out of the patio floor. I held the iron pole beside it with one outstretched arm,

and my other hand on my waist so with hip cocked to the side, I became Marilyn Monroe until I tired of it. Usually when I played Monroe I was in my suit, but not always. For in the summer I was mostly, freely, happily, obliviously naked.

3   Our house was long and flat-roofed. It meandered down a sloping hill that was our front lawn. The lawn stretched on in every direction until it met with several different barriers: a wall of trees, a gravel drive, an apple orchard. My parents, sister, and I were entirely secluded, and I thought, self-sufficient. We rarely met with the outside world—save trips to the dump via Dairy Queen with Dad. I was, therefore, immodest, and associated summer, early fall, and spring with nudity.

4   In the fall, my older sister would go to school. She would wear her hair in two braids, put on dresses, and carry a lunch box. In the afternoons she came home with bright paintings under her arm, and stories about apple seeds. I would play in my toy box while she'd sit in the rocker and read.

5   I was fascinated by the idea of school, of a place where my sister would go and always return with new things. When she left in the morning, she would walk importantly down the drive to Plympton Rd. where the school bus would pick her up. And on this particular morning, I was outside when she marched off to school. As she disappeared between the leaves, I started to follow, slowly keeping my distance. My bare, soft feet pressed into the gravel, and I was slightly chilled with goose bumps. It was a long drive, and I walked it without the air of determination my sister always had. I was curious. With my stomach poking out, I reached the mouth of the drive where the bus was just stopping. My sister turned and saw me standing there, mute and bashful, and cackled. I looked into the bus, through the windows that reflected the turning leaves, and saw the huge, open mouths of the students, climbing over each other to get to the window, their bodies shaking, their faces pressed to the glass. As the door folded open, there was a burst of sound escaping suddenly like the whistle of steam from a kettle. Once my sister had stepped up into the bus, and the door had closed off the noise, it pulled away. I hurried back up the drive, just until I was between the trees, just so long as I was inside the barrier.

6   That was fourteen years ago. But last summer, I was naked. At eighteen I stepped out of hiding, on purpose.

7   I had a boyfriend. As far as boyfriends go he was all right. He said a lot of nice things, made a lot of stupid mistakes, and was usually there when I wanted him to be. I suppose I loved him, though that's hard to say now. I used to say it all the time. It was an easy thing for me to yell after him as he left my doorstep. I never understood why my friends couldn't tell it to their boyfriends when they wanted to. It was a "stupid mistake" to speak the truth at the wrong time. I always stripped down as soon as I could. I just said it one day, he said it too, and we were happy.

8   Then summer came. We were separated by vacation plans. He was a counselor at a tennis camp, and I was living with my sister. For weeks we accepted our parting with optimism, like two children before Christmas, knowing it wouldn't be too long. I tried to hurry it along by taking a bus up to Vermont to see my Grandparents, who live near the camp. I told him I was coming, to take two days off. But when I got there, he couldn't get away. He had no transportation. He had no time off. We spoke on the phone from a distance of thirty miles.

9   "I think we should break up," he said.

10   "What?"

11   "It's ridiculous to keep this up. I never see you."

12   "That's your fault."

13   "Maybe."

14   "I can't believe you're saying this. Over the phone."

15   "How else could I? I never see you. . . . I can't love someone I never see."

16   "Right."

17   "I'm going to be in California for four years, we'll never be together for more than three or four days again. Do you want that?"

18   I was crying.

19   "Look, I've gotta go, it's 6:30. Dinner."

20   "Uh huh."

21   "I'm gonna go."

22   After two days I wrote a letter. I mailed it the day I left for Europe. It was eight pages of words I had never been able to say to him; more than "I love you." They explained things, told him exactly how I felt. They were soft words, and so honest that I surprised myself. They remembered times we spent in high school, waiting to graduate together. They were sad words, admitting the loss I felt. They told him he was right. And they told him I still loved him.

23   In three weeks I got back from Europe. There was no letter.

24   This fall, sitting between the pillows on the futon, my roommates discussed art. We were hanging posters and I tacked up Matisse postcards on my bulletin board: a woman reclines on a chaise lounge in red harem pants, naked from the waist up. The walls of the room are orange and yellow flowers, and a blue and white patterned screen surrounds her. Her hands are behind her head and she is resting, calm. One roommate caught sight of a bared breast, and stopped.

25   "What is that?"

26   "What?"

27   "That's naked!"

28   "I know it's naked. Haven't you seen a nude before?"

29   "Not in a painting. I've seen myself."

30   "You've never seen nude painting? Aren't there museums in Newfoundland?"

31   "Yes but they don't exhibit that."

32   "But it's important, it's beautiful."

33   "That's not beautiful, it's disgusting."

34   "It's art."

35   "It's disgusting."

36   I wondered if I had unconsciously taped the centerfold on my wall.

37   I see others carefully covering up their tracks like criminals, spreading the dust thin over the unique grooves they refuse to leave behind. They twist words into measured speeches, keeping silent the taboo feelings. They do it out of fear. They do it out of habit. They learn it young on school buses. They create barriers and never cross them. Because when we see nudity, when we hear nudity, we turn away, close the door to the dressing room in awkward haste or simple ridicule. So I keep reminding myself: I was born naked. I was born naked.

China Forbes uses a number of interesting techniques in this essay that help her weave her reconstructed memories into a coherent whole.

"Scene-by-scene construction" works well because she constructs the scenes economically: they are compressed and full of energy; she mixes narration and exposition very well within a scene or paragraph without overdoing her explanations. In paragraph 5, for example, she merely suggests what happens when a naked, curious, carefree child dares walk outside the barriers of her own yard into the company of older children; she creates other scenes that depend on dialogue (paragraphs 8–21 and 24–36), giving us variety; throughout the essay she also makes good use of her own images—the Marilyn Monroe pose, the child with the stomach poking out, the breast on the Matisse postcard.

One of the most striking aspects of the essay is the way China varies the length of paragraphs. The two-sentence opening that indeed constitutes the *beginning* of her essay explains very little but suggests a great deal. It is so perfect in its simplicity that to tamper with it by adding explanation might be to ruin it. Her longer *ending* is reflective and explanatory yet still restrained and suggestive. What is most interesting about this essay is that we see several versions of the writer in this piece; she appears twice as a child, once as a high school student, and once as a college freshman. Outside all these scenes is the writer, China Forbes, reflecting, shaping evidence, creating meaning out of the materials of her life.

Essays such as "Naked" seem to have been written easily, without difficulty. Reading them we think they must have fallen in place effortlessly. Rarely, if ever, is that the case. Although China came to freshman composition with a love of language and a good sense of how to create scenes (she acts in campus theatrical productions), she nevertheless spent a great deal of time as she prepared to write and as she wrote, examining related moments from her life, making sense of those moments in an essay that focuses on nakedness. She also listened to peer evaluations in the classroom, exchanged her work out of class with another student, and had one lengthy conference where we discussed rhetorical strategy. The essay developed over two weeks of give and take. It evolved slowly from a single moment of recollected experience, from that piece she called "Bus Stop."

Students retain from these writing exercises a sense of how to shape personal experience and turn it to the service of an idea. They know, of course, that the general shape of the personal essay—beginning, middle, and ending—defines other essays as well. They discover too that all essays evolve in much the same way that personal essays evolve, from a consideration of evidence, from exploration, from letting the mind play against the grain of an idea.

But the most important thing they learn from writing personal essays is that whatever form and shape their essay takes, the first person is always doing the writing, always doing the thinking, always shaping experience, whether that experience be gained from personal interactions, from reading, or from solitary thinking. We may choose to disappear from our texts as characters or as the pronoun "I," but we can never actually disappear. We are the intelligence behind the text; it is always ours and no one else's. We must choose what to put in, what to leave out. We are the shapers of experience, we the fashioners of texts. Those texts, our arguments in whatever form, gather force as the depth and variety of our impressions increase, as the quality of our education begins to play itself out in the words we choose to express ourselves.

Works Cited

Baker, Russell. "Life With Mother." In *Inventing the Truth: The Art and Craft of Memoir*. Ed. William Zinsser. Boston: Houghton Mifflin, 1987. 31–51.

Didion, Joan. "The White Album." In *The White Album*. New York: Simon & Schuster, 1979. 11–48.

—. "On Keeping a Notebook." In *Slouching Towards Bethlehem*. New York: Farrar, Strauss, Giroux, 1968.

—. "Why I Write." *The New York Times* 5 Dec. 1976, sec. 7: 2, 98–99.

Dillard, Annie. "To Fashion a Text." In *Inventing the Truth: The Art and Craft of Memoir*. Ed. William Zinsser. Boston: Houghton Mifflin, 1987. 54–76.

Eiseley, Loren. *All the Strange Hours: The Excavation of a Life*. New York: Scribner's, 1975.

Eliot, T. S. *Selected Prose of T. S. Eliot*. Ed. Frank Kermode. New York: Harcourt, Brace, Jovanovich, 1975.

Hillman, James. *Anima: An Anatomy of a Personified Notion*. Dallas, TX: Spring Publications, 1985.

—. *Archetypal Psychology: A Brief Account*. Dallas, TX: Spring Publications, 1985.

Hoy, Pat C., II. "Mosaics of Southern Masculinity: Small-Scale Mythologies." *The Sewanee Review* 97 (1989):220–37. Rpt. in *Located Lives: Place and Idea in Southern Autobiography*. Ed. J. Bill Berry. Athens: U. of Ga P, 1990. 152–166.

Morrison, Toni. "The Site of Memory." In *Inventing the Truth: The Art and Craft of Memoir*. Ed. William Zinsser. Boston: Houghton Mifflin, 1987. 101–24.

Newman, John Henry. *The Idea of a University*. Ed. I. T. Ker. London: Oxford U. P., 1976.

Pater, Walter. *The Renaissance: Studies in Art and Poetry*. Ed. Donald L. Hill. Berkeley: U. of California P., 1980.

Sanders, Scott. "The Singular First Person." *The Sewanee Review* 96 (1988):658–72.

Judith Beth Cohen

🐦 *Confronting Ethical Issues*

Here are some recent lessons our students have learned in ethics. When you own the Empire State Building, you don't pay taxes. In between sermons about other people's sins, TV evangelists embezzle from their flocks and sleep with their secretaries. Or frequent brothels. Wall Street millionaires trade tips under the table to become billionaires. Government officials trade arms for hostages to maintain illegal armies. Those in charge of justice flout it, those in charge of nature despoil it, those in charge of sheltering the poor despoil them.

We sit and watch it all on television.

If, in the middle of this *danse macabre,* our students become cynics and moral relativists, taking refuge in privatism and personal achievement, washing their hands of questions of the greater social "good," we can scarcely blame them. How can we help them to engage the social and ethical problems of this era when so many of their elders refuse to do just that?

Nor are the young failed only by contemporary values. The very language with which they might debate these values fails them too, a fact reflected back to them and reinforced by "the media." Ours is an inarticulate society.

As witness the low level of discourse during the 1988 presidential election campaign. Questions about capital punishment and prison furloughs, to mention only one area of debate, were not addressed in light of the principles of justice. Neither candidate discussed what penalties would best suit a democratic society; neither urged us to consider the relationship between prisoners' rights and safeguarding everyone's rights. In fact there was no debate. In its place, the electorate was offered mute manipulative images: black criminals, waving flags.

Or consider abortion. I can think of no more lifeless writing assignment than "Write an essay that argues for or against legalized abortion." And yet. This is one of the great social and ethical issues of our time. We must talk about it, we must think about it. Yet most of us simply cannot locate language that is fresh enough to do the job—that is, language that *means*. Mention the word "abortion" and what instantly spring to mind are "phrases tacked together like the sections of a prefabricated hen-house" (Orwell, 159), along with, perhaps, the gruesome, wrenching, televised photographs of murdered fetuses held up outside abortion clinics by "pro-life" supporters.

I do not think the paucity of our values and the paucity of our vocabulary are unrelated. It seems to me there is a direct connection between our inability to discuss social and ethical issues and our impotence to do anything about them. In order to act, we must be able to think; in order to think, we must be able to speak, to write, to articulate our thinking. As Orwell pointed out years ago, "language . . . becomes ugly and inaccurate because our thoughts are foolish, but the slovenliness of our language makes it easier for us to have foolish thoughts" (157). "Foolish" being too gentle a term, to my mind, for the current age.

Our task as instructors, then, is twofold: it is, on the one hand, to engage our students actively in thinking about social and ethical issues, to help them to forge a direct and living connection with the great questions that are central to our citizenship and to our humanity; and, on the other hand, to help them reinvent a language in which to make this connection. A first-year writing course that draws its topics from current social debates can provide the ideal setting for both these struggles. At its best, the class becomes a laboratory for exploring conflicts between personal problems and ethical principles. Telling their own story and listening to other people's stories and other people's voices on issues that touch their lives—drugs, discrimination, the environment—can help students to overcome the mute isolation and self-interest that our society has modeled for them. Students then become able to speak rationally on difficult, emotionally charged topics in a voice that is still, unmistakably, theirs.

This last point is crucial. I believe that a writing course on social and ethical issues, if it is to be effective, must take as its starting point a paradox: if our students are to transcend privatism, they must begin with what is private to them. In order to take their subjectivity and transform it into a means of understanding the human condition, they must begin within that subjectivity, in the foul rag-and-bone shop of the heart. If they are to develop a voice capable of speaking for others as well as themselves, they must first learn to speak with their own voice.

Years of teaching and writing have led me to believe that the road best taken to rational research-based essays, which make principled arguments about some of the complicated ethical and social questions we face, begins in personal narrative. It seems to me that the way to help our students get past a myopic obsession with personal rights is to begin, precisely, with the self, gradually moving out of the solipsistic, in the course of the semester, via readings, dialogues (both spoken and written) with other students, and serious research, into the larger human story.

It took me some years to develop the sequence of assignments I now use to help students move from the narrative of a personal issue to a closely reasoned argument about the social implications of that same issue. Initially, a month or so into the semester I and my fellow instructors in "Writing About Social and Ethical Issues" simply assigned a research paper, urging students to choose a topic of real concern to them.

One of my colleagues had a student named Laurie. This young woman began with a troubling personal problem. She knew that her parents had picked out the name "Dennis" for the baby they were expecting, when she turned up instead. Deeply marked by their obvious preference for a male offspring, she decided to research the new birth technologies that now make it possible for parents like hers to get their wish. Although she began her paper by recounting a lively exchange with her mother about her name, Laurie's tone and diction changed abruptly as soon as she began to report on the scientific literature ("If the sex is the desired one, then the blastocyst is reinserted into the mother . . ."). For the rest of the paper she lifelessly summarized her readings. She offered no reflection, no judgment, no commentary on material that had been so charged with meaning when she began.

One of her references, a controversial book by feminist Mary Warren, warned about the frightening implications of sex selection, yet Laurie merely restated Warren's ominous prediction that fewer girls would be born, that women would become a minority certain to lose their rights. Why did this student fail to say what she thought of this frightening scenario? Did she consider Warren a reliable source? Given Laurie's initial concern that her own parents were the very people the book worried about, what did *she* make of this problem? Indeed, what did she make of any of her sources? She faithfully recorded what it was they had to say, but she avoided any kind of dialogue with them, she did not seem to have meditated at all on the issues they raised. Her sole response to her research was: "If I were Dennis now, I might be desperate for even a date."

At the end of her paper Laurie reported that, armed with her new information, she confronted her mother again:

"Let's say that all the methods of choosing the sex of the baby existed when I was born. Would you have used any of them to change the outcome of my sex?"

After a tense moment of silence, her mother replied, "Hasn't that college taught you not to ask such silly questions? At least some things will never change!"

With these words the essay concluded.

Although she'd begun with a personal issue and done good research, this student never quite bridged the gap between the two, never made an intellectual connection between her own experiences and the larger ethical questions posed by the new birth technologies. Nor did she dare to take a position on these questions. Instead, she escaped, she fled the obligation to adopt an ethical stance. Her voice was largely missing from the paper. Throughout its long middle section, framed by the two scenes with her mother, Laurie herself was scarcely audible. It was her Sources we heard speaking. And in the end it was her mother who got the last word: Don't ask threatening questions, don't rock the boat.

If you believe that Hamlet's tragedy came from tackling a family problem too soon after college, perhaps you think that Laurie's question about her very existence was too threatening to confront, that her teacher should have advised her to see a counselor or, at the very least, to pick a new topic. But I am convinced that the right assignment could have helped this student to achieve the intellectual distance she needed in order to integrate her intuition with her research and to claim her own voice to establish her own authority in the province of her paper.

This is in itself a startling concept to many of my students, the majority of whom arrive at college with the firm belief that they are not and cannot be the authority in research papers (or anywhere else in college, for that matter) and that a first-person essay and a piece of academic writing have absolutely nothing in common. No matter how much or how little they know about writing, they are all possessed of one rule: "Never use 'I' in a formal paper." And we can understand why their high school teachers have promulgated this rule, as an antidote to self-involved writing that is deaf to any opinion save the author's (the *abortion is wrong because I could never do it* brand of essay). Unfortunately, what often happens to the "I"-eschewing student is that he erases his own voice along with his subjectivity. The tape is blank. And whereas moving beyond solipsism is an intellectual advance, the accompanying loss of voice is frequently a stylistic disaster. If, as soon as he begins to use evidence and analysis, he sounds like a textbook rather than a human being, he loses his reader to boredom and himself to the belief that (1) academic writing is a turn-off and (2) he has nothing to say.

Recent research in developmental psychology can help us to understand this loss of voice. William Perry, Lawrence Kohlberg, and Carol Gilligan have all studied how students move beyond a narrow, self-absorbed orientation to a more sophisticated, more inclusive mode of thinking. And building on their work, the authors of the more recent *Women's Ways of Knowing* have examined the development of self, voice and mind in a series of women they interviewed (Belenky, et al.). The five positions these researchers outline show their subjects progressing from a position of "silence" toward the ability to speak out of a personal synthesis of past experience and new learning. Although based on women, the model in this book seems to me to be applicable to students of both genders. As writing teachers, we are all familiar with the students these researchers describe: the "received knowers," whose voices are lost as they defer to outside authorities, the "subjective knowers," so limited by their personal frameworks that they are unable to hear other points of view, the "procedural knowers," who have mastered the rules and never take a step beyond them.

The latter group tend to perform well in traditional classrooms; their competent but boring papers often get high grades. Even if no teacher ever tells them to get rid of "I," they are highly suspicious of the personal voice. Pleased with their relatively new ability to problem-solve and criticize their own ideas, they often defer exclusively to reason. They quash any intuitive impulses they might have. Ultimately, what they write seems unconnected to who they are. As David Bartholomae has pointed out, these procedural knowers have learned all too well how to parrot the discourse of the university. But it is our task to help them move beyond such "separate knowing," so that they may become "constructivists" (see Belenky, et al.), able to create knowledge by combining their own past experience with the new information they have gathered.

Laurie's paper was an uneasy mixture of subjectivism and procedural thinking, and I as a teacher had to figure out how to help students like her past this stage in their writing and thinking. Were she my student today, I would ask for a written narrative first, thereby obliging her to step back and ask herself: "What story do I really want to tell?" Once she had created a text that her peers and I could help her to read, I think she would have been better able to transform her personal issue into a manageable topic, to abstract from her private question a collective one. And to such a question she might have been able to bring that rich thinking that encompasses the personal narrative inherent in any ethical argument and and to reexamine this "story" in the light of evidence and logic.

I use the term "story" advisedly. As any instructor who has ever taught "Shooting an Elephant" or "Stranger in the Village" or "Letter from Birmingham Jail" knows, narrative is as central to the expository essay as it is to fiction. And the same is true of research papers, although we seem periodically to lose sight of this fact, to distrust the role of narrative in "serious" nonfiction, as though the presence of a good story somehow weakens a serious argument rather than strengthening it. As though the mention of concrete human experience somehow trivializes or invalidates reflective critical thinking. And yet when Camus wishes to explore the existential question of suicide, he tells us the story of Sisyphus; when Plato wants us to understand the world of forms, he makes up a story about a cave. Darwin tells us marvelous stories, and so does Freud. And so do our most articulate contemporary scientists and social scientists. Neurologist Oliver Sacks writes case studies that read like novels: "He reached out his hand, and took hold of his wife's head, tried to lift it off, to put it on. He had apparently mistaken his wife for a hat! His wife looked as if she was used to such a thing" (10). And as William Zinsser points out, in *Writing to Learn*, paleontologist Stephen Jay Gould "never forgets one of nature's oldest laws: that everybody loves a story. Every month [in *Natural History* magazine] he tells me a remarkable story and then tells me why he thinks it came out the way it did" (19–20).

Rather than squelch our students' stories, for fear that they are symptomatic of low-level discourse, we would do better to use them as springboards into high order reasoning. If these stories can be made to serve as the take-off point, not the final product, of our students' writing, that progression described by the developmental theorists can unfold during the course of the semester, in the process of writing and revising. And telling their personal story at the very outset allows students to confront their biases and move beyond them. In my experience, the threat posed to clear thinking is greater when the autobiographical motive remains hidden. Unacknowledged agendas can distort a piece of writing, making the topic unclear and the argument opaque.

Thus, when one student struggled to write about drugs and pregnancy, I couldn't understand what question she wanted to explore, until she told me that a drug her mother had taken during pregnancy resulted in severe birth defects and the ultimate death of her baby brother. Once she had written about this experience, I was able to help her investigate manufacturer liability, government regulation, and individual responsibility for potentially harmful prescription drugs. Another student, who held an ROTC scholarship, protested the unfairness of having to trek all the way over to MIT for compulsory ROTC classes. Not until he investigated why Harvard had banned ROTC, during the upheavals surrounding the Vietnam war, did he have any context for his argument. Having viewed his own problem in perspective, he could then consider whether the fairness principle he advocated was absolute or relative to the historical moment. As these students made the connection between their autobiography and the social and ethical issues at stake, the public/private split so characteristic of student thinking and social life began to dissolve.

Curtis Chang began his first assignment in my freshman writing course as follows:

> When I abandoned speaking Chinese, I abandoned a large part of my ethnic identity. Going to Chinese School would force me to acknowledge that uncomfortable fact. It would force me to decide whether or not I wanted to reclaim a certain part of myself.

I had asked students to reflect on a tough decision they'd had to make, a decision where the opposing choices seemed equally strong. Some greeted the assignment with a challenge: "What does such a personal paper have to do with arguing about social issues?" I explained that their narratives should work as an argument does, convincing readers that their personal dilemma was real. As writers they would have to summon sufficient details to take readers through the experience they had lived. In this paper the evidence to support their argument would come from experience and memory. Later, they would be asked to draw on primary and secondary research to make their case, but the use of compelling, concrete details would be necessary in both papers.

Thus we began the process intended to lead them from narrative to research and argument. First, they would work at establishing a strong personal voice, a voice I hoped they would not feel compelled to silence when they moved into more formal, academic writing. By writing about a personal issue, they would practice dealing with dialectical tension in their own lives before tackling a social problem. A problem that might seem as private or idiosyncratic as Laurie's name or Curtis's struggle with language could lead to a topic with broad social and ethical dimensions.

To see how the leap from personal narrative to research is made, consider Curtis Chang's account of his conflict over studying Chinese. Early in his short essay, he paints the scene as two buddies banter on the basketball court: "Duane and I come from similar backgrounds. We both immigrated from Taiwan when we were young, we both were losing fluency in Chinese, and we were both lousy basketball players." At the end of his piece he concludes that sacrificing a few basketball games is worth the price of attending Chinese School: "I was born Chinese and no amount of assimilation could change that."

Once the class had copies of this essay before them, they let Curtis know what questions his story raised for them: What's wrong with assimilation? Why are Chinese students so driven to achieve? Why is there more discrimination against blacks and hispanics than against Asians?

The discussion helped Curtis to put some distance between himself and his own story. His personal conflict over studying Chinese became a metaphor for the larger conflict between assimilation and minority loyalty, and this led to a new question, one that took him from "I" to "we," from his personal problem to its social manifestation. He asked: Are Asian-Americans really better off than other minorities in America?

His research into this question began with the numerous articles in the media that extolled Asians as the model minority. This is how the first draft of his research paper began:

> "Take a look at this." My Caucasian friend handed me the latest copy of a *Fortune* magazine. "Not bad, huh?" He pointed to a headline story titled "Asian Americans: America's Super Minority." It was just the latest congratulatory addition to the media image of Asian Americans as the "Model

Minority." . . . As an Asian-American it appears that I, in the politician's lingo, have been getting "great press."

Though he is to look beyond his own experience, Curtis still frames the problem with a personal anecdote and dialogue, just as he did in his earlier personal narrative. But as he immerses himself further in research, reading sociological studies, testimony before the U.S. Commission on Civil Rights, and the work of Asian-American specialists, his own story gets woven into the larger story in a much more subtle way. Curtis argues that by publishing endless articles congratulating Asian Americans for their material success the popular media perpetuate a false mythology and dupe Asians into believing the myth: "The Model Minority's mythology belies an even more deceptive ideology. It attempts to justify the existing system of racial inequality by blaming the victims rather than the system itself."

To support his arguments Curtis looks beneath the numbers that proclaim a higher median income for Asian-Americans than for other minority groups. He shows how these statistics are deceptive when one considers that Asians have larger families and live in more expensive urban areas. Furthermore, by documenting the widespread discrimination that still operates against Asians, he challenges the assumption that material success is equivalent to equality. His paper makes a convincing, rational argument without losing the passion that led him to the topic. "We Asians are indeed a model minority," he asserts: "a perfect model of racial discrimination in America." And noting how his Asian peers show little concern for other minority groups, he observes: "We 'white-washed' Asians have simply lost our identity as a fellow disadvantaged minority."

Before writing his final draft, Curtis received written responses from two fellow students—responses that raised questions about his tone and his use of evidence. One student wrote: "I'm black and I don't think that Asians experience as much racism as we do. Your tone puts me on the defensive." And another: "You criticize the government and the media for using statistics deceptively, yet you rely on statistics to make your argument. Why is your interpretation of the numbers more trustworthy than theirs?"

These voices and their invocation of conflicting "stories" helped him to clarify and rethink his final version of the paper, whose first sentence now reads:

> Over 100 years ago, an American myth misled many of my ancestors. Seeking cheap labor, railroad companies convinced numerous Chinese that American streets were paved with gold.

We note that here the writer no longer relies on a personal anecdote to introduce his topic. He is still present in the first person, but he now identifies himself with other Asian Americans and looks at the problem with a longer historical view. In its final form, "Streets of Gold: the Myth of the Model Minority" won a Bedford Prize and was published in the *Harvard Political Review*.

Like Laurie, Curtis was driven by the sense of personal loss that, according to Lacan, drives all narratives (Eagleton, 170). But Curtis was able to move from his own discomfort about the potential loss of his Chinese identity to the more generalized identity distortion of Asians in the media. In the process of writing, both Curtis and Laurie reached toward "connected knowing." If the latter did not quite succeed in separating herself from the personal issue to reconnect with it through a social problem, I believe this was largely because she did not have the benefit of the right series of assignments and the right kind of feedback from teacher and peers.

The assignment sequence that led to Curtis' final paper is not the only one that can work to achieve the goal of moving students from a personal issue to a research project on a social or ethical problem. At other times I have asked students to narrate a vivid childhood memory, reminding them of Flannery O'Connor's dictum that anyone who has survived childhood has enough to write about for the rest of her life. After they finish their narrative, they read the work of developmental theorists that I have placed on reserve and then write an analysis of their own story through these psychologists' lenses. Their question: Given the stage they were in or their age at the time of the narrated experience, what psychological dynamics were in play?

This two-part assignment requires the student to look at the same material twice, first from her own point of view and then through the eyes of a theorist. The resulting perspective helps the writer to triangulate, to rethink her first time away from home or her confusion at her grandmother's death. Often the result is research into broader questions: on child-rearing practices, on our culture's attitudes toward death, on hospital policies regarding life-support systems and living wills.

Another assignment sends students to the library to read a newspaper published on the day of their birth. They then write an essay in which they discuss an historical issue or event in light of their own family experience. One young man wondered how his mother had managed to escape the influence of the feminist movement, which seemed so prominent in the newspapers he read. This led him to question the accuracy of the media portrayal of 1970s feminism. The opportunity to compare the birth technologies available to her own parents with those available today might have helped Laurie to gain greater distance on her own story.

Each of these assignments says to students, You can move beyond your personal question, but you need not surrender your own voice; you can rethink your own experience and write about it in a more intellectually sophisticated way.

Despite what the foregoing discussion may suggest, my students are in no way obliged to pick a research topic derived from family or childhood experiences. If a student wants to write about the homeless, let us say, but his family lives in a three-story Victorian townhouse, I don't deny him the topic. I do insist, however, that his research involve him directly in the material. A few years ago, one of my students chose to investigate the controversy that flared up when a group of homeless Cambridge residents created a tent city on the MIT campus. As part of his research, Charles became a participant observer at the site of the conflict, and his writing immediately reflected his personal engagement. After a first visit to MIT, he wrote:

> When I saw the site of the Tent City Controversy, the first two words that came to mind were "urban blight." . . . Bottles, paper, even an old toilet seat littered the boarded houses. . . . Wouldn't everyone be better off if MIT just tore them down and put up its university park complex, complete with swimming pool and squash courts?

Just as Curtis interviewed his fellow students, Asian and white, for his paper on "the model minority," so Charles interviewed the parties to the conflict he was investigating, homeless activists as well as MIT spokespeople. He then wrote up what he heard, so that we hear these multiple voices in his paper. He presents the opposing positions, evaluates them, and takes his stand: "I realized that MIT and other corporations have an obligation to the growing number of homeless in our community." To support his ethical position, he quotes one of the people he interviewed:

> "If you take something out, you have to give something back. You can't grow a crop year after year in the same soil and not fertilize it." Morality and common sense tell us that MIT has a corporate responsibility to give back some of the profit it made.

In questioning and responding to participants in a conflict, students are carrying on a dialogue with living texts, and there is more to be learned from such a dialogue than simple information. I encourage my students to seek out people actively involved in the area they are writing about—not just for the benefit of informed opinion, but also in order that they may begin to recognize the human authorship behind published texts. It is striking that, at the outset, even the brightest and most aggressive students resist this activist approach to learning. They do not want to interview the expert; they would prefer to sit back and read the expert's book. But it is worth pushing them beyond the walls of the university, beyond the "procedural mode" of learning. For once they have ventured to ask an authority to clarify or amplify her statements in a face-to-face encounter, they can no longer ignore the fact that she's human. Then the studies they consult cease to be holy writ; they become human texts—like the students' own essays—subject to bias and error. And the infallibility of any text is open to question.

Write-ups of interviews or site visits are due before the final draft of their papers, and these become sources on the final bibliography. This also goes against the academic grain, for in most of their college courses students will encounter another version of prejudice against the personal voice: a mistrust of the eyewitness account. Authors as ancient and venerable as Xenophon, Thucydides, and Josephus wrote their historical narratives in the third person, despite the fact that they had often witnessed many of the events they wrote about (Scholes & Kellogg, 243). The fictional objective voice they created was meant to make their narratives seem less personal and hence more trustworthy, and this practice of avoiding a first-person account in favor of false objectivity has become a common and accepted form of deception: academics are expected to continue the tradition, hiding their personal involvement with a topic in order to sound dispassionate and unbiased. This is yet another way of masking the fallibility of the text, its human provenance. But if students imitate this falsely objective stance before they have formed a voice and claimed their connection with their writing, I fear they will never forge that voice, that connection.

Beyond the personally charged topic, the primary research, how can we help students further to own their work, to write lively, informative, elegant papers that are distinctly their own? Using the first-person pronoun is neither the only nor the best way to let the writer shine through. When my students are beginning to revise their drafts, we discuss how their prose might be strengthened by the use of imagery, humor, active verbs, and vivid examples—all rhetorical devices that students associate with "creative writing." That's okay for the personal narrative, they say, but not for a paper on medical ethics or homelessness: get *serious*. To convince them otherwise, I point to those serious storytellers mentioned above—Freud, Sacks, Camus. I urge them to develop the moment, the anecdote, the story, to illustrate parts of their argument. As inspirational reading, we consult vivid passages like the following, in which Stephen Jay Gould evokes Mickey Mouse's backward development from man- to child-mouse:

> Mickey has traveled this ontogenetic pathway in reverse during his 50 years among us, he has assumed an ever more childlike appearance as the ratty character of STEAMBOAT WILLIE became the cute and inoffensive host to the magic kingdom. By 1940, the former tweaker of pigs' nipples gets a kick in the ass for insubordination. (98)

If a serious scientist can risk such playfulness, such irreverent language and striking visual imagery, so can they. As Curtis Chang demonstrates:

> Not surprisingly, the dunce-capped blacks and Hispanics resent us apple polishing "well behaved" teachers' pets.

Like Curtis, they will frequently find such images, along with other usable material, in the personal narrative they wrote at the very beginning of the semester. This document will come to serve, then, as one more piece of evidence for the research essay.

The stories our students tell, whether they be personal narratives that help define a research topic or anecdotes that dramatize the topic, can help them make intellectual discoveries. Sequenced assignments like those I have described enable students to move from personal issues to collective problems, thereby promoting some serious matchmaking between subjective and objective understanding. After reflecting on the many voices they have heard, after revising their thinking and their essays, students know how to do research, how to critique their own ethical assumptions, and, most importantly, they see their own story as a living part of the larger human story.

Works Cited

Bartholomae, David. "Working on Texts: Composition, Criticism and the Under-graduate Curriculum." Keynote address, Literacy Conference, University of San Francisco. 9 June 1988.

Belenky, Mary, Blythe Clinchy, Nancy Goldberger, and Jill Tarule. *Women's Ways of Knowing.* New York: Basic Books, 1986.

Chang, Curtis. "Streets of Gold: The Myth of the Model Minority." *Harvard Political Review,* October 1987, 6–9.

Eagleton, Terry. *Literary Theory.* Minneapolis: U. Minnesota P., 1983.

Gilligan, Carol. *In a Different Voice.* Cambridge, MA: Harvard U. P., 1982.

Gould, Stephen Jay. *The Panda's Thumb.* New York: Norton, 1980.

Kohlberg, Lawrence. *The Philosophy of Moral Development.* San Francisco: Harper & Row, 1981.

Orwell, George. *A Collection of Essays.* New York: Harcourt Brace Jovanovich, 1953.

Perry, William. *Forms of Intellectual and Ethical Development in the College Years.* New York: Holt, Rinehart & Winston, 1970.

Rest, James, ed. *Moral Development: Advances in Theory and Research.* New York: Praeger, 1986.

Sacks, Oliver. *The Man Who Mistook His Wife for a Hat.* New York: Summit, 1985.

Scholes, Robert and R (?) Kellogg. *The Nature of Narrative.* New York: Oxford U. P., 1966.

Zinsser, William. *Writing to Learn.* New York: Harper & Row, 1988.

Linda Simon

✌ *Advanced Disillusion: The Writing of History*

The writing of history is the remembering of other people's lives. Whether a historian is writing about a Major Event (the bombing of Pearl Harbor), a catastrophe (the 1918 influenza pandemic), an apparently inanimate object (the British warship, *Dreadnought*), or an apparently intangible idea (futurism, shall we say), he is, of course, reconstructing a peopled world.

These people, these individuals whose lives must be resurrected and whose air must be breathed, necessarily save history from the fragmentation that threatens other disciplines and, as we know, the university itself. One cannot write history, even as a dilettante or a student, without considering the context of lives that were lived. That context includes all human endeavors—art and music, business and recreation, food and clothing, architecture and literature. That context includes physical surroundings—climate, terrain, and even those peculiar factors now known as air quality and wind chill. That context includes psychological theories and medical treatments, the availability of wine, and the occurrence of ergot in wheat.

This interest in context separates historians from many others who write within the academy and makes the writing of history a particularly significant activity for the undergraduates we teach. Although students often mistakenly believe that the historian seeks after Truth or Lessons from the Past, in fact, the object of writing history is much simpler: simply to impose order on seemingly disparate facts and events and, in imposing order, to give meaning.

This desire for order is the essence of all creative writing, within the scholarly community and without. "One of the chief motives of artistic creation," Sartre wrote, "is certainly the need of feeling that we are essential in relationship to the world. If I fix on canvas or in writing a certain aspect of the fields or the sea or a look on someone's face which I have disclosed, I am conscious of having produced them by condensing relationships, by introducing order where there was none, by imposing the unity of mind on the diversity of things" (371). Students rarely have this experience, however, as they move from course to course, from term paper to term paper, throughout their careers as undergraduates.

In most colleges, undergraduates are urged, if not required, to take a course in composition where they are asked to decompose, rather than compose, their thinking and writing into a number of discrete activities: brainstorming, freewriting, outlining, drafting, proofreading, revising. They learn discrete writing tasks: explaining, describing, persuading, arguing, reporting, reflecting, comparing and contrasting, analyzing, synthesizing. They learn that there are different requirements in different disciplines, different methodologies, different writing strategies, different standards for judging the success of the finished product. And after this course, which is, you remember, called composition, they emerge into the university only to confront more differences—between biology and literature, history and sociology, psychology and physiology.

Students rarely see their task as that of imposing order on any material they confront. Instead, when asked why they write papers, students reveal that writing is another kind of test-taking. They are persuaded that in the act of writing it is not they who have any authority, but rather the instructor and the experts upon whom they rely for their information. They write not out of a need to speak in a distinctive voice but rather out of a desire to merge their voices with so many others. They write not because they want to but because we, the instructors, ask them to. They write not to express who they are but to prove what knowledge they have accumulated. They aim to convince their instructors that they have learned—from class notes, from outside reading, from the texts of the course—everything they are supposed to know. The student reads, writes, and reports. The instructor judges.

It is no wonder, then, that students, no matter what the assignment, will summarize rather than analyze; will quote experts rather than venture an opinion of their own. It is no wonder that, set free to choose their own topics, they will choose the safest, least risky subjects, subjects that have been written about time and again, subjects for which there is a long bibliography of books and articles by writers who already have earned their "A" in the world. It is no wonder that when they are asked to think of questions to focus a research project, they come up with questions for which they are certain there are answers.

This kind of writing reinforces the idea that education is accumulation: of facts, of information, of the definitions of key terms, of the memorization of names and dates. This kind of writing focuses on the abstract—the more abstract, in students' minds, the more erudite—rather than on the concrete. Students have a deep suspicion of the concrete detail, as if reconstructing the daily life of one particular woman were less significant than exploring gender-based narrative strategies in autobiography; as if writing about conditions in makeshift hospitals in Georgia in 1864 were somehow less significant than writing about the theoretical basis for an argument in support of states' rights. And surely most of them believe that to fully understand the implications of the Civil War, it is the theory, and not the festering wounds, that will be most illuminating.

We have taught students to define education as linear: they move from one course to another, writing one paper after another, lengthening their list of courses passed, until they graduate, certifiably educated. If they take a course in Colonial American History as freshmen, they do not take it again as seniors. After all, Colonial American History will not have changed in four years. It does not matter if they as students have changed or if they have learned something from sociology, literature, music, or art that may have altered their way of seeing colonial life. Once they have written their term paper, they are finished with Colonial American History.

The term paper, of course, gives students the experience of writing about history, not writing history itself. Students who have mastered the technique of successful term papers tell me they do best beginning with recent secondary sources on their topic. From these, they can compile an up-to-date bibliography of other references, a bibliography that is essential in getting them a good grade. After all, they need to prove that they have read the right material, can cite the most important writers on the topic, have found the very latest revisionist theories.

Most successful term paper writers have mastered the current trends in thesis statements. The historian Warren Susman parodied this process in a guide to students that he included in his collection of essays *Culture as History*. This guide, he said, offers

> a universal model of history yet requires only the most limited knowledge for its implementation. All you have to remember are four major propositions; all you have to have is some fast footwork . . . to get away with it.

> You start (some brief attention to place and time sets the proper tone) with the announcement that this (whatever time and place you are supposed to be discussing) was a time of crisis. After all, historians always are finding crises; some sort of crisis can always be found. . . .

> Of course, the crisis (one should be sure to define it with sufficient vagueness or generality) leads naturally to your discussion of the cause of the crisis. That, too, is always easy: it was a period of transition. Once again, what kind of

historian are you if you can't find some kind of transition? The world, it seems, is always betwixt and between: feudal to capitalist, rural to urban, the possible list is virtually limitless. Transitions seem the one really stable thing in this transitory world in which we live. . . .

The transition, Susman goes on to say, results in "a significant shift in the social structure" that itself leads to the rise of a new class. It does not matter what class rises, "as long as you are aware that sooner or later" (233) it will fall.

Armed with such guidance, it does not take long for experienced students to create a paper according to the requirements of current conventions. Papers can—indeed, they must—be done quickly. It is not unusual for my students to tell me about 12- or 20-page papers, due the next morning, that they have hardly begun. But with the proper format, with photocopied pages from the proper sources, with a deferential attitude, they manage quite well.

Even if students choose to refer to primary material—letters, eyewitness accounts, photographs, maps—they do not venture far from the views of experts. In fact, students, who are supposed to be practicing scholarship, seem instead to be practicing the techniques of journalism, a profession, as one journalist recently described it, "that requires thrusting oneself into one unintelligible situation or topic after another and subsequently passing oneself off as an expert" (Kiefer, 18). It seemed to this journalist that he got his best training for the job in two college literature courses. In other courses, too, students are asked to serve as gatherers of information and as conduits rather than as explorers and scholars.

If we do not want our students to write like journalists, if we know that most of them will not go on to become scholars, then what do we want? And how does writing fit in to their education?

It is unlikely that students, whatever they do in life after graduation, will "take" their cultural life in the form of self-contained courses. Nor will they write anything that resembles a term paper. What they will do, if we have done our jobs, is become autodidacts. They will seek out information about the past; they will examine their lives and their cultural, social, and historical present and try to make some sense of their world. It seems to me that they may as well begin this process as undergraduates; and if I were to devise a new curriculum, its principle courses would be these: Introduction to Discomfort, Development of Empathy, and Advanced Disillusion, or, to combine the three, the Writing of History.

Through the experiences required in history writing, students would be persuaded that they learn not by memorizing data but by questioning with a healthy skepticism; not by skimming the surface of a problem but by delving deep; not by gaining a quick fix but by proceeding slowly. They would find that they must rely on their own authority to decide what is true and what is not. They would see the advantages of looking at issues from different perspectives. They would gain some experience in giving order and meaning to apparently disordered and disconnected facts and events. In all these tasks, the writing *of* history, and not *about* history, would serve them well.

Introduction to Discomfort

Historians are inspired to write out of an intellectual itchiness that cannot be soothed except by deep immersion in primary sources. Here is John Demos, telling us why he decided to write about a particular stage of human life:

> By the late 1970s historians had taken up "life course" studies in a remarkably vigorous way. Infancy, childhood, adolescence, old age, not to mention the special moments of birth and of death: these matters furnished more and more grist for a larger and larger scholarly mill. Curiously, however, one part of the life course remained as yet untouched: the part we call mid-life or, simply, middle age. (114–15)

Here was a gap, a place where there were only scattered bits of information. "Historians decide to study and write about something," Bernard Bailyn tells us, reflecting on his craft, "because they observe that in the present state of the historical literature there is a *need* for such work, a need in the sense that a proper utilization of known resources has not been made" (202).

Students, even without an overview of the state of historical literature in a particular area, can feel inspired to fulfill a personal need for information. One of my students with an interest in the French Revolution felt dissatisfied with presentations of material that characterized the aristocracy as villains and the revolutionaries as heroes. "We should ask ourselves," she wrote in her term paper, "if this portrait is complete, and if it is representative of all, or at least the majority, of the nobles in France at the eve of the Revolution. To balance our opinion, it would be essential to study the writings of one of the aristocrats who was there at Versailles and witnessed these events."

The student found a primary source in *The Journal of a Fifty Year Old Woman*, written by a marquise, covering the years from 1778 through 1815. This source answered a few of her questions about the French nobility: "what values directed their actions, what relationships they enjoyed with their inferiors, and what level of awareness they possessed of the unrest in their land beyond the opulence and gaiety of the court functions"; and it allowed her to assess her own assumptions about the French aristocracy, to draw some inferences, and eventually to evaluate some secondary sources. In the end, she decided that her marquise "and many of her class were not the ogres that they are believed to be. Many of them were well-intentioned people who were, just like so many of us, too wrapped up in their own life styles. . . . The real villain of the Revolution," she came to believe, "turns out to be the separateness of French society."

This experience at writing history satisfied not only a personal need to find information but an even deeper need to gain a sense of confidence in making intellectual decisions rather than recording the decisions made by experts.

Such motivation for research and writing is echoed by practicing historians. John Demos, explaining the genesis of his work on middle age, writes: "I had just celebrated (?) my fortieth birthday," says Demos, "when the idea . . . occurred to me. . . . I wanted, I welcomed, the chance to study the history of middle age." He faced his puzzle alone. "Lacking any other historical studies of mid-life—lacking, too, much overt assistance from the historical actors themselves—I have been forced to read *back* from present-day experience, and *out* from present-day theory. Eventually, it will be necessary to build this history up, piece by painstaking piece, through the study of individual lives" (114–15).

Demos set out to piece together a story about middle age, continually using himself and his own time as reference. Whatever he found would be tested against what he experienced and what he felt. His questions were generated by a genuine curiosity, not by an assignment contrived by someone who already knew the results. How, he asked, do middle-aged individuals act and react; how are they different from what they were before and will be later; what forces work upon them; when does middle age begin; what plots are most typical of that time? Demos knew, of course, that he never could tell the whole story. Unlike students, historians do not complete a job. They only end it for a while.

Sometimes discomfort comes not from what is lacking but from what is known. My own most recent moment of discomfort came when I discovered that late in 1906, two events occurred almost simultaneously: in New York, William James, at the end of a long career as psychologist, philosopher, and teacher, delivered his lectures on a particular way of thinking that he called pragmatism; in Paris, a young, relatively unknown painter began work on a large canvas that he later would call *Les Demoiselles d'Avignon.* Here were two men, James and Picasso, seeking to articulate their particular way of making sense of the world, suggesting a shift in vision that might be required to more effectively apprehend a new age. Here were two men suggesting new responsibilities for the individual seer and doer. What, I wondered, was the connection? Years of research, leading away from and back toward those events, have revealed other connections. Eventually, I will have a tapestry of interwoven stories—and still only a partial answer to my original question.

Connections are vital in the writing of history. There would be no story at all if lives did not connect, if events were not juxtaposed, if one "fact" had no transition to another. We spend time in composition courses introducing students to the notion of transitions. We give them lists of words: "however," "nevertheless," "therefore" . . . that can serve them in highlighting the relationships between their ideas. These are the essential words in the telling of a story, in the writing of historical narrative. There is no more triumphant moment for the historian than when she can say, with some confidence, "Therefore. . . ."

Development of Empathy

We are not talking here about pity or even compassion, only the ability to identify enough with another human being to speculate about what might have been. I had had trouble understanding Henry Adams, for example, who seemed to me altogether pompous and unyielding until I discovered that Adams, being a very short man—far shorter than many of his contemporaries—had his furniture specially built to give him the illusion of normal height. In that moment I understood something about him that his *Education* never revealed: his feeling of being an outsider in his time and culture, his feeling of being unable, somehow, to participate in the considerably noisy political world he watched from his windows on Lafayette Park, had its roots in his visceral and physical sense of being a misfit in his own world.

It is not easy to recreate lives, but it is essential for any historian. I wrote once about Margaret Beaufort, a 15th-century noblewoman who saw her only son, Henry, take the throne of England as the first Tudor king. Beaufort herself, like most medieval women, left few traces of her life. She had been the subject of a few 19th-century hagiographies, but I was trying to understand not so much the good works and religious fervor she demonstrated when she was the mother of a king, but her private life when she was 15, pregnant, and, recently, a widow.

She was in Wales, far from her few relatives outside of London, in a castle where the servants spoke a language she did not understand and where she was about to deliver a child with the help of midwives who bore strange oils, potions, and an oddly shaped birthing stool. It was not so much the oddities of medieval gynecological procedure that helped me to understand that moment in Beaufort's life but the discovery that the walls of the castle were a foot or more thick. The walls were bare. The floors were stone. It was cold, and she was virtually alone. She was thin, frail, small, and, after all, 15.

Happily for her, the birth went well. The child, a son, lived, and so did she. And then, in a moment of rare boldness, she held out against her husband's Welsh relatives and refused to name the child either Edmund (after his father) or Owen (after his grandfather). It would be Henry, she insisted. A good English name. The name of kings. All her craftiness, her manipulation to see her son take the throne began in that moment of naming the child. Later, she gained the reputation of being quietly indomitable and, in a self-effacing manner, quite shrewd. For me, she became vivid when I saw her in a room of bare stone, with walls a foot thick, at 15.

Barbara Tuchman calls these facts "corroborative details." When she once read about a party given at the Museum of Modern Art in New York, the most telling detail, for her, was a reporter's note that there had been 80 cases of wine—906 bottles of 7,680 three-ounce drinks. "Somehow," Tuchman wrote, "through this detail the Museum's party at once becomes alive; a fashionable New York occasion. One sees the crush, the women eyeing each other's clothes, the exchange of greetings, and feels the gratifying sense of elegance and importance imparted by champagne—even if, at one and a half drinks per person, it was not on an exactly riotous scale" (33).

History is about human lives in their total complexity, and in no other discipline are those complexities so relevant to the decisions scholars make and the conclusions they draw. "There is the conflict of characters," writes British historian A. L. Rowse, "the mutual likes and dislikes, the loves and hatreds; the conflicts within one person, the irrationalities, the divided loyalties; there is the subtle complexity of motive; the strange patterns that our lives fall into, the drama and tragedy of so many of them upon the public scene" (37).

What student papers are about in any discipline rarely has to do with life as it is felt as one lives it, nor even ideas as they are felt as one thinks them. What students rarely demonstrate as they write about the past is a sense of historical-mindedness, an empathy with times that were. They are encouraged to think of their writing as assessment of other people's views rather than as narrative. I have never known a student who has set himself the task simply of telling a story. Yet telling a story requires one to ask, again and again, who were these people? What do I know about them? How do I know it? What do I believe? How can I persuade my audience to believe me?

Perhaps the most significant question concerns the writer herself. Who am I in this story? Where am I? "The writing of history," Warren Susman admitted, "is as personal an act as the writing of fiction. As the historian attempts to understand the past, he is at the same time, knowingly or not, seeking to understand his own cultural situation and himself. When I began my own studies of the 1930s, a most distinguished historian in the field of cultural history praised me for my willingness to undertake such a serious intellectual struggle with my father and therefore my immediate past." Susman was naive enough to be "stunned by the suggestion" (xiii). But he soon learned that of the many assumptions a historian must question, foremost among them are assumptions about his own beliefs and perceptions. The historian, George Kennan says, has to take "personal responsibility for the product. This was the task of analysis and interpretation. And this meant that the fixed point from which one viewed history was actually none other than one's own self—one's self in the intimate personal sense" (272).

Quite awhile ago, when I wrote a biography of Alice B. Toklas, I realized that many questions I asked about Toklas's life were generated by my own life and the lives that I observed. When I anticipated her actions and reactions, when I speculated about how she felt, I relied on intuition based partly on the information I found, partly on what I believe about women, rebellious women, cranky women, intrepid women, ambitious women. Inevitably, a biographer, drawing upon her own life, daringly suggests "what must have been" in the life of her subject and speculates about the forces that shaped a life in the past. Just as inevitably, the subject's life urges the writer to question forces that shape her own life and times. Only through such questioning does the writer manage to define and redefine her own authority.

Students are timid, of course, about asserting their authority, but they relax visibly when they believe that they are required only to *essay*, to try, in their writing, rather than to complete and conclude. In analyzing a primary source, for example, they try, many of them for the first time, to find answers that the text does not readily yield. I give them, sometimes, a copy of Christopher Columbus's letter to Isabella and Ferdinand describing his first landfall in the new world. Who, I ask, was this man, Columbus? What were his motivations? What is the subtext of this document?

At first, many students are uncomfortable. Where is Samuel Eliot Morison when they need him? What can they remember of the Nina, the Pinta, and the Santa Maria that will enable them to fill up three to five pages? But when I encourage them to read closely, to pay attention to language, to be aware of contradictions, they are surprised at their success. What kind of man was Columbus? Here is one student's conclusion:

> Despite what he claims his goals to be, the nature of the facts that Columbus chooses to report in his letter reveals that he was greatly more interested in conquering territory and stimulating commerce than he was in saving souls. Never does he comment on the religious beliefs of the natives. He certainly never asks whether these people need saving at all. If he thought that the king and queen were sincerely interested in the spiritual welfare of the natives, wouldn't he have reported on their present religious practices? These seemed to be of no interest to him. Instead, he chooses to report on the existence or lack of towns and cities (to facilitate commerce and diplomacy, no doubt), the fertility of the land, and the accessibility of the harbors. He even makes an attempt to investigate the natives' economic system. He reports: "I was not able to find out surely whether they have individual property. . . ."

What students discover about Columbus comes as much from their assumptions about human nature as from their reading of the text. When they ascribe feelings, motives, and ambitions to the explorer they cannot help but identify with him as a human being. His landfall becomes not a historical fact, but a moving, exciting, and even controversial event.

Advanced Disillusion

Students confronted with fragments of the past often are uneasy. I remember the freshman who came to see me during my office hours, toward the end of a semester course in Writing and History. He understood me to believe, he said gloomily, that there was, historically speaking, no Truth. "There is your truth," I said; "and it is a truth that must be proven and defended. Instead of thinking about Truth," I suggested, "try thinking about what can be substantiated and what cannot." This was not what he wanted to hear. He subscribed to the illusion that the historian's task is to discover right answers, and he had no patience for the exercises in historical writing that did not seem to point to those answers. He left our talk, I am glad to say, disillusioned.

The illusions lost in the process of writing history have little to do with preconceived notions about particular events or particular people. What is lost, again and again, is a belief in certainty and in answers. No matter how small and circumscribed his subject, the historian never can know everything, never can see everything from every perspective. One never can be sure; just sure enough, at least for the moment. One begins any historical study—and any other kind of writing, as well—with questions. And one ends, inevitably, with more questions.

"I had naively supposed, ..." George Kennan wrote not long ago, reflecting on his first book, "that there was a body of unrevealed or unappraised historical fact lying scattered around, like so many archeological fragments, in the archival and bibliographical sediment of the ages, and that the historian's task was only to unearth these fragments, to order them, to catalogue them, and to arrange them in a manner that would permit them to tell their own tale" (271).

Of course, he found out otherwise. Facts and fragments do not speak. And as for their order: "They could be arranged in an infinite number of ways," Kennan discovered, "and each had its specific implications." Writing history, he soon decided, was an effort far more arduous than the mere accumulation of notes. It required imagination and empathy; it meant, he said, "that if you really wanted to get near to your subject, it was yourself you had to change" (272). You had to enter another world and another time, to recognize the differences between what you might believe now and what you would have believed then, to learn to look and to listen in a new way.

Once the illusion of certainty is lost, the writer no longer tests his work against an absolute Truth, but against his own sense of logic, his own priorities of importance, his own way of shaping reality. If the writing of history is undertaken with integrity, if what is asserted can be substantiated, the writer is able to exert authority even if she must work within the boundaries of limited knowledge. Biographers who cannot have access to sequestered letters, historians denied a crucial interview are not paralyzed—as students sometimes are—by their limitations.

Authority is gained even as illusions are lost. Students, though, desperately seeking certainty, will not allow themselves to take charge of their own writing. They prefer, and it is understandable, to let experts write their papers; they merely provide the text that intersperses long quotations or paraphrased passages. The reason for our discontent with students' papers, for our impatience over their tepid assertions and weak theses, is their evident failure to exert authority. But how are they to develop authority if they write with experts always looming over their shoulders and whispering pithy conclusions in their ears? If they are asked to construct a historical narrative, they cannot resort to other people's ideas. Instead, they need to confront the most frightening and intimidating of all scholarly material: the primary source.

If they are not asked to make their own decisions, unaided by experts, in the sheltered confines of the university, then how will they manage on their own in the world, faced with such sources of information as *The New York Times*, where they might find a transcript of a political speech or a news conference. Will they have the courage to go it alone, or will they wait for Dan Rather to tell them what it means?

Finding meaning is a slow process, despite the exigencies of college courses, where meaning must be found in two weeks. The writing of history requires a good amount of patience. "In the beginning there are the words," Warren Susman wrote, and each word is an historical problem in itself. There are "all kinds of words," he continued, "from all kinds of places: words from philosophical treatises and tombstones, from government documents and fairy tales, from scientific papers, advertisements, dictionaries, and collections of jokes." There are other sources of information for historians, of course: photographs, for example, or maps, account books or uniforms, corset stays or hairbrushes. But, as Susman points out, these are "analyzable only when translated into words" (xi).

And words are not easy to understand. They are, as Oscar Handlin said, "slippery." In some freshman composition classes I ask students to examine a 1908 Lincoln penny and make some inferences about ways in which the images and inscriptions on the coin reflect the culture of the time. The only background information they have is knowing that the Lincoln penny replaced the Indian-head penny in that year, a deliberate decision by Theodore Roosevelt and his administration.

Lincoln himself, of course, features emphatically in their essays, and students speculate about why, decades after the Civil War, his image would grace the most widely used coin. Perhaps, some assert, domestic problems caused Americans to look for a strong leader. After all, they say, Lincoln seemed so paternal.

But what of that term? Students are content to describe Abraham Lincoln as "paternal" until I ask them for a definition. A lively, even passionate, discussion follows. Does paternal mean "comforting, nurturing, compassionate"; or "strict, demanding, and stern"? If today's students cannot agree on that term, then how are we to understand what it meant to contemporaries of Lincoln or to the men and women who were children when Lincoln was killed and who grew up revering him as the spiritual father of the age of reform and progressivism?

"Few discoveries bewilder the teacher more," Handlin noticed, "than the revelation that students can more easily learn to read a book than a chapter, a chapter than a sentence, and a sentence than a word" (165). But it should not be bewildering if we remember that students have been encouraged to read not just one book at a time but many and to take courses in "reading strategies" rather than etymology.

Stopping at words slows down the process of writing instant papers, many of which are due at the same time during the semester and all of which are about different subjects. When historians talk about what they do, they chronicle a slow and cautious journey on unpaved roads, with frequent junctions and not a few blind alleys. Yet they have some exhilarating trips.

We can set our own students on this journey as we give them opportunities to write. They will be uncomfortable, of course, but that is a requirement.

Works Cited

Bailyn, Bernard. "The Problems of the Working Historian: A Comment." In *The Craft of American History*, vol. II. Ed. A. S. Eisenstadt. New York: Harper, 1966.

Demos, John. *Past, Present, and Personal: The Family and The Life Course in American History*. New York: Oxford, U. P., 1986).

Handlin, Oscar. "How to Read a Word." In *Truth in History*. Cambridge, MA: Harvard U. P., 1979.

Kennan, George F. "The Experience of Writing History." In *The Craft of American History*, vol. II. Ed. A. S. Eisenstadt. New York: Harper & Row, 1966.

Kiefer, Michael. "Down to Size." In *New York Times Magazine*, 8 January 1989.

Rowse, A. L. *The Use of History*. New York: Colliers, 1963.

Sartre, Jean-Paul. "Why Write?" In *Twentieth Century Literary Criticism*. Ed. David Lodge. New York: Longman, 1972.

Susman, Warren. *Culture as History: The Transformation of American Society in the Twentieth Century*. New York: Pantheon, 1984.

Tuchman, Barbara. "History by the Ounce." In *Practicing History*. New York: Ballantine, 1981.

Eileen Farrell

🙞 *From Critic to Colleague: Transforming the Internal Dialogue*

In the late 1970s, L. C. McDermott and D. Trowbridge made a distressing discovery. College students in an introductory physics course, they found, could define velocity as distance per unit time, but they did not really understand the concept. For example, they said that ball A was moving faster than ball B because it was "ahead of" ball B—even though they had seen the experimenter release ball B farther back than ball A (1022–23). Their intuitive idea of speed was, presumably, based on a great deal of previous experience: most races, after all, start with all the runners standing on the same line. Most intuitive concepts contain similar assumptions about conditions that may vary but are so uniform in everyday experience that the possibility of variation is overlooked. Research in cognitive development suggests that to learn physics, students must uncover their misconceptions and replace them with expanded concepts like "velocity" as understood by physicists.

The students' misconception was rooted in their own physical experience, not in previous classroom learning (they could parrot the correct verbal definition and had even seen the experimenter start one ball farther back than the other). Real change requires students to experience the new concept for themselves. For example, the teacher has pairs of students roll the balls themselves: student A is told to start his ball from the center of the room while student B is told to start her ball from the wall. The students are then directed to start their balls rolling at the same time but to make sure that both balls hit the opposite wall at the same time. They quickly realize that student B must roll her ball faster than student A and that even though both balls end up in the same place—at the opposite wall—student B's ball travels farther in the same time than student A's ball. Having done the demonstration themselves, the students now understand that distance and time, not position, determine velocity.

This story has a twofold moral: the students' task is to transform their concepts, and the teacher's task is to provide them with the kinds of experience they need to do so. The moral is also relevant to writing teachers, because students enter our courses trailing equivalent assumptions about writing. More important, their assumptions are based on equally pervasive experiences—not on the playground where racers start from the same line, but in classrooms where students read textbooks and poems, and write to have their competence evaluated by a teacher. These assumptions—about the student's identity as a writer, about the purpose of writing, and about the relationship between writer and reader—may be so taken for granted that their limitations, indeed their very existence, often pass unnoticed. And they are often quite as misleading as the idea that relative position reliably indicates relative velocity.

By the time students reach our writing courses, they have already experienced a scene of instruction that too often resembles a courtroom drama: the teacher, a combination of prosecuting attorney and hanging judge, ferrets out and condemns violations of the rules; the student, a hapless defendent, defines his task as answering the prosecutor's questions while avoiding self-incrimination as far as possible. This scenario distorts the real range of relationships between writers and readers, just as the image of racers starting at the same line provides a false model for the physics of bodies in motion. To write more effectively, students require new experiences in the external world, experiences vivid enough to transform their sense of identity, purpose, and relation to the reader.

In talking with students about their papers, one can often glimpse their misconceptions. Asked to explain an elliptical phrase, the student writer replies "What I *meant* was . . . ," and the aggrieved tone hints at an underlying assumption: the teacher should be able to read his mind, or at least share with him her own idiosyncratically enriched interpretation of the phrase. And in fact his assumption makes sense when we consider his previous experience. Teachers do know more about most subjects than their students, and they often take over to finish the sentence for a student who falters when speaking in class. Why shouldn't the student writing a paper expect the teacher to do the same thing? Or consider the long-suffering student whose habitual good cheer finally deserted her during one conference about half way through the semester. "Why do you keep talking about 'clarity'?" she exploded. "In my Lit courses they keep telling us that the most obscure poems are the greatest ones. And you're supposed to spend hours interpreting a short story; a good story isn't supposed to just come out and say what it means." She was perfectly right, of course. When a writer is telling yet again the familiar story of a son in conflict with his father or a woman in search of her true self, complexity in the telling is a virtue. But what of the scientist who is trying to explain that string theory, simulated on a computer, produces the same galaxy clusters when the dark matter forming the background of the universe is "hot" as when it is "cold"? In this case, difficulty is also a virtue, but it inheres in the argument, not in the way the writer uses language to convey it. My student had taken a truth about literature to be a truth about all writing, just as some physics students take the rule of thumb "the one that's ahead is going faster" to be valid for all bodies in motion.

The student nonetheless had a point when she reproached me for my stress on clarity. In fact, the idea she was writing about—the role of competition in science—was familiar to us both. She knew that she didn't need to write clearly to make me understand it. The scientist writing up research for a journal, in contrast, undertakes a more challenging task. (I use this example for the sake of simplicity, not because I think published scientific prose good or because I expect all our students to become researchers. Like the concept of a body falling in a vacuum, the concept of the scientist writing for a professional journal is an abstract ideal useful for thinking through a complex problem.) No matter how much background knowledge his readers have, the scientist knows more than they do about the results of his latest experiment; if he didn't, he wouldn't be writing the paper in the first place. Although some of his statements rely on others' work, his purpose in writing is to announce his own findings.

This purpose—to announce a discovery—determines the scientist's identity as a writer: he is an expert. When it comes to writing about his own research, he is more expert than even the most competent of his peers in that field. The scientist expects his work to be evaluated, but he also hopes to participate in an ongoing debate, to get into the action, to add a piece of his own to a jointly constructed edifice. The self-centered goals—getting tenure or winning a prize—are important, but so is the feeling of being part of an enterprise larger than oneself. In this case, the relationship of writer to reader is that of teacher to student or explorer relating discoveries to stay-at-homes. For the student, the roles are reversed. Having no independent authority for anything he says, he is a defendant facing as judge the teacher who examines his writing for infractions of the rules. Of course the scientist too expects to be evaluated, but the role of defendant under scrutiny by the scientific community is only part of his identity. He is also a puzzle-solver, a revolutionary, a discoverer. Because his own identity lacks these dimensions, the student is likely to overemphasize correctness, and once again the limitation breeds misconceptions—for example, the idea that "revision" means proofreading for mechanical errors.

The contrast in purpose also affects the experience of the writer-as-reader. The student writes to be evaluated, not to inform; consequently, she reads to absorb facts and ideas that she will then repeat to the teacher who assigned the reading and, presumably, already knows everything it says. In contrast, as a reader the scientist does not passively absorb facts; unlike the high school student, she does something I call "quarrying." When I read as an anthropologist, for example, I have some research problem of my own in mind—explaining spirit possession among the Swahili women I studied in Kenya, perhaps. I might be trying to decide if they were protein deficient or suffering from the same kind of hysteria Freud described among 19th-century Viennese women or protesting against ill treatment in the only symbolic language available to them. As I read, I look for facts and ideas I can use to develop my own theory and meet the objections to it. This purpose affects my demands on the writer whose article I'm reading. I don't want to waste energy trying to figure out what the writer means or admiring her style; I want to use that energy to make connections between what she says and what I already know or surmise. My student, intimidated by the expert articles she reads, seeing them as the authoritative truth about the subject rather than as raw material for her own project, can scarcely be expected to value clarity the way I do.

Like assumptions about style, assumptions about organization emerge from the writer's sense of his identity and purpose. For example, the introduction to a scientific paper usually outlines the problem the writer has been working on, mentions previous attempts to solve it, and explains both how these came to grief and how he managed to go beyond them. This history-of-the-problem opening can be dramatic indeed to readers working in that field, holding all the fascination of a quest romance, with problems in measurements looming large as dragons and solutions greeted with all the excitement due a Galahad arriving back at the castle, grail in hand. The student, lacking a real problem to solve, is often reduced to conjuring up significance out of such hallowed phrases as "Since primitive times, man has tried to conquer disease." The student's instinct is sound: history is relevant. But since he feels himself more akin to primitive man in his ignorance than to the experts he will soon be citing, he feels more comfortable invoking the former in his introduction. Similarly, when urged to write good transitions, the student writer often balks: "It sounds too dry," she says, by which she seems to mean pedantic, authoritarian, obnoxiously hitting the reader over the head with the main point. Again, the student's instinct is sound. A theme sentence like "The second major advantage of this drug is X" does in fact exhibit all those faults. But when a journal article numbers its points, provides strong guidance in the first sentence of each paragraph, and stops at the end of each section to briefly summarize the argument so far, it does so because the argument is far more complex than the one the student is constructing. The student's paper is likely to summarize all the advantages of a new drug—effectiveness, low toxicity, low cost—while discussing each in fairly general terms. The journal article, in contrast, will focus on only one of these, toxicity for example, and it will present evidence that using another drug along with the first reduces some harmful side effects. In doing so, the article may have to deal with such technical details as sample size, dosage, the possible effects of past drug usage, and the implications of all these for interpreting the results of the study. When the material presented gets this complicated, the reader needs and welcomes strong guidance; rather than feeling pushed around, she feels grateful. The student who has never written such a complicated argument himself, and had equally expert readers fail to understand it, has a concept of "smooth transitions" that differs as much from mine as the physics student's concept of velocity differs from the one his teacher has, and for similar reasons.

Finally, given their experience, the students' favorite conclusion, the pious exhortation—as in "Society must act now to reduce carbon dioxide in the atmosphere before the greenhouse effect destroys all life on earth"— makes perfect sense. It is just the tone taken in editorials and political speeches to endow an argument with lofty significance. Watson and Crick could end their classic paper announcing their discovery of the structure of DNA with a chaste understatement: "It has not escaped our notice that the specific pairing we have postulated immediately suggests a possible copying mechanism for the genetic material" (Watson, 139). The student, in contrast, has no real discovery to announce, no reason to feel that the audience will find his paper impressive, and no other way to end. The scientist often ends by suggesting future directions for research: applications of his theory, or new puzzles posed by his findings. His readers, peers working on the same project, find such an ending satisfying enough. The student must use rhetoric to manipulate the reader into feeling that he hasn't wasted his time. If the student knows that the teacher couldn't possibly have learned anything from the paper, it's no wonder that the rhetoric sounds half-hearted.

If I am right about the way scientists' experiences shape their assumptions about scientific writing, our task can be summed up as helping the student to change the way she experiences her relationship to the reader. This relationship itself has, of course, two aspects: the student's experience of herself as a writer and her experience of the reader as a particular kind of other. The student needs to experience herself as a writer who possesses authority—the authority of an expert who knows more about the subject she is writing on than the reader does. The new identity I propose for the student writer is one I call "the comparative expert." That is, the student needs to feel that her argument has something new to teach the reader, no matter how much more knowledgeable the reader may be in general—just as the scientist writing for a journal tells her colleagues something new, even though they may know more about the field as a whole. This sense of authority also transforms the student's experience of the reader. As an authority the student is now dealing with a reader who needs help in following the student's argument. The reader presupposed by the typical classroom assignment can be expected to read the student's mind. (I think of this figure as the "omniscient parent.") The new reader, in contrast, is a figure I call "the needy reader," defined as someone who has something to learn from the student's paper. Experiencing the reader as needy rather than omniscient sets up progressive pressures towards elaboration of meanings, in contrast to the regressive pressures set up when the student experiences the teacher as a mind reader akin to the mother of infancy, who is expected to sense empathetically what the infant means by his inarticulate cries.

How, then, can we enable our students to write as comparative experts? In the standard freshman composition course, this challenge is met by assignments like the personal narrative. When a student writes about his own life experience, he writes as an expert; he knows more about it than the reader does. Because personal experience is by definition unique to the individual, the student is telling the reader something new; progressive pressures are built into the logic of this situation. The teacher reading the essay can ask the student to explain the experience more fully, to describe it in concrete detail, to be more precise. And the teacher can do so as a needy reader who cannot in fact understand the experience without such elaboration of meanings—rather than as a judge applying external "rules of good writing." [Composition teachers recognize the powerful leverage provided by such assignments, hence their popularity.] The personal narrative goes beyond the familiar injunction "Write about what you know" in one crucial respect: it enables the student to "Write about what you know better than your reader." After all, the student who writes a boring essay about minimum wage laws is also writing about what he knows: he knows all the facts and arguments that he has read. The real problem is that the teacher reading the essay knows them too. The personal narrative provides leverage because personal experience adds something the reader doesn't yet know—what a familiar kind of experience looks like from the student's point of view.

But how can we get this sort of leverage in teaching other kinds of writing? Consider, for example, scientific writing, which poses the problem in its most extreme form. Science values objectivity; it rules out of court precisely the kind of subjective experience that gives us leverage in the personal narrative. In science, experiments must be replicable, meaning that all observers of the alleged phenomenon must experience the same thing. Authority in science comes from observing a new thing, not from observing a familiar thing from a uniquely personal perspective. We might try to solve the problem by expanding the personal narrative to include interviewing a scientist, but such assignments are also limited. Only a small part of science writing deals with the familiar features of character, action, and setting that take center stage in both the interview and the personal narrative. Compared to literature or history, science writing is remote from the familiar stories about human conflict that students have been reading and telling each other all their lives. Instead, science writing requires describing inhuman entities interacting in unfamiliar ways or manipulating abstract concepts whose ties to sensed reality are remote. After the first simple assignment asking the student to describe a microscope, where do we go? In fact, that assignment also fails to give the student any authority, unless the reader has in fact never seen a microscope. Saying "Pretend that you are describing a microscope to somebody who has never seen one" creates more problems than it solves: the student knows that he is really writing for his teacher, who cannot reliably impersonate ignorance, if only because the tacit assumptions we rely on to understand things ramify so widely that ultimately they involve our whole experience. To gain a genuine experience of authority as a writer, the student needs a genuinely needy reader, just as the physics student needs a ball that will really roll across the room, not a ball that pretends to roll across the room.

To cope with this dilemma, one strategy I've tried is designing assignments that ask the student to choose a concept from the assigned reading and apply it to a topic of his choice. One student might use Karl Popper's concept of "testability" to figure out whether the theory of the greenhouse effect described in a recent article in *Discover* is really scientific; another student might try to decide whether current attempts to detect proton decay fit Thomas Kuhn's concept of normal science as "puzzle-solving." These assignments allow the student to write from a position of authority because, although I know the concept well, I have never bothered to figure out how it applies to theories about the greenhouse effect or the search for proton decay. Such assignments also get around the students' lack of specialized knowledge, since one need not understand the mathematical formulas for proton decay to apply Kuhn's concepts at this level. And since every month brings new scientific discoveries, I am never without new problems for the students to solve; I can respond genuinely as a needy reader who depends on the student's paper to tell me exactly *how* the current experiments measure up to Popper's criterion or fit Kuhn's description.

Another assignment that casts students in the role of comparative experts is the research paper. Although a student explaining how researchers use monoclonal antibodies to prevent rejection of bone marrow transplants has done no original experimental research, she does tell me things I myself didn't know. The standard worry about such teaching is that it cannot elicit from students a sufficiently rigorous level of analysis, since the writing teacher may fail to recognize errors in a student's interpretation of the data. Scientists, like students, make mistakes, but they can expect their readers—colleagues in the same field of research—to spot the errors. The writing teacher must rely almost entirely on logical coherence. Fortunately, students make enough errors of this kind—inconsistent statements, non sequiturs—that the writing teacher can easily demand greater rigor. Our goal, after all, is not to elicit a publishable paper but to provide a transforming experience, and the errors we can spot are frequent enough to allow that. The more important point is that when I do say "On p.5 you say X, but that seems to contradict what you say about it on p.3," I don't myself know which statement is correct. The student is the one who has to clear up my confusion by deciding which is right. This experience—of being confronted by a reader who spots an error but doesn't know how to correct it—is what helps the student to transform his identity as a writer. After all, in science a researcher's peers frequently point out that something won't work, and leave it at that, sending the researcher back to the lab. It is this similarity with the scientist's experience of writing that is most crucial to the college student's growth as a writer, rather than some unattainable mirage of complete freedom from factual error.

Learning to experience himself as one who writes from authority is, however, only part of the student's task. The other half is transforming his experience of the reader. The key to making the student's experience of his new authority (and responsibility) vivid is the reader's response; and as I have come to appreciate how essential this experience is to my students, I have changed the way I comment on papers. I used to enact the role of judge, evaluating the paper according to standards of good writing: clarity, smooth transitions, supporting detail. Now I enact the role of needy reader, using comments to record my experiences as I seek to learn something from the paper. In other words, I define problems not as infractions of the rules but as obstacles that tripped me up as I was trying to understand what the writer had to teach me. Instead of saying "This transition is too abrupt," I say "I expected you to keep on talking about sample size, but now you seem to be talking about the placebo effect, and I didn't really figure out that you were talking about a new idea until about sentence 5 of this new paragraph." Or I may say, "Paragraph 8 says that Wilcox's data don't support his theory about sunspots, but I can't see that he has any theory at all. When you talked about his article on p.7, all it seemed to amount to was a bunch of statistics about solar wind. Does he have a theory connecting solar wind to sunspots? If so, what is the connection? How do sunspots cause solar wind?" I build revisions into the syllabus, so that students have a chance to answer such questions in the next draft, thus reinforcing their internalized image of the needy reader.

Reinforcement is essential, since most students have firmly internalized a vastly different function: the internal censor. It is clear from talking to them that this function is hyperactive. When I ask "What did Wilcox say about how sunspots cause solar wind?" the student says, "Well, I was going to put that in, but I thought that would be getting off the track." It is discouraging to realize how many of the omissions I spot turn out to be things the students thought of doing but censored. Similarly, when we discuss a paper, students are always coming out with fascinating ideas that would have generated a much more challenging argument than the one they actually wrote—and when I ask, "Why didn't you write about *that?*" they reply with some appeal to the omnipresent official censor, that internal critic instilled by years of having their papers criticized for violating the rules.

Transforming the internal censor into a needy reader also requires a different approach to the rules themselves. I tend now to define them as hypotheses about what readers expect and need. "Readers expect the writer to keep on talking about the same thing unless they get some signal that she is about to change the subject; that's why some logical signal like 'However' is needed here." And rather than saying "Put statements in positive form," I say that most handbooks include this rule because readers seem to find positive forms easier to decode. And I mention Noam Chomsky's theory that the deep structure of a sentence is positive, so that readers have to do extra work to transform a negative sentence into a form the brain can use easily. From this perspective, the old rules appear as a handy set of rules-of-thumb worked out by generations of writers; they are rough-and-ready guides, not sacred commandments.

Similarly, in class discussions of student papers, I used to ask questions to which I already knew the answer, questions like "Which version is more confusing?" Then I learned (by watching a videotape of my class) that such questions put the student on the spot—he could give the wrong answer, and I would end up replaying the defendant-judge relationship. Then I tried to ask only those questions to which I did not already know the answer: "What do you think of this paper?" "It was confusing." "Where did you first start to feel confused? What were you confused about?" I found, however, that such questions were too global—discussion ground to a halt fairly quickly. Now I ask the students to read through the paper and record at least one spontaneous reaction to each paragraph: "I really agree with this because . . ." or "I really don't believe this because . . ." or "glitch" (I got confused here) or "neat!" (I wish I'd written that). By enabling students to play the role of needy reader themselves, this discussion strategy reinforces the effect of my comments on their own papers. It works especially well when we apply it to professional papers as well as student papers. I used to use only model papers, on the assumption that students were only too familiar with bad writing. But I found that students benefit from disciplined analysis of bad professional writing. Professional models of excellence tend to intimidate them ("I could never do that," they say, or

"I could never get away with saying that"); in contrast, analyzing bad professional writing tends to increase students' sense of their own authority. Painfully aware of their own ignorance, they find it hard to take the role of judge vis-à-vis a professional writer, but they can and do adopt the less threatening role of reproachful needy reader.

Unfortunately, this needy reader, however helpful, is a one-dimensional character. Readers may be relatively ignorant on some points, but they are not complete dolts. In science particularly, they are apt to be contentious—ready to use the knowledge they do possess to challenge the writer's argument at every turn. A teacher who does not prepare students to cope with this side of the reader has done only half the job. The challenge here, of course, is to help students anticipate the objections of a critical reader without raising the ghost of the internal censor we have just labored so hard to exorcise.

The following story suggests one possible model. A friend of mine, an atmospheric physicist, was explaining how he writes articles for the professional journals in his field and referred several times to his "internal critic." When I asked him about this term, he launched into a vivid description of the birth of this personage. It began in graduate school, when his advisor and mentor would tear to shreds every claim he made. This ordeal went on for what seemed like years, until he was about to give up in despair and quit graduate school for good. Many of his friends, he said, did quit at this point, their self-confidence damaged beyond repair. But he was too stubborn to quit, and finally he started to "fight back"—he found himself able to anticipate and refute his advisor's criticisms. At that moment, the internal critic was born, an external adversary tamed and transformed into a sparring partner. Rather than censoring his ideas, as before, this new part of his mind sharpened and strengthened them; it had become a valued part of his thinking and writing. As an established member of the professional community, my physicist friend now spars with others besides his advisor. Before publishing a paper, he presents his ideas at conferences and seminars, where his peers test his arguments and he does the same for them. In fact, for him, half the fun of doing science comes from this lively debate; he values the fierce joy of intellectual competition at least as much as the excitement of making an important discovery.

My friend's account brings out especially clearly the way the imaginary reader can function as both adversary and ally. But it also brings out something even more important: the way the imagined reader is born out of numerous experiences of face-to-face debate. Scientists' published accounts of their working lives reveal that such debate is pervasive and that it can be supportive as well as critical. Books by biologist James Watson, physicist Luis Alvarez, and psychologist Jerome Bruner abound with accounts of conversations—in pubs and offices, on the beach and in the corridors at scientific conferences. As Alvarez puts it, "Since most physicists find they don't really understand a subject until they've discussed it with their colleagues, talking physics is essential to doing physics" (47). The flavor of such talk emerges vividly from his description of one arena for discussion, Robert Oppenheimer's "bullpen," where the Berkeley theoretical physicists "crowded with Robert into one of the rooms at Leconte to watch and comment as someone worked equations on the blackboard"—and Alvarez characterizes these comments as "helping each other happily with criticism and advice" (48).

If professional writing grows from a rich substratum of discussion, then students need to experience equivalent kinds of response to their writing. To write an argument that is "rigorous," they need a chance to see what it feels like to explain an idea, have the reader respond, "But A doesn't lead to C," and then expand the account to show that A does indeed lead to C, by way of B. In other words, they need experiences that will enable them to internalize a more complex and responsive internal reader, a more productive inner dialogue. They need to receive comments that are not negative or vaguely encouraging but stimulating—responses designed to elicit further explanation or suggest fruitful new lines of thought. Alvarez's description of "talking physics" captures the kind of experience students need as they attempt to balance the reader's need for guidance against his power to criticize.

That students have trouble achieving this balance is shown by their reluctance to follow the handbooks' advice to "anticipate and refute possible objections to your argument." To most students, this advice makes no sense. "Won't that just weaken my case?" they ask. "Maybe the reader won't notice that weak link, so why should I help him?" At the root of such objections is an image of the argument—and by extension, the writer himself—as a vulnerable creature whose safest course is to hide. If the student's internal critic seems a predatory beast, as often it does, this impulse is understandable. The professional writer, whose internal critic is more benign, reacts differently. Many of his most effective devices can be seen as healthy responses to an internalized needy reader. Take, for example, the device of clarification by contrast. One day several years ago, I decided to sit down and try to find out what sort of things good professional writers do that my students do not. I picked up Stephen Jay Gould's *Ever Since Darwin*, and the first thing I noticed was how often he clarifies a new idea by contrasting it with other ideas with which it might be confused. "The essence of Darwin's theory lies in his contention that natural selection is the creative force of evolution, not just the executioner of the unfit" (11–12). Or "Our uniqueness arises from the operation of ordinary evolutionary processes, not from any predisposition to higher things" (14). These local contrasts almost never appear in student papers, yet they occur on almost every page of a writer like Gould. It is easy to imagine them growing from an internal dialogue with a reader. Gould writes, "Natural selection is the creative force of evolution," and the imaginary reader says, "Oh, sure, survival of the fittest," and Gould then corrects this limited notion by calling natural selection "the creative force of evolution—not just the executioner of the unfit."

Many of the devices we label "development"—not only local contrasts but also specific examples, concrete details, spelling out the chain of reasoning—probably originate in such internal dialogue with a responsive inner reader. Indeed, I was led to this hypothesis by the unanswerable objections of my students when I first pointed out to them the way Gould uses clarification by contrast and other such devices. "Wait a minute," they would say. "When Gould is sitting there writing, does he really think to himself, 'Well now I better put in a clarifying contrast'?" And I had to admit it seemed unlikely. Indeed, I was reluctant on principle to envision the writer as a technician systematically applying a set of rules. On the other hand, I didn't want to have recourse to some explanation like "He has good instincts" or "He has a feeling for what will work." After all, if I appeal to some mysterious inborn talent or intuitive feel for what's good, I undermine my own claim that writing can be taught. The hypothesis that effective strategies emerge from the writer's dialogue with a responsive inner reader seems equally plausible and certainly more helpful.

The student whose internal critic is irrationally aggressive tends, I think, to hear the same objections from the imaginary reader as Gould, but he responds by freezing; he deletes the idea and looks for another one. I know this because often when I am talking about a paper with a student, I will say, "Why didn't you just say that Watson was being dishonest?" and the student will say, "Well, I thought of that, but then I thought that would be too negative." Further questioning shows that by "too negative" the student means "too arrogant" and that he had in mind some unfriendly reader saying, "Who are you, a mere freshman, to criticize a famous scientist like Watson?" Many missing links and patches of convoluted prose can be traced back to just such bits of internal dialogue. Rather than attacking these problems piecemeal, it seems more sensible to try to reach the root cause, by helping the student to change the identity and tone of that internal critic.

Here, a new model of the writer's situation may prove helpful. In the arena of intellectual controversy—as in that of bureaucratic policy disputes, competition for funding, and routine engineering reports—people write as participants in some ongoing debate over what the problem really is and how it may best be solved. They write to urge that the problem be reformulated in some particular way or to insist that solution A is better than solution B. And they address what they write to colleagues engaged with them in some larger project. Consider, for example, a debate in the Correspondence section of the 1983 *New England Journal of Medicine* ("Coffee and Cholesterol"). Researchers wrote in from Boston and Kentucky, from the

Netherlands and Australia, to challenge the previously published findings of some Norwegian researchers, who had claimed to show that coffee drinkers had higher cholesterol levels than people who didn't drink coffee. Some of the letter writers objected that the elevated cholesterol levels might be caused by the cream in the coffee, not the coffee itself; others suggested that the culprit might be stress (with coffee drinking just another symptom of that stress); still others reported research showing no such correlation at all. Unlike the student who reacts to criticism by giving up on the idea and looking for another topic, the Norwegian researchers responded in several different ways. They began by elaborating on their original article, explaining that they had looked at other dietary sources of cholesterol, such as cream and steak, and found that they made no difference. Then they countered the suggestion that stress might be the culprit by reporting that other factors related to stress—such as cigarette smoking—had been investigated and found not to alter the association between coffee drinking and elevated cholesterol levels. Finally, they agreed with a new explanation suggested by one of the letters, that the key factor might be the way the coffee was grown, roasted, or brewed.

The important feature of this debate for my purposes is the way a shared project shapes the way each party in the debate responds to the others' proposals. These researchers are not engaged in a classroom exercise called "spot the faulty assumptions"; they are trying to find out whether drinking coffee is harmful. My problem as a writing teacher is to bring the interchange between me and my students, and between them and their peers, closer to this kind of debate. They need to experience the give-and-take that occurs between colleagues, where debate is less a test of personal competence than a test of the solution proposed. Only when the comments on a student's paper can be oriented to some problem of joint interest will they sound like the kind of talk shared by colleagues.

Theme courses, in which students choose a writing section on a topic that interests them (creativity in science, the image of the city, the stranger in modern American fiction), provide a natural setting for this kind of discussion. Students in such a course can expect to learn something from another student's paper that will help them in their own writing projects; they can respond as colleagues rather than enacting a junior version of the teacher-as-judge. From the perspective of the student whose paper is being discussed, her classmates are readers who genuinely need to understand and test her paper's ideas, to help them develop their own ideas further. They are not "peer critics" but colleagues, whose responses grow from a shared commitment to the same problem-solving project.

The undergraduates in our writing courses occupy a peculiar transitional status, betwixt-and-between the docile pupil and the professional expert. The arguments that sound best to the professors who read their papers are the kind that those professors read and construct themselves, the kind they find in their professional journals. But to produce that kind of argument, the writer must be a comparative expert on the topic; he must be able to tell the reader something new. Few college writing assignments allow the student writer to do that; instead, by requiring the student to tell the professor something she already knows, they reinforce all the regressive pressures on writing that the student experienced in high school. What the student needs are assignments evoking the same kinds of responses that the professional writer depends on to guide her work—the kind that shaped her own internal dialogue.

Few of the students we teach will end up doing original scientific research, and a course focused on some specialized product—the professional journal article, for example—is too narrow. But a course focused on the writing process, defined as what goes on in the mind of an individual writer, is also too narrow. In science, the writing process begins with "talking physics"; for the journalist writing about science, the world of responsive colleagues may include editors and interview subjects; for a consulting engineer, it may include the city manager seeking to discover what has contaminated the town's water supply. In any case, the final written product, and even the internal dialogue that goes on while it is being written, is only the tip of the iceberg. Students need to experience what goes on beneath the surface appearance of the articles they read. They need to begin to participate in the kind of give-and-take that shapes an article by shaping the identity, purpose, and relationship of writer and reader, who are colleagues, or adversaries, or consultant and client, before they begin to write or read this particular text. As Wittgenstein remarked, a rule does not itself tell us how we are meant to apply it, and before students can apply the excellent advice in their handbooks, they need to start experiencing the life-worlds that give the rules their point.

Works Cited

Alvarez, Luis. *Adventures of a Physicist.* New York: Basic, 1987.

Bruner, Jerome S. *In Search of Mind.* New York: Basic, 1987.

"Coffee and Cholesterol." In *New England Journal of Medicine* 309 (1983): 1248–50.

Gould, Stephen J. *Ever Since Darwin: Reflections in Natural History.* New York: Norton, 1979.

Trowbridge, David E. and **Lillian C. McDermott.** "Investigation of Student Understanding of the Concept of Velocity in One Dimension." In *American Journal of Physics* 48 (1980) 1020–28.

Watson, James D. *The Double Helix: A Personal Account of the Discovery of DNA.* New York: Mentor-NAL, 1969.

Maxine Rodburg

🕭 *Workshops in the Teaching of Writing*

> So, as my classroom experience as a teacher
> has taught me, there are hipper ways to get
> to gut and brain than with hot pokers and
> pincers.
>
> *Toni Cade Bambara,*
> *The Writer on Her Work*

For fiction writers trained in university graduate programs, the use of workshops in the classroom is not foreign. A writer/teacher with an MFA or MA in writing will surely have participated in workshops as a matter of course. The Writers' Workshop at the University of Iowa, the oldest and still among the most renowned of the MFA programs, has used workshops since its inception in the 1920s. So too do all other current graduate writing programs.

In the fiction workshop, a small number of student writers—let's say 12—meet with an established writer and spend their time critiquing student work, with the established writer serving as anything from a discussion leader to a preacher to a role model, from malevolent dictator to non-threatening peer. The strengths and weaknesses of a piece of student fiction are noted and scrutinized; attention is paid to the basic elements of the genre—character and dialogue, setting, plot, the handling of time.

"I don't think someone like John would react in this way when his wife picks up the kitchen knife—he's tightly wound, not likely to start screaming quite yet," says the shy young woman at the far end of the table.

"That's just the point," counters the burly young man who last week submitted to the workshop a piece in which the protagonist interrupted a symphony by playing three-card monte in the center of the stage. "John is so rigid, he's got no other recourse—words elude him."

The discussion continues, at the end of which the student writer staggers home to marvel and ponder. During a weekly three-hour session, the group might "workshop" (the noun is freely used as a verb in such settings) two to three pieces of writing—generally short stories, perhaps a chapter of a novel-in-progress. And so it goes.

Yet the emphasis on workshops in the teaching of fiction writing may be a result not of careful pedagogical choice but of frustration—the frustration inherent in writing fiction itself. Traditionally, the act of writing fiction has been perceived as both wondrously and stubbornly impervious to external input. The fiction writer toiled alone, accomplishing literary creation through a private process involving much trial and error. Fiction obviously wasn't grammar, and when writers began to tentatively consider "teaching" fiction, they certainly didn't imagine it could be done by standing at the front of the classroom, imparting a body of knowledge to passive students. (Not that grammar is or should be taught this way.) For one thing, that body of knowledge was not entirely known. For another, fiction writers have traditionally given at least lip-service to the notion of community—the inherent value, both intellectual and therapeutic, in getting together to talk about writing. And so, graduate writing programs do not necessarily rely on teachers with traditional academic credentials as workshop leaders, but on established fiction writers. Sometimes these writers have academic credentials, sometimes they do not. But presumably they all know something about the process they go through in writing their own fiction.

We can think of the teaching of fiction writing as a kind of arranged marriage between the academy and the writer, who until then often has been virginal regarding institutional settings. That marriage, it seems to me, is enlivened by the interaction and implicit tension between two such odd bedfellows. After the contract with the academy is signed, the fiction writer keeps not only her maiden name but to a large extent her previous identity. That is, she becomes a writer who teaches, rather than a teacher who writes. Her idea of relaxation doesn't often involve cooking up gourmet classes based on pedagogical theory, or vacuuming student work for grammatical errors. The fiction writer who teaches comes in from the cold of her private preoccupation to the warmth of the populated academic kitchen and, flesh atingle, begins to talk about writing with the students gathered there. Fiction, not pedagogical theory, is what she knows. If time remains when class is done, she spends it at her own writing.

As a spouse, the academy must worry about the rituals and nuances of running the household: the organization and content of the classes; assuring student mastery of specified skills; and the big bugaboo, grading. The writer may or may not be interested in these issues. If not, then usually, for the sake of domestic peace, she secretly regards them as irritating or tolerably eccentric, maybe even imagines them as exotic—for imagining is what fiction writers routinely do.

In temperament and in training, fiction writers who teach are content to be hired hands: they have no trouble believing that if you want to learn plumbing, the best thing to do is apprentice with a plumber. For fiction writers, the notion of workshops has always been linked to the notion of apprenticeship—working, perhaps alongside but generally a few steps behind and beneath the sometimes benevolent, sometimes harsh wing of an acknowledged expert. In this sense, every published word is a potential for apprenticeship. *Read, read, read some more* is what fiction writers have always advised. *Read everything.* Such advice, more often than not, is superfluous; scratch an aspiring fiction writer and usually you'll find someone who grew up reading and loving fiction. Now, in the workshop, the aspirant can sit beside others who share and indulge and are eager to talk aloud about the same passion.

Historically, composition has been taught not by writers but by scholars. Despite the recent proliferation of PhD programs in composition, even today its teaching to undergraduates often is the bottom of the English department barrel in terms of status and pay; many institutions rely solely on adjunct instructors to teach the course, thus freeing the *real* academics for what is considered more seemly and challenging work. So it is not surprising that the use of workshops in college composition classes has evolved quite differently than in graduate fiction programs.

As originated and developed for the composition class, workshops have been associated with what is termed "collaborative learning." The various practices that comprise collaborative learning began with peer counseling (one student tutor working outside the classroom with one student tutee in need of extra help) and today include small groups of students discussing one student's work; peer editing (two students in the same class editing each other's work); and workshops that involve the entire class.

As it did in the teaching of fiction writing, frustration with existing educational strategies helped bring about the various techniques and modes of collaborative learning. In the early 1970s, college faculty and administrators across the country looked around their campuses and became increasingly aware that new students were not achieving at the expected levels. Students were offered all sorts of extra assistance but rarely took advantage of those offerings. So, from a kind of practical desperation, "some college faculty members guessed that students were refusing help because the kind of help provided seemed merely an extension of the work, the expectations, and above all the social structure of traditional classroom learning"—which had originally left those students unequal to the tasks at hand (Bruffee, 1984, p. 637). New strategies seemed necessary, and the first collaborative models were born.

Yet fiction workshops had been in existence for nearly half a century; they had produced an honorable cadre of graduates, many of whom went on to successful writing careers. The faculty of fiction-writing programs was often located within the English department, so presumably there had been possible some intermingling of pedagogical approaches—at least, the opportunity was there. But, like many composition teachers, fiction writers have an ambiguous, if not tenuous, relationship with the academy. Rarely are these positions tenured; in terms of title, rank, and status, fiction writers are *in* but not *of* the academy; an uneasy truce often exists between them and it.

Yet surely clarity, precision, structure, shape, and careful strategy are common to both fiction and nonfiction. Of course, we say. Nevertheless, powerful notions and myths have surrounded the writing of fiction and therefore its teaching. When we thought about fiction we imagined solitary toil in dusty garrets, midnight vigils in quest of the elusive muse, a left-brained and somewhat irrational venture at expressing a personal vision: creation, the unteachable art. All this was romantic, exotic. Nonfiction, in contrast, implied work-a-day craft, the teachable mastery of canonized basics—organization of ideas around a solid thesis and expression of these ideas with clarity and precision: the diminution of the personal voice to highlight whatever was the subject matter.

But on the level at which we increasingly understand it, writing is writing—a private process made public when another person reads the product. And this product, regardless of genre, prizes the implicit relationship between writer and reader. Recent interest and scholarly study of the *process* of writing no longer sever the body of a student writer's work into heart, soul, brain, limbs; not into nonfiction versus fiction (or, worse, "creative" writing—as if there exists a sort of writing that is not creative). And these distinctions have also blurred in the world of professional writing: note, for instance, the (today, not-so) "New Journalism" and the increasingly fluid shape of the personal essay.

What distinguishes the various genres is their genesis toward something more powerful and shared than whatever may separate them. All writing requires reflection, a sort of conversation with oneself, an internalized version of what Bruffee calls our "direct social exchange with other people":

> If thought is internalized public and social talk, then writing of all kinds is internalized social talk made public and social again . . . We converse; we internalize conversation as thought; and then by writing, we re-immerse

conversation in its external, social medium . . . The point is not that the particular thing I write every time must necessarily be something I have talked over with other people first, although I may well often do just that . . . The point is . . . that writing always has its roots deep in the acquired ability to carry on the social symbolic exchange we call conversation . . . our task [as writing teachers] must involve engaging students in conversation among themselves at as many points in both the writing and the reading process as possible . . . The way they talk with each other determines the way they will think and the way they will write. (641)

If we agree with Bruffee that writing is reverberative communication, then as teachers it is necessary to assist in making the atmosphere in which the writer works less rarified: to disabuse students of the notion that writing must be only a lonely, arduous process at the end of which they submit the work and await our unguessable opinion about it. If writing is dynamic interchange between writer and reader and back again, and back again *ad infinitum*, then the workshop setting can give real shape to this model. Seated around a table of peers, a crucial component of the writing process beyond that which the student experiences in the lonely act of creation is specifically and intrinsically attended to—the role of the audience.

My students of composition or expository writing are often surprised to consider that writing is not only self-expression but also an implicit relationship between writer and reader. But for years they have themselves been puzzled, wearied, angered by enforced reading of texts that do not seem to consider them. For years they have received back from their teachers writing that has been evaluated, graded, checked, or marked according to a set of standards that too often seems to vary year by year, as the student proceeds through the school system. So they quickly embrace the idea that audience is crucial: they like to be able to hear the hosannas or see the thumbs down. They like being reminded that writers and readers are human. My students are consistently stunned and intrigued when I say, "Remember those of us who will be reading your work—there are all sorts of ways to do this, but try starting out by making your work interesting and comprehensible: imagine how you would feel reading it." Make an essay interesting because other people will be reading it? Because their peers will be? The teacher as reader, as *person?* They never had been advised to think of that.

Still, it took a while before I tried workshops. As a new teacher, learning to write on a blackboard without making the chalk screech, I was eager for and uneasy about establishing some sort of control in the classroom. So it was difficult to contemplate changing my still uncertain role in a traditional classroom to one that relied heavily upon workshops. How could beginning writers serve as a sophisticated audience for each other? Worried about my own performance, I felt they might only reinforce each other's "weaknesses" (never thinking that they might reinforce each other's strengths) and be unable to effectively criticize. If I was anxious about my credentials to give feedback, how could students be prepared to do so?

Part of this fear might have derived from my own training in an MFA program, my own commitment to apprenticeship. How could a beginning plumber learn how to plumb from another beginner? Indeed, had I then been acquainted with the theory of collaborative learning, I suspect I would have found the word "collaborative" a bit unsavory, nearly smarmy, as it related to the process of writing. For me, "collaboration" conjured images of Vichy France. The teaching of writing through collaboration, then, posed a moral affront to my rigorous belief in solitary struggle at writing, never mind my own patriotism to the nation of apprentice-oriented workshops.

But once I began using collaborative workshops I learned that, far from being ill-suited to the task of serving as each other's audience, my students were ideally prepared—regardless of their talent for or previous training in writing. Because when they walk into the classroom, those students already are members "of several knowledge communities, from canoeing to computers, baseball to ballet. Membership in any one of these communities may not be a resource that will by itself help much directly in learning to organize an essay or explicate a poem. But pooling the resources that a group of peers brings with them to the task may make accessible the normal discourse of the new community they together hope to enter" (644).

This is not to suggest that merely having a peer point out that baseball does not involve touchdowns or that ballet dancers do not wear tap shoes will lead students to learn how to organize and make interesting an essay on either of these subjects. Yet surely such an essay will profit somewhat by this sort of input. And surely, as experienced readers and thinkers, students are capable of articulating their responses to work that is disorganized or uninteresting—surely they've come across such work before, often in published form. Sometimes all that is necessary to hone essay-writing skills is for someone to note that an essay as is doesn't make sense. Sometimes more concrete suggestions are needed. To those of us who have experienced the relative ease of critiquing another person's work compared to the difficulty of critiquing our own, it will come as no surprise that students can appreciate and suffer from the difference, too. And they, like us, learn much about what comprises effective writing by commenting on other people's work.

Since I began using workshops, I have discovered that, along with my students, I too am a member of certain "knowledge communities." One is that of the professional writer, another that of the teacher. I fit into the classroom group well, and my own resources easily pool with those of my students. I have learned new respect for the audience that, together, we constitute. So have my students—not to say they don't find the process of sharing their work initially unnerving. They find both workshopping and being workshopped very unnerving novelties, as did I as a graduate student. But in a workshop, the audience is there, it is visible and known, often intimately so. The students quickly gain appreciation of E. B. White's dictum that "no writer can improve his work until he discards the dulcet notion that the reader is feeble-minded, for writing is an act of faith, not a trick of grammar. . . . a writer who questions the capacity of the person at the other end of the line is not a writer at all, merely a schemer" (949). At our first workshop, my students look around the table and realize something crucial: people have read what they wrote. Real people, with needs—the needs of real readers to understand the writer's intentions. They hadn't thought of this before. Seeing a reader is talking to a reader; the reader's physical presence makes the concept of audience real. Like all writers who write to communicate rather than solely to express themselves, my students have no wish to pointlessly puzzle or weary or insult each other—either in person or through creation of their own tedious or incomprehensible texts.

Without such a forum, learning to value the audience is an intellectual exercise very difficult to master. In composition classes where I have not used workshops but have nevertheless tried to introduce the importance of audience, the legitimate questions students asked were consistently impossible to answer. Are we writing for you? Are we writing for the world out there? Are we writing for ourselves?

In those classes, I never came up with a response that made any sense—to me or to my students—though I tried many. And yet a perfectly appropriate audience was with us right there, in the classroom. They were freshmen or sophomores sitting in the chairs in front of me, slouched or alert but in any case passively awaiting The Word. My Word, speaking often of the need for them to develop their own voices. But what better way to hear your own voice—or to finally notice and attend to its inadvertent muffling—than in a group: a group in which all voices are equal, and the teacher's does not overpower?

In his introduction to *Writing Without Teachers*, Peter Elbow lays a framework for rendering the teacher as indistinct from the student as possible. In so doing, Elbow is "not trying to deny that there are good writing teachers. I know a few and it is impossible to miss them: they are people who simply succeed in helping most of their students write better and more satisfyingly. But they are exceedingly rare." What Elbow *is* trying to do is "deny something—something that is often assumed: *the necessary connection between learning and teaching*." In his class the students, along with the teacher, wholly and equitably participate as peers, for it "is possible to learn something and not be taught. . . . if the student's function is to learn and the teacher's to teach, then the student can function without a teacher, but the teacher cannot function without a student" (ix).

So when we think about the use of workshops in the classroom, we are challenging ourselves to "teach" in a very different way. But still, having accepted the evolution of the noun into the verb, how, specifically, to workshop?

It is one thing to hope to empower student writers with their own voices and their own suitability as audience and quite another thing to learn what, as a teacher, to expect and to do in a workshop: where, even, to sit during the discussion. The issue of seating in the classroom, as in any social situation, may appear insignificant but is in fact no small matter. The physical structure of the workshop simultaneously reflects and engenders the possibilities that occur there. What every student viscerally knows is that no one else in the workshop has the teacher's opportunity to render it a useless, even painful experience for students. For sheer valor in survival, few students can compete with one who has lived through a semester of workshops "facilitated" by someone who has botched the job. As a teacher, I started out at the head of the table and have since moved toward the middle; the student whose work is being discussed sits at the head and conducts the discussion. I decided to move from the head of the table, both literally and figuratively, because I wanted to make a clear statement to my students regarding my position on our relative power.

A brief horror story will prove the point. During the second year of my MFA program, a writer I very much admired routinely conducted a workshop for first-year students in a classroom directly above ours. Afterwards, a few students from each workshop would meet for a beer or a coffee at one of the local campus hang-outs. The first-year students rarely spoke about what happened in their workshop. They were more reticent, or perhaps more professional, than us second-year students, who typically hashed and rehashed everything that had gone on in our workshop. But for several weeks over beers, I had begun to detect an increasing anxiety whenever one of us asked, "So what happened tonight in your workshop?" Still, the first-year students didn't report anything of particular interest—just a vague angst: "It was okay, I guess. I survived. I'm not sure if so-and-so did."

Because it served several other purposes, the classroom in which the first-year workshop was held contained a small microwave oven in the far corner. One evening, frustrated with a student's work, the writer who taught that workshop began the session by turning on the microwave and placing the student's story in it. When the edges of the paper had begun to brown he turned off the microwave and held the story out to the class. "Half-baked," he pronounced. "That's what this is." The students, of course, said nothing.

That night, over beers, we didn't have to pry news of their workshop from the first-year students. They were, in a word, devastated. So were we. For all of us, it was as if our worst collective nightmare had come true. No matter that, the following week, the microwaver—having been confronted by a delegation of his students—apologized in class for his excesses. The fiction-writing community in any university generally is relatively small, nearly incestuous. Add to this that beginning writers tend toward a raw sensitivity, and the result is that what one teacher does in a workshop invariably effects other students and colleagues. The rest of the semester, we second-year students waited for the other shoe to drop on *us*, though the leader of our workshop was, for all her foibles, not nearly so narcissistic.

Enough said about the power to brutalize, except to underscore that the teacher who hopes to enable a successful workshop must think hard about issues of authority. For the sake of our own students as well as our colleagues, we must find ways to encourage students to trust the workshop as a generic entity: to feel when they enter it that the workshop is by reputation a safe, dependable, worthwhile place to explore the possibilities of their writing. In the academy as in the rest of the world, bad news travels fast—perhaps faster.

I began trying workshops by trying to "run" them because, in addition to having sat in chilling proximity to the above-mentioned microwaver, my own experience had initiated me to the tyranny of fellow students who were entirely unguided by any professorial expectations, reflected in comments like these: "This doesn't do it" (no explanation offered or required as to why not, or how to make "it" work); "I don't like that" (ditto); and "You can't write about a character who thinks this way" (ditto again, with the student whose story was "up" by this time completely silenced and glazed). Or, as a friend and fellow workshop veteran, now a published writer and teacher, sarcastically scribbled to me during a petty, interminable, and anarchic evening in which only the most minor aspects of a student story, rather than its essence, seemed to concern my fellow students: "What color were the pea pods?"

As it turned out, the teacher who was running that workshop was too timid to confront and become comfortable with her role as teacher. By her own admission, she disliked and was anxious about the teaching of fiction writing. So the atmosphere in that workshop became chaotic and adversarial rather than constructively supportive: that is to say, helpfully critical. (Or she was anxious about and therefore disliked teaching—I cannot remember her exact words, but I do remember that as a student eager for her interested input about my work, I didn't want to hear either explanation of her choice of profession and was sorry that I had.)

But there are also workshops, of little more use, in which the "helpfully" dominates the "critical," and the workshop becomes a mere support group. In these workshops, the comment considered most appropriate is something like "I loved what you wrote. So many strong points here! I guess there's stuff that could be improved—there always is—but basically this is really good."

Well, yes. But.

I am thinking, in particular, of the evening when my MFA workshop took on a story in which the protagonist, a young American woman visiting Germany on a Fulbright grant, dreamed that she was enjoying rambunctious, and graphically described, sexual intercourse with Adolf Hitler. Many problems afflicted this story, not least but perhaps the most obvious of which was that the Christian protagonist, a self-avowed Semitophile, seemed untroubled by the dream and the deep, unambivalent pleasure she took in it. At the start of the workshop, everyone except the story's writer appeared to be uncomfortable and awkward. But in the absence of any guidance from the teacher, several students—as if by silent agreement—began to locate the story's few sentences of scenic description and hold them up for prolonged praise. Finally, one or two people confessed to having taken deep offense at the subject matter. Not only that, but the dream about Hitler didn't arise from any connection to the protagonist's other aspects of character—so it seemed, at best, in sensational bad taste. Eventually, someone brought up the deeper implications of the issue—that some subjects, like the Holocaust, are too fraught with import to be used as metaphor for trivial events. But because most of the students were frightened by such unfriendly talk, and because the teacher remained mostly silent, the discussion quickly veered back to the overblown attributes of those one or two sentences of scenic description. It was safer that way.

There will always be students who, if they must be in a workshop, long for one of this touchy-feely kind. In an undergraduate setting the longing is understandable, given the youthfulness of the egos involved. Nevertheless, students must be weaned from this longing and learn to treat their work as work rather than cling to childlike awe about their written creations—what I think of as the beginning writer's "Mudpie Syndrome": yes, you are a writer; but at the moment, this is still a mudpie, and just because you made it doesn't mean it's beautiful. As John Gardner has said, a poor workshop results when "there are no standards for goodness . . . . If the teacher has no basic standards, his class is likely to develop none, and their comments can only be matters of preference or opinion. Writers will have nothing to strive toward or resist, nothing solid to judge by . . . undue rigidity can be destructive; but even a rigid set of standards, if it's clear and at least more or less valid, can be useful in giving the student something to challenge" (84).

This is not to suggest a parallelism between *personal* rigidity and "good" workshops—in other words, let us agree that at minimum the microwaver-teacher clearly forgot, or never realized, what Gardner has astutely noted: "the extent to which aesthetic standards are projections of one's own personality, defensive armor, or wishful thinking about the world" (84). But whatever the differences in precipitating psychologies, the results in all three of these workshops were not dissimilar. The business of the workshop was not being attended to. And this business of workshopping is for the students and the teacher together "to figure out (or if necessary ask) the purpose and meaning of the piece and only then to suggest carefully, thoughtfully, why the purpose and meaning did not [or did] come through" (82).

Elbow offers more specific guidelines for workshop members, advising readers to give writers "movies of your mind" (85). Readers should point to and summarize the text under discussion, tell and show how the writing made them experience whatever they experienced while reading it. In other words, it is not enough for the student reader to say to the writer, "I didn't understand a lot of this. I just couldn't get into it." A close reading and reference to the text is necessary. What might be said is, "After you finished talking about the woman on the flagpole, I was lost when she wound up at the roller skating rink—it's over here, in the middle of the third page. I found myself day-dreaming at that point." Guidelines for appropriate responses to student work may—indeed, should—be articulated by the teacher before the workshops begin. Such a practice gets the students thinking about their own goals and expectations for the workshop and helps ease their fear of the unknown; they feel safer knowing that the workshop is not a metaphor for anarchy, that someone is in caring charge, though this someone—you or I—may not particularly resemble the authority figure of the traditional classroom. Without clear ground rules, those who venture into any new enterprise tend to flounder, not knowing how to start. As Portnoy says at the end of his *Complaint*, "Now vee may perhaps to begin."

To clarify my expectations for the workshop and help prepare my students for it, I give them a chunk of Elbow to read and discuss, and I don't begin workshops until several weeks into the semester. Those first few weeks, we discuss examples of professional writing—also in the workshop format. We look at the anatomy and physiology of the particular essay or short story we are reading, try to understand if and how and where it works (What is this essay about? What is the author trying to say? Do all the parts serve that intention?)—how the so-called rules of a particular form of writing are impeccably followed or brilliantly foiled. By the time we begin workshopping the students' own writing, we have developed a mutual vocabulary suitable to the task.

Student essays in my class are never workshopped anonymously because the students lead discussions about their own essays and because I believe strongly that writers must sign their own names and take or enjoy the consequences, as is the case in all matters of import. I feel strongly too that students have a responsibility and a right to prod and question their audiences; this is not possible when the essay is anonymous, for the student whose work is being critiqued feels too keenly the risk of exposing his or her authorship by speaking out. I want my students to know the pleasure and frustration of coherently writing and speaking to an audience.

Generally, I "run" the semester's first workshop—not for a last fling at exerting my professorial control but to help guide the students through a new experience about which, after all, I already have familiarity. By this point, besides reading Elbow, the students know what *I* expect in the workshop: that they will, simply, continue to treat each other according to the Golden Rule—and in addition to common civility, this means that they have a mutual responsibility to speak up and help their peers by offering whatever insights they have. In a classroom where time is limited, silence is not golden, though a certain amount is inevitable and must be accepted as part of the process. My students also must be concrete in their comments—point to the text or to where something crucial is missing from the text. Beyond this I don't harp; they get it. Probably they would have without my sermon, but as a teacher whose occupational anxiety is never fully dormant, I tend to repeat myself.

In this sample workshop, as in all others, the student writer first reads aloud a paragraph of the work so that members of the class can hear the writer's voice. During the discussion that follows I try to keep us focused on the text (monologues forbidden, pea pods always are green), pointing out why I am saying whatever I am saying. My standard opener: "It would be useful if, before you [the writer] explain what you were trying to do, we listen to what your readers thought you were trying to do. You'll get a cleaner read that way." At the end of the workshop, the readers pass to the writer their copies of the essay, along with the comments they wrote before class. These comments help the writer later, in revision, and have helped the readers to begin thinking hard about the essay before they get to class. In my experience, when students read aloud work that others hear for the first time, the ability of everyone in the room—myself included—to give thoughtful feedback is seriously undermined. In such cases, shooting from the hip becomes the norm, and instead of gaining understanding the writer must spend every moment ducking bullets: some of criticism, some of praise, but all half-formed.

I always keep in mind that the workshop is a writer's group. Here, as always, the noun is stronger than the adjective: group dynamics, while mercifully vibrant and impossible to control, may be crucially influenced. Vigilance is too harsh a goal, but the teacher must be attuned not only to comments about the writing but also to what goes on interpersonally among the students. Though the need rarely arises if the workshop is constructed with care and clear guidelines, the teacher must intervene if intervention becomes necessary. For beginning writers in particular, the wounds of indecent exposure take a long time to heal.

As leader of the semester's first student workshop I avoid commenting on the writing itself, but in following workshops—when the student writer leads the discussion—I do, with greater ease and thoroughness than in the days when I confined my remarks to scrawlings in the margins of the paper. I take comfort in knowing that, when faced with a criticism particularly difficult to raise, several students invariably will back me up: more often than not, they were waiting for me to make the tough comment. (There is no such thing as a true democracy. This is fine. It's my job, and my skill.) I also am comforted by knowing that, if my comments on a given day are off the mark, other students will not hesitate to tell the writer to take what I say with a pound of salt. Which has happened. I was tired. One of my buttons was pushed. I misread.

Or I am just, as my students tell me, hopelessly old-fashioned. We laugh a lot during workshops. Once, when a protagonist in a student story spent the night "pounding a few," I asked the writer, "Is that something about sex?" I had read the story as if it were, but I was wrong, and was duly informed with much rolling of the eyes that at least in Cambridge, "pounding" means drinking beers very quickly. No use arguing that my generation had a different term for the same activity.

But I'm glad to have my students flanking me. Freed of the traditional authoritarian role, the teacher may respond as a human being to student work: as writer to writer. Acknowledging our human fallibility—the fact that each of us is one voice only, with no hotline to The Truth—encourages students to trust us at the same time it teaches them to depend more and more on their own critical abilities: to serve as their own teachers, critics, and editors. Most students leaving the composition classroom rarely will be back to take another writing course; yet they will be writing for the rest of their college careers, often for the rest of their professional careers. We must give them their own internalized teachers, critics, editors.

Some teachers who use workshops select or ask a few of their students to volunteer to be workshopped during the course of the semester. I structure the syllabus so that each student is workshopped once—given the inherent teacher/student disequilibrium, I can at least minimize that of student/student. But there are many variations to the workshop. One that I especially like is useful when working on openings and closings. Then, instead of one or two students "being up," each student reads aloud the first or last paragraph of her essay and receives a few minutes of peer feedback, limited to specific criticism—for instance, Did the opening grab your attention? Did the ending satisfy your need for closure? During these all-class workshops, the students who read near the end of the hour invariably are seen furiously editing before then, having decided while their peers were reading how to improve their own paragraphs. In any case, however the workshop is formatted, by midpoint in the semester quite a few students often are disappointed that because of time constraints they cannot go "up" again.

And I am sorry too, because I worry that they may never have another opportunity to sit at a table of similarly concerned, knowledgable peers and say, "Tell me what you think my essay is about." For when they hear the responses, the writing of students invariably improves. One young man had meant to write a personal essay about mourning the loss of a friend from cocaine overdose. But too many people at the table in our classroom— not all the people, it's never all—experienced the essay as a polemic to "Just say no." They did not detect or feel moved by the personal origin of the writer's anger about drugs; they felt that they were being preached to through a sermon, in which the dead boy merely was another statistic.

The value and heft of this feedback is something that, as a single voice, I alone cannot offer. My own voice, while important, is not as important as that writer's personal discovery that his intent did not sufficiently surface to the page: sufficiently in this sense—that he cared deeply about his essay, so deeply that he wanted *everyone,* or at least more students than did, to "get it."

I never mastered the screeching chalk. So I gave up the blackboard.

Works Cited

Bambura, "What It Is I Think I'm Doing Anyway." In *The Writer on Her Work,* Ed. Janet Sternburg, New York: W.W. Norton & Co., 1980.

Bruffee, Kenneth A. "Collaborate learning and the 'conversation of mankind.'" *College English* 46 (7)(1984): 635–652.

Elbow, Peter. *Writing Without Teachers.* New York: Oxford U.P., 1973.

Gardner, John. *On Becoming a Novelist.* New York: Harper and Row, 1983.

White, E. B. "Calculating Machine," in *The Dolphin Reader,* Douglas Hunt, ed. Boston: Houghton–Mifflin, 1986, p 949.

Alex Johnson

Why Isaac Bashevis Singer, Truman ☙ Capote, Joseph Conrad and Virginia Woolf (Among Others) Were Having a Bad Morning

And so I begin:

"I sit down religiously every morning. I sit down for eight hours and the sitting down is all. In the course of that working day I write three sentences which I erase before leaving the table in despair. Sometimes it takes all my resolution and power of self-control to refrain from butting my head against the wall. After such cries of despair I doze for hours still conscious that I am unable to write. Then I wake up, try again, and at last go to bed completely done up. In the morning I get up with that horror of the powerlessness . . . *The ideas and words creep about my head and have to be caught and tortured into shape.*" (Olsen, 156)

It's that final sentence that always does it. Not a single yawn; not a pair of eyelids fluttering asleep in the overheated lecture hall. The faces stare in recognition. Undergraduate misery. It's all there in those words: the heroic self-despair, the frustration, the well-intentioned effort doomed to failure. The quotation, I tell them, isn't from a sleep-deprived student, but Joseph Conrad.

As the collective gasp settles I'm reminded of what it was really like to be in college: the intellectual excitement of discovering Conrad, the dull panicked despair of having to write a *paper* on him. The horror. The horror. Yet, like these students, college presented its own obstacle course for me. How in a seminar on image systems in George Eliot or moral imperatives in Mill could I ask the real questions that nagged me term after term: Why is writing so hard? Why does it take me so long? Why do I need to do so many drafts? Why can't I do them faster? Will the process ever be less agonizing?

I never figured these out as a student. Like the Furies, these questions haunted me from college to graduate work to my first job. This was particularly inconvenient as my first job was as a writer. In print. Often. My first editor was no help at all. She had sold her first short story at 16, her first novel at 21. She was 71 when I met her: novelist, biographer, woman of letters. I could no more ask her than my college professors. My luck, though, was soon about to change. Together we devised a series on creativity, profiled interviews with famous writers, which she called "Artists and Their Inspiration," and I, *sotto voce*, "Artists and Their Perspiration." Writing was still very hard work for me. I'd come to agree with Thomas Mann that "a writer is someone for whom writing is more difficult than it is for other people." (Plimpton, vi). I longed for and dreaded this series. I knew that while the interview with Elizabeth Bishop or John Fowles would take only four hours, crafting the finished piece could take me weeks.

My first interview was with novelist Isaac Bashevis Singer. I had barely arrived at his apartment on Manhattan's Upper West Side when Singer himself opened the door. The face, of course, I knew. It was the expression that startled me, one I recognized instantly: Isaac Bashevis Singer hadn't had a good morning writing. His face was like a crumpled piece of paper. I followed him into the living room where he writes. The wastebasket was full, the Yiddish typewriter covered. Was it possible that Singer, six months away from winning the Nobel Prize for Literature, wasn't immune to these same questions? Apparently. Singer, I soon learned, wasn't wearing a coat and tie just for the interview. He wears them daily as if when writing he's preparing himself for a strenuous job interview or a difficult dinner guest. I'd found my man. "Mr. Singer," I began, "on days when writing isn't going, say, perfectly well . . ."

In that series and elsewhere I discovered what I had suspected intuitively: writers have some very odd work habits to help with the exacting business of writing, of getting ideas on paper. Saul Bellow, for example, writes on two typewriters: one for fiction, the other, nonfiction. John Updike writes in four rooms, each corresponding to a different genre (fiction, reviewing, nonfiction, letters), with different writing implements (typewriter, legal pad, computer). Anne Tyler writes only on one end of the same sofa. Fay Weldon writes in her kitchen; Singer in his living room with the telephone constantly ringing.

Of all the stories of writers coping with the vagaries of the writing process, my favorite is Truman Capote's from *The Paris Review*'s series *Writers at Work*. Capote, it seems, had stern ritualistic prohibitions about where and when he could (and couldn't) write best. Other people's homes were most problematic. "I have to add up all the numbers. There are some people I never telephone because their number adds up to an unlucky number. Or I will not tolerate the presence of yellow roses which is sad as they're my favorite flowers. I can't allow three cigarette butts in the same ashtray. Won't travel on a plane with two nuns. Won't begin or end anything on a Friday. It's endless, the things I can't and won't. But I derive some curious comfort from obeying these primitive concepts" (Cowley, 298).

In over *eight* years' teaching at Harvard, I've discovered that undergraduates have superstitions that rival these. Among the most sacred:

I can only write well just before the paper is due.

If I start early, the paper loses all its life.

There's not enough time for more than one solid draft.

Anyway, I can't undo my first draft once it's done. That's it.

I can only work at 2 a.m. with my radio on and my roommate out.

My favorite scenario, though, goes something like this: the student sits down at his desk, hands poised on the keyboard. The moment he touches the keys (as it's described), someone else inhabits his body, a kind of literary poltergeist: dimwitted but determinedly strong-willed. Incapable of original thought. Who else was responsible for writing this badly? Obviously someone else. This is confirmed the following week when the tutor, holding up the offending essay, asks: "Who wrote this?" With total candor the student replies: "I dunno."

Flannery O'Connor was once asked if she thought writing courses stifled college students. "Not enough," she replied. (Hersey, 56) The question, it seems to me, isn't how to stifle students so much as how to prevent them from doing it to themselves. When we tell students "just write . . . ," it's not ourselves that we're opening up to a chaos of incoherent writing, but them. Those two words, so deceptively simple, self-evident in their very command, are often a kind of Pandora's box for students. We tell them "just write," but have we shown them how? We assume they know how to work, but do they? Too often are we guilty of the very error they make: stressing writing as a product, not a process? Writing as a seven-page paper rather than a two- or three-stage process, multifaceted, richly creative, strewn with frustration, full of false starts, ultimate solutions, unexpected connections? Writing.

At some point every writer inevitably grapples with the vagaries of how she works. As I learned from Singer, it is often a lifelong process, one that shifts with each new level of writing and expertise. Yet while there is everything deeply mysterious about the creative process, there is less so about the actual stages of writing itself. (Here I'm addressing nonfiction exclusively. Fiction is its own kingdom, its path requiring its own compass.) This, then, is an essay about process, creative and structural. It's a step-by-step look at the writing process itself: from the moment a student learns she has to write something till the moment it's handed in. It is *not* intended to be prescriptive. Rather, it's a way to reflect on the writing process, specifically, the creativity of thinking, of connections, that happen in those early stages. Call it making peace with those questions, mine and those I hear each term. I want to honor those questions—confessed rather than asked, it seems— questions strategically timed at the end of conference or when shuffling out of class, questions disguised as spontaneous afterthoughts, questions that invariably follow: "I know this sounds stupid but . . ." It shouldn't take me so long. I write too many drafts. I'm smart, so why is writing still so hard?

Unlike most students, I now know that these questions simply don't disappear after graduation (or publication). The questions seem to be an integral part of the writing process. My favorite definition of writing, in fact, comes from a colleague, Doug Bauer, who says you know that writing is starting to happen the moment you start feeling the resistance to it. Indeed, don't be misled by the anthology you now hold. These essays, full of wit and insight, were not effortless. Or quick. I'd wager that at some point every single author here, to varying degrees, experienced frustration, boredom, panic, loathing: a collective *Why* did I ever agree to do this? (Why? Our editors blithely said, "Just write . . .") And so, like Forster's Adela Quested in the Marabar Caves, we, just like *all* writers, entered fresh with hope, began groping in the increasing darkness, only somewhere in the process to find our minds ricocheting with panic and emptiness, panic and emptiness.

As writers we often forget how long it took to formulate our own ways of working. I certainly did. I spent the first two years of my teaching wondering why students' shoulders would bunch up around their earlobes everytime I announced a new assignment. I never made a connection between "just write . . ." and the often miserable "products" I got. Nor had I made the connection that I spent all term telling them what they weren't doing rather than how, possibly, they might write.

That changed one spring term. After a particularly long weekend of my own writing, I introduced them to the voices that, like some deranged *a cappella* group, had vied for my attention as I worked. Voices, no doubt, that echoed within them. I introduced them to my internal board of directors, so-called as, historically, mine have had such endless funding and re- sources it could only be corporate sponsorship. These, I told them, were the real poltergeists homesteading in their bodies as they tried to write. These were the culprits who were forever carping and interfering, whispering the most dubious advice. If you were to write, you had to wrest control back from them. I'd narrowed the worst perpetrators to four: the internal critic, the saboteur, the procrastinator, the perfectionist. I then asked students— and have been asking them ever since—if they recognized the following situations.

──────── *The Internal Critic* ────────

Scene: Two days before a paper is due the student sits down to work. He stares at his computer but does nothing yet. He is haunted by a small voice inside that tells him his idea isn't original, that, somewhere, there's a "right" answer to the essay.

IC: "And you, idiot, don't have it. Everyone else in the class does, but, of course, they're *smart*."

Undeterred, the student starts with the idea he has. He's halfway through the first sentence when he hears:

IC: "Wrong word!!! Number four, the verb. Wrong, wrong, wrong. Stop and cross it out. Look up a better word. *Yes*, better means bigger. Of course it's okay to interrupt yourself here. Go on, go on."

The student obeys, thumbs through a worn thesaurus and inserts "contraindicated" for "opposed." He finishes the sentence and rereads it immediately.

IC: "Let's face it, it doesn't have the ring of 'Call me Ishmael' or 'In mid-journey along the path of our life, I found myself in a dark wood and the true way was lost.' "

The student heaves a small sigh.

IC: "Scrap the sentence. It sounds too studenty. Go on. You've got to sound intelligent. Imitate what writing should sound like. Try to get 'the writer's voice.' Imitate James Joyce. Orwell. Kafka, even. Anyone but *you*."

Subtext: A belief that, like some Platonic ideal, there's only one right answer to any given assignment. A belief that the "original" (and final) idea automatically comes in the first draft. A belief that it's productive to interrupt yourself constantly, writing and editing simultaneously. A belief that making a sentence different is always the same as making it better. A belief that your own voice has to be airbrushed out of any piece of writing in favor of that nebulous "writer's voice." (We all know those papers where students have opted for some imagined writer's tone. It's like Muzak in prose: distorted, eerily distanced from the original source, annoyingly ever-present.)

──────── *The Saboteur* ────────

Scene: 10 p.m. The student has just returned from the library. All the books on his subject have already been checked out. Maybe he should have gone earlier. Not the night before the paper is due.

S: "You know, you're probably a journalist. You thrive on deadlines! Nah, don't worry. You do your best work right before a paper is due. You *need* deadline pressure. Can you feel that tension? Whoa, it's going to be some paper."

10:30 p.m.

S: Okay, big deal. So you knew you were meeting friends at 10:30 for a pizza. You deserve a break. You'll pick up right where you left off. It's no easy thing what you've just done. And it *is* a great title."

12 a.m.

S: "Is it your fault that place is so criminally slow?"

The student rereads his class notes and pulls out a sheet of paper.

S: "An outline?? What are you doing!! Do you realize what *time* it is? Who has time to organize? Relax. You've got all the ideas in your head. No prob. It's a cinch to get them out."

1:30 a.m.

S: "A quick nap always helps. I mean you've got the first page out of the way. The other six will flow better when you're not so sleepy. Better order a medium next time. Without onions."

7:30 a.m.

S: "Damn. Numero uno today: get a new alarm clock."

9:30 a.m.

S: "So the main idea is on page four—at the bottom. What are they going to do, *sue you?* The argument does skip around and you could use a bit more evidence. Don't worry, they'll get the basic idea. They only read the first and last pages anyway. Proofread? No time. Turn it in like it is. Anyway, professors don't mind a few typos. They probably don't know how to spell Madagascar either."

Subtext: The first-as-final draft syndrome, that hothoused all-night assault, which mistakes deadline pressure for inspiration, a single-night effort for efficiency. Since he's never worked any other way, the student has yet to find anything to contradict his experience that writing is agonizing, something to be gotten over as quickly as possible. Writing as product, never as process. Seeing that he got a C−, the student rationalizes: "I could have gotten an A if I'd had more time." (How many times have you suspected that you've spent more time correcting an essay than the student spent writing it?)

—————— *The Procrastinator* ——————

Scene: a room so neat that a passerby suddenly wonders if it's Parent's Week already. In June? Oh, the history paper is due . . .

Pro: "There's so much to do!!!"

Variation One
"Clean out the closet. Again. Alphabetize the medicine chest. Make a fresh cup of coffee. This time you can grind the beans with your desk stapler. Iron your shoelaces . . ."

Variation Two

"You have a whole week before the paper's due!"
"You have three whole days before it's due!"
"You can get a lot done the night before it's due!"
"You can set your alarm for 3:30. That's enough time!"
"You can ask for an extension!"

Subtext: If only any of us could harness the creativity we expend avoiding writing on actually writing, we would all be in great shape.

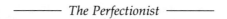

The Perfectionist

Scene: The student knows she has a week to write the paper. That's good. A brittle voice inside tells her she's going to need every single minute of it. She's been through this before. As she faces her computer she wears an expression seen only on PhD candidates, nuclear fission experts, and test pilots.

Per: "You know the rules: you cannot possibly go on to the second sentence until the first is perfect. Perfect idea, word choice, style, grammar. You can't go on to sentence three until number two is perfect. You can't go on to . . ."

The student tenses and hazards her first sentence.

Per: "Let's get this right. The *whole* paper hangs on it. And what do we mean by right, missy? Perfect, perfect, perfect. Polish, polish, polish. Make that sentence shine. It doesn't sound like a Pascalian epigram to me yet."

The student stops. The voice is oddly familiar. Somehow the tight, practiced smile of her sixth-grade teacher comes to mind, the one who taught how to do outlines that looked like Bauhaus models.

Per: "Of course it's normal to spend four hours getting the first paragraph absolutely right. And, yes, it *was* necessary to retype the entire paragraph every time there was one of those very nasty, messy little typos."

The student rereads the paragraph and groans. It doesn't sound like Pascal. It sounds disturbingly like her. It must be wrong.

Per: "Odious, dull, trite, banal. Horrid. This definitely won't do. *Imagine* if they chose to read this in front of the entire class. All your peers laughing. Just like in 'Dumbo.'"

Silence. And then, a small thudding sound, remarkably similar to someone hitting her head against a computer screen. Silence. The student narrows her eyes. The perfectionist, correctly guessing her thoughts, shrieks:

Per: "SHOW this to someone? ARE YOU CRAZY? And reveal yourself? No one has these problems. No one. Let's start again. Yes, from the top, literally. Sentence one. Practice makes perfect."

Subtext: Perfect makes paralysis. The student is crippled by unrealistic standards (wanting to write just like Proust) and unrealistic expectations (writing like Proust *in her first draft*). Unfortunately, "first" and "draft" aren't taken literally. The perfectionist is the internal critic gone wild. A belief that everything in the first draft must be tightly locked into place: thinking, writing, style. A mistaken emphasis on polishing style rather than loosening thinking. The polishing not only flattens the writing but inhibits the creative connections in thinking. Failing to live up to some preconceived (and self-imposed) standard, the draft(s) is usually abandoned. The perfectionist usually has five versions, all unfinished, littering the desk. When such a student finally turns in the paper, I'm always surprised to see it's typed. It feels as if it should be chiseled in marble with that strange Roman lettering you see over post offices or federal buildings.

For Gail Godwin all these voices coalesce into one ogre: the watcher. "My watcher," she writes, "has a wasteful penchant for 20-pound bond paper above and below the carbon of the first draft. 'What's the good of writing out a whole page,' he whispers begrudgingly, 'if you have to write it over again later? Get it perfect the first time!' My watcher adores stopping in the middle of a morning's work to drive down to the library to check on the name of a flower or a World War II battle or a line of metaphysical poetry. 'You can't possibly go on till you've got this right!' he admonishes. I go and get the car keys. On a very bad day I wrote my watcher a letter. 'What is it you're so afraid I'll do?' Then I held his pen for him and he replied instantly and with a candor that has kept me from truly despising him. 'Fail,' he wrote back" (Godwin, 1977, 31).

Let me confess. I have often misjudged students' failures. One example from this last term. Reading a student's first essay I muttered, "All the telltale signs: repetitions, poor evidence, even poorer writing. Obviously a charter member of the saboteur-procastinator club." He wasn't. He had tried hard. He simply didn't know how to write. Or work. He had gone to a school where writing was minimal, revision nonexistent. He simply needed someone to show him the writing process. I did. But I never would have known any of this had I not questioned him about how he worked. Oddly, he was far easier to work with than his classmate who, potentially, ranked among the top three in the class. Her problem was perfectionism. (She was a walking embodiment of Gene Fowler's quip: "Writing is easy; all you do is sit staring at a blank sheet of paper until the drops of blood form on your forehead." (Metcalf, 1987, 273)) Her work suffered from a tight, overconstricted focus. Learning to loosen her grip, to break up the writing process and experiment was probably the most invaluable part of the course for her.

Like Godwin, I tell my students to write their watchers a letter. Some send telegrams, others pink slips. One wrote a parody of a Raymond Chandler murder where the very dead bullet-ridden corpse was the late internal critic. Another student wrote a lengthy Rothian dialogue between procrastinator patient and analyst who advised: "Ya vell, so perhaps, *now* we begin?" The assignment, while creative, isn't an exorcism so much as an exercise in self-awareness: of how their habits aid or abet work. Above all, that they are responsible for the act of writing. I then ask them to draw up a list of ten (or so) writing resolutions, a kind of Martin Luther edict of dubious habits, that will glare from their desk. ("Thou shalt not sit down to work at 10 knowing thou art hotfooting it out for pizza at 10:30 . . .")

But, of course, even the best resolutions are born to be broken. At some point we all get lazy and once again the board members are loitering in the hall. They gang up. The result? After "just write," the *other* two most dreaded words: writer's block. The classic symptoms we all know: the page or screen as white as our knuckles. Terror. Boredom. A carpet worn in a crescent pattern from pacing. Yet there are more subtle versions: the stalled second paragraph rewritten for the tenth time; five variants of the same essay on the desk; the essay that changes its idea page after page, orbiting its subject in some ghastly Flying Dutchman nightmare. Writer's block.

In my lecture "Inspiration and Procrastinat ion: Everything You Wanted to Know About Writing, but, Like Me, Were Too Embarrassed to Ask in College," I ask students if they know why they get this. They do. Like drowning sailors, the hands go up one by one: *fearing you have the wrong thesis* ("I just know it has to be more complicated than this"); *terror of grades* ("If I don't get an A, I'll never get into med. school"); *boredom* ("Who cares about Tamil linguistic theory?"). *Audience.* Oh yes, I sigh. I tell them about my college history professor, a horrid, illustrious man who would spasm a smile every time I came to conference. "I have your latest effort here," he'd say wearily, stressing effort—his not mine. He was my internal critic externalized. Made manifest. Writ large. It took me years to get him and his thin smile of toleration out of my mind as I sat down to work. Whoever our own version is—professor, parent, peer—it has to be exorcised if we are to work well.

While all these contribute to writer's block, there are four real reasons it occurs. One is purely mechanical: writing and editing simultaneously, compulsively. I liken it to driving with a hand brake on. You can move—but not very fast. Writing: one inch forward; editing: two inches back. The constant push-pull is fatiguing. As a consequence, the writer gives up sooner. The three most common reasons for writer's block, though, are:

Not understanding or having a full grasp of the subject yet

Not generating out enough material on that subject to begin writing

Not sufficiently organizing the material at hand

Whenever I get stuck I try to identify which of these is the culprit. However perversely, the mind here is doing the writer a favor. Heed it. It's trying to tell us that we're not prepared to write yet, that if we start now we'll invariably do draft after draft after draft. Why? Because we're still using writing to find out what we think about a subject. This seems to make a lot of sense to students. They always copy it into their notebooks. So, too, when I mention that we all do so many drafts to refine the *thinking*, not the writing. Indeed, the hardest part of writing isn't writing *per se*, but the thinking behind it, the exacting business of making ideas and words and images concrete. And the hardest, most agonizing, least efficient way to write is first-as-final draft. Students never copy that down in their notebooks. It's sacred, the college credo: I first-draft, therefore I write. If it's so effective, I always ask the sea of faces in the lecture hall, why did you all petition to get into this writing class? The pens tilt back to full mast again.

Yet the question still looms: How to get the thinking out? It took me years of trial and error to learn the obvious: writing is best and most satisfyingly done in stages. Like Truman Capote's not writing on Fridays or Singer's working in a coat and tie, I have learned to obey my own writing process faithfully. It has helped me do what my student have signed up to learn: to write faster, do fewer drafts. I now know and trust completely that writing happens long before I ever type a word; that my best thinking and writing will happen before and after the first draft but not necessarily during it; that by seeing writing as a process, I now know the pleasure of making connections: ruminating on a subject, seeing patterns emerge, watching an argument evolve, evidence cohere. In short, that glorious territoriality of staking and claiming a subject as my own.

Just as a writer makes a subject his own, so must he with his own writing process. It is as individual as writers themselves. The following five-stage process works for me. It is not meant to be prescriptive. Rather, it's more of a working guideline, a way of breaking down the writing process, a way of respecting that each stage has a unique and powerful purpose. Moreover, each has simple methods to facilitate writing to its next stage. (The following steps are spread over a week, the normal span a student has between hearing of an assignment and having to turn it in. The days alter according to individual process.)

──────── *Stage One: Ruminate (Day 1)* ────────

We have all had the experience: while taking a shower or on an afternoon walk the very idea that eluded us all morning at our desk suddenly looms: vivid, concrete. There. Virginia Woolf captured this phenomenon in her journal: "I walk, making up phrases, sit contriving scenes; am, in short, in the thick of the greatest rapture known to me." (Olsen, 173) Like so many writers, Woolf had long discovered a secret to her own work process: it was on walks or while writing in her journal—not at her desk—that inspiration often struck. The axiom is simple: when the critical guard is relaxed, the mind is more apt to produce a great tumble of ideas and fresh phrasing. As Rebecca West once noted: "My memory is certainly in my hands. I can remember things only if I have a pencil and I can write with it and play with it. I think your hand concentrates for you" (Plimpton, 64).

26: *Copy of First Draft, p. 16*

~~As I write the steps on the board I always say.~~

~~Process, like a subject~~, claim as ~~your~~ own. ~~Process~~ is

an individual as writers themselves. As I write steps, not

intended to be prescriptive but a working guideline, a way of

breaking writing into stages, each with its own, simple exercises
to facilitate ~~each~~ stage.

Stage One: Ruminate

(Day 1)

"I walk, making up phrases, sit, contriving scenes; am, in short,

in the thick of the greatest rapture known to me." When Virginia

Woolf recorded this in her journal she had long since discovered

a secret to her own work process. Her best ideas and phrases often

happened not while sitting at her desk but on her daily walks or
when the critical guard is relaxed
when writing in her journal: a great tumble of deas.

We have all had the experience: while taking a shower or on

a walk the very idea that had eluded us all morning at our desk

suddenly looms up: vivid, concrete. <u>There</u>. Virginia Woolf captured

this wrote in her journal: "I walk, making up phrases, sit, contriving
: Tantalus-like ~~logic~~: not at her desk on walks, writing in her journal.
scenes; am, in short, in the thick of the greatest rapture known to

me." ~~She had long discovered;~~ when the critical guard is relaxed,

the mind produced a great tumble of ideas or inages.

Do not wait till the night before a paper's due to introduce yr mind to
The moment you hear you have to write something walk away it.
Students underestimate this stage.
from it, sleep on it. Make procrastination work for you. (Anne Tyler

has notecards house so when idea) Write it down. It will have

How first phrasing idea was correct. ~~Don't wait to introduce your~~

~~mind to your subject the night before a paper is due.~~ Even in late

stages--especially revision--ruumnate. Finger it like worry eads.

~~Start the moment you hear it's due.~~ The satisfaction of tucking

found money into a savings account.

The secret is keeping the internal critic out. (If you jot ideas on the back of an old Visa slip, you can fool him into thinking you're not working, which, of course, you are.) The real point is letting the mind work creatively *for* you. Do not wait till the night before a paper's due, I always tell students, to introduce your mind to a subject. Make "procrastination" work for you: sleep on it, walk away from it. Literally. Gail Godwin keeps note cards all over her house. She knows that it is often while she's doing something else—cooking, reading, exercising—that ideas surface from the sub-conscious. They're usually the ones that are still there in the final draft. Write them down immediately when they come. It's the satisfaction of tucking found money into a savings account.

──────── *Stage Two: Generate (Day 2)* ────────

While reading Schiller's letters Freud came across a sentence that fascinated him. Advising a frustrated young writer, Schiller observed: "You reject too soon, you discriminate too severely." For Freud it identified the root of literary paralysis. Yet it is precisely what most students do before ridding themselves of their watchers. No wonder writing is allotted only one night. It helps stem the chaos, the frustration. The judgment.

Ironically, it's that so-called chaos, the having to sit with inchoate, unstructured material, that needs to be tapped. The process is generating. By suspending critical judgment, ideas are allowed to pour out and connec-tions to be made before ever writing a single sentence. The problem Schiller cites isn't what to alter in the writing process so much as *when*. By going straight from vague ideas to first draft, students reverse the natural order of work: trying to write logically before they've thought intuitively about their material. Again, without knowing it, they are using draft(s) to find out what they think.

Draft ideas, not sentences. This is the key to generating. Use the freedom of the legal pad—not the formality of a first draft—to get the initial thinking out. Generate first, write second. Unfortunately, in the rush "to get writing" (mistaking typing as writing), it is the step most often skipped over. Ten minutes of freewriting saves literally hours of false starts in drafts. By concentrating on ideas—not on how they're expressed or spelled—generating not only silences the watchers but sparks the material that allows the writer to begin properly.

The easiest way to generate is freewriting. Da Vinci did a similar exercise every morning upon rising, writing thought after thought to limber up his mind. Many writers, notably Gide, Woolf, Chekhov, Tolstoy, have used journals for the same purpose. Relieved of the burden of correct phrasing, the mind concentrates on ideas instead. One idea triggers another and another again. It is what Woolf called finding "diamonds" amid "the dustheap." (234)

If you work on a computer, simply turn off the brightness light and begin freewriting on your topic. Many people prefer working on a legal pad first. Once you get going—and it will happen quite quickly—don't stop. The temptation is to break off the moment the first plausible idea occurs and start the first draft. Don't. Probe the connections further, push the associations. When the topic is exhausted, print out or go back over the material, highlighting the good ideas (and phrasing) with a yellow marker.

Listing is my version of freewriting. I dispense with sentences altogether. I usually begin with something concrete from my subject: a fact, a quotation, a source comment, something that my mind can work like a worry bead. I then jot the ideas in respective groupings. At the end, the page looks like a map of ancient Egypt: small pyramids of material over what had once been a wasteland of white paper.

Generating is the one step I insist students do before starting a first draft. (Almost invariably, the paper without solid connections or clear argument has skipped this stage or done it only briefly.) The real dividend, of course, is a sense of confidence and control. Seeing how much material they've generated, and how, in the process, a pattern has emerged from it, they can begin the first draft with a degree of control.

――――― *Stage Three: Organize (Day 2)* ―――――

Nothing makes me more nervous than hearing a student say, "The ideas are all in my head." Writing is that problematic physics of getting ideas from gray matter to white paper. The single most important change in my own writing since undergraduate days is the amount of time I spend organizing material before writing. So too my students. By the end of the term, they spend more time organizing for the simple reason that it saves them unnecessary drafts. Organization techniques vary greatly. I simply number my freewriting pyramids in logical sequence, jotting support or evidence under each heading. John McPhee prefers notecards for both his freewriting and organizing stages. Each idea is allotted an individual card. He merely orders them according to the shape he wants a project to take. Whether you use these or a traditional outline (now available in software packages), organizing safeguards against interruption while writing. If you have to stop, when you return you can pick up directly where you left off—an impossibility if the material is still free-floating in your mind.

――――― *Stage Four: First Draft (Late Day 2; Early Day 3)* ―――――

During college years this is usually step one. No wonder so many students get stuck and frustrated. Why is writer's block so common at this point? Look at what's being asked: to think, write, organize, *and* make connections about the material simultaneously. Four separate activities, each challenging in and of itself. To work effectively, the writing process needs to be broken up into manageable stages.

What should one expect from the first draft? A controling idea. Period. The most common misconception is that the first draft is about writing *per se*. It's not. It's about thinking. If you've managed to turn out felicitious phrasing, I always tell students, it's icing on the cake. The real concern is how your idea evolves and sharpens, how its deeper structure emerges. To help this process along, don't agonize over word choice. Underline a word or simply leave a space and go back in the revision stage to get it right. Use momentum. Gag your internal critic and perfectionist when they report, correctly, that the draft seems sketchy. That's why it's called a first draft. Don't be too wedded to getting it "perfect" since it will inevitably change and deepen in revision. (See page 167 for a sample copy of my first draft of pages 166–169.)

———— *Stage Five: Revision (Day 5 on)* ————

In terms of the writing process, revision is where the best work—specifically, the writing—gets done. If the previous steps are the foundation and framing work, revision is the interior completion. The intricate wiring; the connection of loose ends; the completion of circuits. It is where process finally yields to product.

As the term goes on, most students shift their work habits by doing quicker first drafts and more serious revisions. They see that when they write they tend to memorize. What had sounded wonderful was merely familiar. A day later the same material suddenly has obvious and needed angles to rework. Here, at last, is where the internal critic has his place. If the creative, intuitive work has been done beforehand, let the internal critic loose with his gleaming machete.

Yet even with this guideline and the miracle of computers, writing can still be sabotaged. Often it is not the writer's fault. One of the great ironies of educational life is that a college environment isn't always conducive to writing. Stereos blare, printers crank out, roommates distract, telephones ring. A writer's nightmare. I've often suspected that the reason so many students work in the dead of night is that it is the only time it's quiet and concentration is possible.

I advise students to draw up a positive corollary to their Martin Luther edict of poor work habits. The premise is obvious: Where do you work best? A quiet nook in the library? In your own room with the telephone turned off? To this I add the questions an English friend of mine asks fellow writers: Are you a morning or a night writer? A window or a wall writer? An at-home or office writer? (I am, unrepentantly, a morning writer who insists on a window. Skylights will not do. It's as if I want my sentences to shimmer with that hard shiny concreteness of the world just outside my window.) And my colleagues? Victor Burg didn't begin writing in his new study until it looked as though he'd been there for years. Linda Simon and I spent a sultry July afternoon painting her study a satisfying lavender. Nancy Kline, our nearest to the John Updike paradigm, has two separate studies (fiction/nonfiction) and is thinking of colonizing a third. Judith Beth Cohen, by contrast, leaves home altogether, preferring to work in writers' colonies.

At the end of my lecture on writing I always pass on some of the more theatrical props writers have used to get themselves working. Balzac worked in a white monk's robe with a pair of gold scissors (for editing?) suspended from his neck. Conrad *asked* his wife to lock him in his study and ignore his shouts to get out. Colette, unsolicited, was locked *in* her study by her first (read: ex) husband.

However strange these habits, they helped the work. They conferred, as Capote suggested, some "curious comfort." These—and our own—personal idiosyncrasies reveal a deeper literary truth: the habit of writing requires a comforting uniformity, what Flaubert meant when he suggested that to write well one must think like a radical and live like a bourgeois. Or as my first editor reductively put it "Same desk, same time, same you."

Let me be clear. Despite the guidelines here, despite knowing if you're a wall or a window writer, despite living like a bourgeois with or without lavender walls, writing can still be a very difficult business. No one thing magically makes it easier. Listen:

> I have never produced anything good except by a long succession of slight efforts. No one has more deeply meditated or better understood than I Buffon's remark about patience ["Genius is but a greater aptitude for patience."] I bring it not only to my work but also to the silent waiting that preceeds good work. André Gide (207)
>
> If only I can *concentrate* myself: this is the great lesson of life. I have hours of unspeakable reaction against the smallness of my production; my wretched habits of work—or unwork; my levity, my vagueness of mind, my perpetual failure to focus my attention, to absorb myself, to look things in the face, to invent, to produce, in a word. Henry James (40–41)
>
> Distractedness, weak memory, stupidity. Days passed in futility. Kafka (Olsen, 17)

One reason I always insist students read writer's journals is to see that inner perceptions and outer reality don't always match. When each of the writers above recorded these entries in his journals, he had produced great work. And would produce greater still. So too Virginia Woolf when she wrestled with the problem of pleasing others, the strenuous accommodation of the self and the time one doesn't have. She resolved this deeper question of writing and vocation, writing *as* vocation, in her essay "Professions for Women." She writes:

> "It was she (the watcher) who used to come between me and my paper . . . who bothered and wasted my time and so tormented me that at last I killed her . . . or she would have plucked my heart out as a writer. She died hard. It is far harder to kill a phantom than a reality. She was always creeping back when

I thought I had despatched her. Though I flatter myself that I killed her in the end, the struggle was severe" (Barrett 59–60).

I used to end my lecture with this quotation. With a kind of evangelical urgency, I'd exhort students to be patient with themselves and with the writing process. Several years ago as I was gathering my notes, a student who had been very attentive throughout the lecture raised his hand and, utterly without guile, asked: "If writing is so difficult why do any of you do it?" It was a stunningly obvious, maddeningly logical question. I looked at my two colleagues for help. The satisfaction of doing something difficult, of doing it well, Carl Nagin said. Making connections in thought and language, Nancy Kline replied.

I answered something similar. But now I would read that student a passage by Gail Godwin that I came across only recently. She observes:

> Once I begin the act of writing, it all falls away—the view from the window, the tools, the talismans, even the snoring cat—and I am unconscious of myself and my surroundings while I fuse language with idea, make a specific image visible or audible through the discovery of the right words. . . . One's carping inner critics are silenced for a time, and, as a result, what is produced is a little bit different from anything I had planned. There is always a surprise, a revelation. During the act of writing I have told myself something that I didn't know I knew. (Godwin, 1987, 18)

It's that final line that, for me, is the essence. I'll incorporate it into my lecture. Next time that's how I'm going to end.

Works Cited

———— *Books* ————

The Diary of Virginia Woolf, Vol. 1, ed. **Anne Olivier Bell.** New York: Harcourt, Brace, Jovanovich. 1977.

The Journals of Andre Gide, ed. **Justin O'Brien.** New York: Vintage. 1956.

The Notebooks of Henry James, ed. **F. O. Matthiessen.** New York: Oxford University Press. 1947.

Penguin Dictionary of Modern Humorous Quotations. Compiled by **Fred Metcalf.** New York: Viking/Penguin, 1987.

Silences, **Tillie Olsen.** New York: Delacorte. 1978.

Virginia Woolf: Women and Writing, ed. **Michele Barrett.** New York: Harcourt, Brace, Jovanovich. 1979.

The Writer's Chapbook, ed. **George Plimpton.** New York: Viking. 1989.

The Writer's Craft, ed. **John Hersey.** New York: Knopf. 1974.

Writers at Work: the Paris Review Interview Series, First Series, ed. **Malcom Cowley.** New York: Viking. 1958.

———— *Periodicals* ————

"How I Write," **Gail Godwin.** Boston: *The Writer.* October, 1987.

"The Watcher at the Gate," **Gail Godwin.** New York: *The New York Times Book Review.* January 9, 1977.

Nancy Kline

𝕫❧ *Writing as Translation:*
The Great Between

At the end of my first semester as an expository writing instructor, after my class had composed the requisite number of essays—six, as I recall—I offered them the chance to write an optional short story, a bonus. In reponse to the assignment, one of my students handed in a perplexing tale about a chicken farmer obsessed with maximizing egg production. This farmer kept the lights on in his sterile modern henhouse 24 hours a day to fool the hens into thinking it was always morning, time to lay another egg. He gave his birds no rest, he was a driven man. His Rhode Island Reds were driven chickens.

I didn't know what to make of the story. I didn't understand it, it was (I thought) totally foreign to the experience of its author, Norman, who came from upper Manhattan. And yet the prose had an edge to it . . .

"What is this all about?" I asked Norman.

"Isn't it obvious?" he said. "It's about Expository Writing!"

I was not amused.

But my education as a writing teacher had begun.

I had not scheduled revisions into my syllabus, I had given my students no sense that words are as mobile, as changeable as thoughts. In my rush to page production (40 pages per semester per student were expected in my department), I had not really allowed them to *write* one essay—had, rather, forced them to lay a series of first drafts. Despite the fact that I myself am a writer and know that writing is revision, as a beginning instructor I had played into the tendency of beginning writers to see a text as a complete and intact entity, immutable. A stone, a stone tablet, a sterile egg. Something that falls out of the sky onto the page or, as in Norman's vision, passes through the writer, taking nothing from him, both parties to the interaction virtually inert.

This misconception on the part of our students, this inflexible vision of the text, has all too often been nurtured in high school by a reverential emphasis on the books of Great [Dead] Writers, books that look to students like tombstones, all of a piece, their words carved in marble. All too many college freshmen confuse what Rainer Schulte calls "the fixity of print" ("Translation and Reading," 2) with language itself, that least fixed of entities. They have not been taught to experience published texts as dynamic—as written—as groups of words chosen by living human beings, words assembled, rearranged, discarded, fabricated in an active struggle by their maker, not delivered whole to his or her door by some muse or god. Students do not picture George Eliot tentatively trying out a phrase then scratching it, they do not think of Shakespeare at a momentary loss for words, they are amazed to find out that John Updike doodles in his margins. They haven't been told what Henry James knew (Freud knew it too, in his own domain): that a book (an analysis) is never finished, it is simply abandoned.

But, then, instructors are not immune either to the fixity of print. In the face of a printed text, especially a classic printed text, instructors are as likely as students to forget the fluidity of language itself. Which is precisely what the translator deals with, always—and precisely what needs exploring with our students, in the context of the composition course. For learning to write is inextricably bound up with learning to read, and if students have been taught to see published writing as finished, fixed, immobile—as inhuman—what can it give them as writers, other than an inferiority complex and the mistaken notion that once their first draft has been typed or printed out, their essay is done? How can the "static appearance of the great work" (Mann, 15) teach them anything about the act of writing? How can they possibly deal with the mercurial qualities of language that they will necessarily experience, once they turn to the making of their own texts—the dizzying play of words like atoms in the seemingly still page, the active struggle of linguistic choice?

"What a bitch of a thing prose is!" comments Flaubert. "It is never finished; there is always something to be done over" (328).

Rainer Schulte has argued eloquently that our reading of texts would be enriched if we were to approach them with the translator's eye, the translator's intimate knowledge of "the inherent uncertainty of each word." Writes Schulte,

> In the translation process, there are no definite answers, only attempts at solutions in response to states of uncertainty generated by the interaction of

the words' semantic fields and sounds. . . . Applying the translator's eye to the reading of a text changes our attitude toward the reading process by dissolving the fixity of print on a page into a potential multiplicity of semantic connections. ("Translation and Reading," 1–2)

To translate is to work, hands-on, with the interaction of words, not simply to plug one (English) word into the hole left by another (French) word. Nor is it to perform an act of veneration before an already existent monolithic original text. To translate is, rather, to place two sets of words—indeed, two entire sign systems—in the presence of one another and to watch as their proximity transforms them mutually. The new text in its unfinished state illuminates the original text, to show us what we had perhaps forgotten: that it too is made up of language, in its very essence unfinished, multiple, ambiguous:

Ultimately, [the translator's] concern does not reside in the transferral of meaning but in the dynamics of situations. He approximates in his translation what he sees in the original text by creating linguistic situations in the new language that allow the reader to find dynamic spaces into which the possibilities of ambiguity have been transplanted from the original. (Schulte, "Translation and Literary Criticism," 4)

Let me give one brief, complicated example.

(And two caveats: my example is brief; my discussion of it is not, cannot be—which is, I suspect, central to the point I'm trying to make: namely, that language is multiple, the single word contains a universe [or at any rate a country and culture]. And then, my intention below is not to deliver a lecture on French feminism; what interests me here is how to translate French into English.)

I have just finished translating Claudine Herrmann's *Les Voleuses de langue*, a work of feminist literary criticism. The first problem the book presented was its title, which is, in a word, untranslatable. *Langue* means both "language" and "tongue," the latter in its literal as well as in its figurative sense. But the real richness of the title lies in the word *voleuses*, the feminine form of the noun (no such thing exists in English) which derives from *voler*, a verb meaning both "to fly" and "to steal." *Voleuses* means, then, at one and the same time, "women who fly" and "women who steal," and to the feminist ear it suggests those medieval ancestors claimed by modern-day feminism, witches. To further complicate and enrich matters, Herrmann's full phrase—(The) women who fly in (steal) language (tongues)—is resonant with another celebrated text in French women's writing, "The Laugh of the Medusa," by Hélène Cixous.[1]

The English translator cannot be expected to inscribe Cixous in the English title; she's gone. But still the problematic terms *voleuses* and *langue* must be dealt with.

A reading of Herrmann's book makes it clear that she emphasizes the second meaning of the verb *voler* (while implying, always, its first meaning): Herrmann's *voleuses* are more involved in theft than flight. Thus, my working title for the translation was *The Language Stealers*. Incomplete, genderless, and colorless into the bargain. When the author herself suggested *The Tongue Snatchers*, I liked it. It was more graphic than the French title, less abstract, but it caught the book's wry humor. It was spunky, and somewhat shocking. Besides which, for some reason that eluded me, the phrase suggested women: "Tongue snatchers" sounded feminine to me. English has its own echoes. It took a disgruntled feminist to point out that these two words contain within them "snatch" (she could hardly bring herself to say it), a term which Claudine Herrmann, being French, probably does not know. Perversely, the title pleases me all the more.

But the point here is that there is no definite answer, no absolute solution to the translator's state of uncertainty, no way to capture in its entirety the richness of the original phrase—not that I could find.

I came away from my protracted, intensive reading of these four words with a provisional translation and a thrilling, somewhat humbling sense of (some of) language's multiple possibilities. What Rainer Schulte urges is that we read, always, with this fundamental semantic multiplicity in mind.

He further develops the theme of the translator's-eye view of language as follows:

> When a translator encounters a word in the text, especially a word that by its very nature does not yield immediately to a clearly defined boundary of connotations, he has to free himself of the notion that words are entities of fixed meanings. . . . The translator, in his desire to recreate a text, must unlearn language. . . . [He] focuses on the dynamics of change that reveal themselves in any prolonged act of interpretation. Through reading and interpretation the translator discovers those elements that constitute the dynamic process of how a text might come to mean rather than what a text means. ("Translation and Literary Criticism," 3–4)

How a text might come to mean—that is what I try to teach my writing students to focus on in other people's written work, since what writing is about is the making of meaning, the coming to mean.[2]

By which I do not wish to suggest that we or our students must eschew interpretation of any given literary text, not at all. Simply let us begin by talking about the published work as dynamic and its author as human, as choosing one word over another. Let us try to talk about the published text as we try to talk about a student essay: as work in progress, never still. Or, better yet, as one still shot, one frame of a movie, which freezes a single moment in what we know to be a dynamic and ongoing situation (I am speaking here not of the characters' situation within the fiction or essay being read but rather of the writer's situation; I am speaking here of the ongoing drama of alternate verbal possibilities). Let us focus on "the dynamics of situations" within the text, on how its pieces (words, paragraphs, sections, image systems, etc.) relate to each other, call each other into being, change each other, resonate with each other. And then, having articulated "how the individual parts of a text contribute to its overall effect," *how the text works*, let us attempt an (interim) interpretation.

Interim because texts change over time and change too with each reading that we give them. This is so because we are changed by each reading we give them, by each reading they offer us.[3]

Poets, of course, know that the written text is as mobile as a flame—and as inflammatory—despite its apparent stasis. In his wonderfully titled poem "The Library is on Fire," René Char juxtaposes the immobility of the book with the dynamism of the human speech it contains:

Motionless books. But books which find their way lithely into our days, cry out in lamentation, begin dances.

[*Livres sans mouvement. Mais livres qui s'introduisent avec souplesse dans nos jours, y poussent une plainte, ouvrent des bals.* (379)]

For Char, in this same poem, the writer is a torch, waltzing with his reader (*Torche, je ne valse qu'avec lui*, [378]).

If we ourselves can conceptualize the text as mobile, then we can begin to communicate its mobility—its moves[4]—to our students. And our reading (and theirs) will become "the making of meaning and not the description of already-fixed meanings" ("Translation and Reading," 1).

But how, exactly, shall we teach this kind of reading? Primarily, it seems to me, by exploring the effect on the reader of the writer's choices in any given text: e.g., what is the effect on you of George Orwell's painstakingly minute description of a dying elephant? What if he'd been briefer? How does Flannery O'Connor's narrative voice make you react to murder? Frank O'Connor's? What if Flannery O'Connor had told her story first-person? What is the effect of Philip Roth's metaphor here? What if he hadn't alternated between biblical diction and 13-year-old American diction? *What if?* "Reading institutes the making of meanings through questions in which the possibility of an answer results in another question: What if?" ("Translation and Reading," 2). And then, Why not? Always there is the return to the effect of the particular paragraph Orwell or Roth or O'Connor(s) finally settled on, allowed to stand. What does this particular (chosen) sentence feel like to you, and how does this particular word reverberate along the length of the whole work?

In order to get my students to focus on these questions and to enter into a dialogue with another writer's choices, the first assignment I give in any writing course at any level is an explication of a text.

To further communicate the feel of the fluidity of language and the multiplicity of choice it offers the writer, we might fruitfully examine different drafts of a professional writer's manuscript (as well as different drafts of student manuscripts). If a translated work appears on our reading list—"The Lady with the Pet Dog," for example—we might compare several different translations of the same (brief) passage in class. We might read with our students professional essays like Joan Didion's "Why I Write," which define writing as exploration, and, in conjunction with these, might ask our students to explore stylistic pastiche and their own fiction (or historical writing or whatever genre is being read in class). Such experimentation, within the context of an expository writing class, is a way of turning reading inside-out, of giving students a glimpse at fiction, for example, from the writer's point of view. Students then return to their reading of professional fiction (or history or science or sociology) with a new perspective.

And if this new perspective allows them to conceptualize other people's texts as written, living, dynamic documents, then they can begin to feel a fruitful kinship with the authors of these texts, rather than an estrangement from them. And then their reading of professional writers will truly begin to inform their own writing. We know that our students learn from reading each other and talking together about how to deal with a particular rhetorical problem. We know this is so because they identify with one another and feel that if a classmate has experimented in a given way or struggled in a given way, they too can do this, risk this. If students can perceive George Orwell as a colleague, then what he has invented or discovered in his writing will become more available to them for their own (tentative, perhaps) use. If they can perceive Flaubert as a fellow writer, not just as a Great Artist (he can be both), then they can come to think of his struggles with his own prose not as some weird ritual reserved for Genius, but as a model and an enticement.

Which brings us to the experience of writing itself. Translation makes palpable the fluidity of the written text. But what can it tell us about the act of making that text?

The eminent translator Helen Lane characterizes her craft as follows: "One is constantly trying one's best to 'bring over' meanings from one language to another. The *primary activity* of translation thus takes place somewhere *between* the source language and the target language" (cited by Christ, 7; Lane's emphasis).

Let me try to describe what it feels like to work in that *between* evoked by Lane, suspended between two different languages, two sister texts that mirror one another

$$\textit{voleuses de langue}] \qquad \text{[Tongue Snatchers}$$

yet remain profoundly, radically distinct from one another. I want to evoke the translator's stark encounter with the arbitrary nature of words: how she is forced to feel to the very marrow of her bones that words are not attached to things, that she might have said everything differently (and thereby seen everything differently?); that the words we possess, the words we think of as *true*, are accidents—wonderful, powerful because "intensely conventionalized" (Steiner, 240), but unrooted in any objective reality, rooted only in the human creature, arbitrary signs suspended over nothing, held up as mysteriously as are the planets by the forces existing between them in that "closed system in which all parts are interrelated," which is language, according to Saussure. When we translate, we find ourselves floating, weightless, back and forth in the infinite Pascalian spaces between two such closed systems like spaceships, between individual words, between the signifier and the signified, the utterance and its reception.

Then, if we are also writers, we realize that *all writing occurs in fact in the Great Between*: that space between the source and the target, between the text I am interpreting (whether it be my own as-yet-unarticulated experience of the world or a piece of writing) and the words I am attempting to formulate it in, between what George Steiner calls my "personal thesaurus" and "the current vulgate" (46), between the books I've read in my life—all the texts of others—and the book I want to write,[5] between my initial draft and my subsequent draft and the drafts after that. Always in the dialectic of writing there is the source and the target, and in the space between them— here—deep in inner space, is the writer, here is where the writer spins, writes, must remain, suspended, till the work is completed.

This is just as true of expository prose as it is of fiction. And it is just as true of student writing as it is of professional writing. The student essay, like any translation, comes into existence in the dizzying, spacy *between*. Not a comfortable location, though it is exciting. This weightlessness, this lack of gravity is unnerving. And so is the solitude. As Proust knows:

> As for the inner book of unknown signs (signs carved in relief, it seemed, which my attention, exploring my unconscious, sought out, bumped against, felt its way around, like a diver taking soundings), no one could help me read it with any rules, its reading consisting of a creative act in which no one can take our place nor even collaborate with us. No wonder so many turn away from writing it! (879)

When beginning writers find themselves afloat like this, they think there's been some terrible mistake. This can't be right, this galactic (oceanic) ambiguity. This suspension in the eternal silence of infinite space. They wish devoutly to be done with the task, the trip.

No wonder it reassures students—and the rest of us—to think of composition as formulaic, arithmetical, earthbound, a skill akin to driving a car. No wonder so many instructors cling to the thesis-driven essay (it can be neatly taught) and students to the egg-text (you can only be expected to lay that once, then you get to go home [until it's time for the next]).

I am aware that in certain subject areas, especially the sciences and social sciences, there is enormous pressure to teach thesis-driven writing.

And, obviously, we have to try to give students certain basic tools: it is our job to help them learn how to reason and argue in their pages, just as we must help them learn how to analyze what is going on in the pages of other writers. It is our job to teach them how to formulate, develop and support a thesis (although because of its rigid connotations for most of my students I am careful to call this term into question, even as I use it). But as my colleague Eileen Farrell, who teaches science writing, puts it: even a thesis, like any other "move" in the text, can be seen—and taught—as provisional, fluid, subject to "What if?" Even thesis-driven writing need not be taught as though it were mathematics or egg farming.

My point is that we know the inexactitude of language, know words to be as profoundly ambiguous as is our experience of the world itself. My point is that this information belongs in a writing course. Commenting on the "messiness" of language, George Steiner writes:

> At every level, from brute camouflage to poetic vision, the linguistic capacity to conceal, misinform, leave ambiguous, hypothesize, invent is indispensable to the equilibrium of human consciousness and to the development of man in society. . . . Human speech conceals far more than it confides; it blurs much more than it defines; it distances more than it connects. (228–229)

This is information worth exploring. For in this fact, this profound and complicated ambiguity, this paradox at the heart of language, lies the writer's limit and the writer's freedom. And I think we owe it to our students to talk about these things, in relation to their writing, as in relation to their reading. About how unruly, how unmathematical language is and about the possibilities this offers to the writer—for cumbersome obscurity, certainly (we see this often enough), but equally for richness of allusion, richness of discovery. We owe it to our students to point out how language's capacity to be opaque, to conceal, can actively enhance the written work (as in a Hemingway short story) or, on the contrary, can offer us—by yielding, suddenly—one of those extraordinary moments when we *understand*, when the text that was opaque comes clear and suddenly we find out how to read it, or how to write it. This opening of language like a door can happen in the work of others and it can happen in our own—usually in moments to be reached only by writing and rewriting and rewriting again—to let us into places we did not even know were there. There is so much to be explored, uncovered, in the act of writing itself. Might it not be our job to guide students beyond formulas, toward the essay as exploration: of their own thinking, of the limits of their own language (which like any limits are expandable only if tested)? Essays, even if they have a clear point to make, can begin with questions instead of solutions, with a troublesome problem, a mystery. I try to urge my students to risk starting out without all the answers, to risk venturing into the spacious and intoxicating *between* I have just been describing; I try to encourage them to risk staying there awhile, in weightlessness and uncertainty, "cultivating a 'careful disorderliness,' learning the uses of chaos," as Ann Berthoff puts it (212).

It is a question here of teaching students a new way to conceptualize writing, just as it was a question earlier of teaching them a new way to conceptualize reading.

All writing is a high wire over darkness (those vast spaces, glimpsed in the mirror of the empty page) that does not—cannot—exist until you put your foot out and step forward onto it. Or, if this image is too dizzying, then let us stay closer to the earth's surface at the outset, defining the essay as a path that gets created, or cleared, only as the writer steps forward to explore the unknown terrain of his or her own thought.

It is a risky business to begin to speak, not knowing where our words will take us. Risky, but thrilling. ("Roads that do not promise the country they are destined for are the roads we love," writes René Char [*Les routes qui ne promettent pas le pays de leur destination sont les routes aimées*] (466)].)

Thrilling to find out what I think, to compass my experience of the world, make sense of my life—or of your book—by speaking them.

Nor is the writer's pleasure isolate, masturbatory. It passes into the text, to be experienced by the reader. As Roland Barthes has pointed out.

I think we have to articulate these things for our students. I think we have to give them permission to run the risks inherent in writing—which they know are there, whether named or not. I think we must acknowledge the risk of starting to write before you have all the answers and the further risk of exposing yourself to the reader's eye at that very moment of vulnerability when you are finding out what you think.

Not that students must show us their initial struggles, their preliminary drafts. Like any writer, they have to be granted some kind of immunity. But it seems to me crucial for them to know that they can allow themselves to be seen in the page of one unfinished draft or another and they will not die of exposure. Knowing this, perhaps they will stop misusing language's capacity to be opaque. Perhaps they will dispel some of the smoke that characterizes so much student writing and begin to experiment openly with their own thought and their own prose, and to show us the experiment. Then a dialogue becomes possible—with us and with their classmates—which will send them back, once again, into their dialogue with themselves, back into the risky Great Between for still another draft, another translation, another set of discoveries.

In the composition course I most often teach, my students read and write about other people's texts, specifically, short fictions. And the question that arises now is what can translation teach us about written textual interpretation, about "a reading that is also a writing"(Mann, 14).

In the fifth chapter of *After Babel*, George Steiner articulates what he sees as the four steps in the translation process. His four-part hermeneutic goes like this: to begin a translation you have to trust that there's something there to be translated. You have to put your trust in the foreign text while it is still opaque, untested, closed to you. Without this initial leap of faith, this "initiatory trust," there can be no translation. Then comes an aggressive, "incursive" second step, which cracks the foreign text open and yields a literal, clumsy, word-for-word translation. Not a pretty step, but crucial. In order to make an omelette, you have to break eggs; in order to make a translation, you have to break texts. In Steiner's third step the translator performs an "incorporative" move, embodying the shreds and shards of the old text in its new language—making French, let us say, sound as English as possible and the text as whole as possible in its new tongue. And finally, in the fourth step, comes "restitution." The translator distances herself from her work, reconsiders the original text, and makes every possible effort to be faithful to it in its final foreign rendering.

There are other ways of talking about the translation process. Robert Bly, for example, identifies *eight* stages of translation in his book of that title. But in the context of the present discussion, Steiner's four steps are particularly striking by their similarity to the steps my students take—sometimes willingly, sometimes not—in their analysis of texts. And I think a consideration of the "fourfold hermeneutic" I've just outlined can help us to understand and, more importantly, to teach the beginnings of textual interpretation.

In the beginning there is the leap of faith. When faced with a new text, any new text, but especially a deceptively simple, elliptical one that seems to be so obvious as to preclude analysis (e.g., William Carlos Williams' "The Use of Force"), or, on the contrary, a particularly difficult one that requires active translation if it is to make sense at all (e.g., Robert Coover's "The Babysitter"), students express skepticism that there is anything there to understand. Or they claim that all readings may be seen as equally valid (and therefore no one of them is). Students are quick, that is, to withhold their trust. They are afraid the emperor has no clothes, afraid of being duped, of appearing ridiculous. This interpretation is all just bullshit, they say, isn't it? Where'd you get all this? Do you really think he meant to put all this in? If we invoke the analogy of translation and urge them to make the leap, to lend the new text "initiative trust," then they will perhaps consent to take a long look at what is in front of their eyes.

Trusting attention must be paid, if one is truly to read a text.

And it is not just a question here of trusting the text and its maker. Students must also suspend their disbelief in their instructor, as a teacher of reading and a guarantor of deeper textual meanings. And they must have faith in themselves—in the significance of their initial reactions to the text and in their own ability to figure out how the text caused these reactions. If they laughed at Cheever's "The Fourth Alarm," they must be urged to trust their laughter and to take it up like Ariadne's thread to lead them through the labyrinth of the interpretive act: What did Cheever do to make me laugh? What choices did he make in the telling of his story? How does his story work, and what does this have to do with its meaning (that is, with my interpretation)?

But these questions take us already into the aggressive second step of Steiner's fourfold hermeneutic: decipherment, dissection. And here too apprentice interpreters frequently resist. Who has not heard from his or her students that they feel they are doing violence to a text by analyzing it? That they fear explication will strip it of its vitality, its truth, its intactness. Students are afraid of destroying something irrevocably by too intensive an act of interpretation, and I have never found an answer to this fear that satisfied me, have always felt I responded with vaguenesses, knowing that interpretation does not destroy but not knowing how to explain that, exactly. The analogy of translation offers me a way of answering. Which begins with an admission: yes, at one point in the hermeneutic motion, we break things. During one tricky, sustained—and perhaps uncomfortable— moment in our interpretation, the shambles of the work we are taking apart lie around us. Cheever's jokes are ruined (temporarily) if we explain them.

Let us acknowledge this and move on to the next step in the translation/interpretation process, which is incorporative. This step involves embodying the text in a new language—for our purposes here, in our own spoken and written understanding, our own essay. Interestingly enough, it is this third step that George Steiner feels to be threatening, the danger he identifies: that we will somehow lose our own speech by taking into it someone else's, that "we may be consumed . . . we may be mastered and made lame by what we have imported" into our own language (299). I believe it was when I read this remark that it really came home to me how male Steiner's model of translation is.[6] I doubt that many women would be threatened at the notion of incorporating someone else's speech, or thought, or anything. To incorporate is not to be made lame, it is to be made fuller. In this connection, Steiner himself quotes Heidegger as saying, "We are what we understand to be" (299). How can we lose by taking Cheever into our universe, our discourse? Like my students, I find the aggressively penetrative second step more threatening: *What if the text I've broken turns out to be Humpty Dumpty, what then?* (Does the fact that my students share my fear of "appropriative penetration" [Steiner, 298] more than of embodiment indicate that they've been feminized—that is, made to feel powerless—by their education? All kinds of feminist meditations suggest themselves at this point . . .)

These speculations aside, I often tell students (and it's true) that I can accurately guess, when reading the fiction they themselves write between each expository essay, which author they have written their most recent analytical essay on. If they have just analyzed a story by Updike, their own fiction will be remarkably Updikesque; if they then go on to analyze a story by Welty, their next fiction seems to hail from Mississippi. Nor is this a bad thing. This is how students grow. They are what they understand to be, and each incorporative act enriches them. Which is why I encourage them especially to become aware of the cannibalistic aspect of interpretation to fatten up their own *expository* style: if they are writing about "Everything That Rises Must Converge" (for example), they can fruitfully echo O'Connor's use of metaphor and humor in their own prose, vivifying their dialogue with her and her text by imitating her sardonic voice, and simultaneously embodying—demonstrating—with this gesture their understanding of her art. If they choose to write about "Hills Like White Elephants," on the other hand, let ellipsis rule. And so forth.

For beginning writers, this is not to be "mastered and made lame by what we have imported." This is to begin to find out what the masters know, to be given license to play with their toys, to borrow their formidable means, on the path to finding out what kind of writers our students themselves can become.

And this gesture of imitation/incorporation moves us toward the final step in Steiner's hermeneutic, the step he calls restitutive. This is the moment when the student-interpreter must finally pull back from his or her close reading and try to see the text whole once again, must try to reintegrate into it whatever aspect has been under discussion (dissection). But to this reintegration will be added the student's new understanding, the student's own growth as a reader and writer—which has occurred in the process of writing about this other written text. In the literal act of translation, this is the moment when the translator must strive to be faithful to the original text. But how are we to understand and apply the concept of fidelity to literary interpretation? What the term suggests to me in the present context is that a successful interpretive essay will leave us feeling the writer has taken apart and understood the text he or she is analyzing, and then given it back to itself, but changed; that text and writer can now be seen to separate, each of them transformed by their encounter. And we who read the essay are also transformed. Our encounter with the metatext will have illuminated and changed our own reading of the text it interprets, so that we will now understand (as does the writer of the essay) how humor functions in "The Fourth Alarm," how Cheever's humor means. And then, and only then, will we really *get* Cheever's jokes.

"Reading," writes William Gass, "is reasoning, figuring things out through thoughts, making arrangements out of arrangements until we've understood a text so fully it is nothing but feeling and pure response, until its conceptual turns are like the reversals of mood in a marriage—petty, sad, ecstatic, commonplace, foreseeable, amazing" (57).

When students are worried about impoverishing or permanently breaking a text in the early stages of their analytical reading, perhaps if we forecast this final step for them, it will ease their mind.

Translation is an "essentially ephemeral activity" (Maier, 5), translations are always superseded, it is the rule of the game; and written texts—published or otherwise—are in process, writing is provisional; and so are writing courses.

"Every serious translator," writes Helen Lane, "realizes, I think, that despite his sincerest efforts, his translation as a whole has somehow fallen short, been unfaithful to *something*, despite what I might call 'local successes'" (Christ, 8; Lane's emphasis). This poignant statement applies to most writing, I suspect, and to most writing courses. And just so, the writer (the writing instructor) fits Lane's description of the translator as Don Quijote, stubbornly pursuing the impossible goal of "THE ABSOLUTELY FAITHFUL TRANSLATION" (Christ, 8; Lane's capitals). Faulkner has commented that a writer keeps on writing because each work is a failure, so he has to go back and try again—indeed, "if he ever wrote one [work] which suited him completely, nothing remains but to cut the throat and quit" (32). The fully realized text or composition course—the absolutely faithful articulation of what we want to say—eludes us. So we abandon the text we've been struggling with (as I am about to) and start on another. And "the act is virgin, even repeated" (*L'acte est vierge, même répété* [Char, 186]).

When I began teaching composition, I wanted to leave my students at the end of the semester with a sense of closure, as it had seemed possible to do when I was teaching French literature courses. One could always say (one was always lying, but nevertheless): "Now you've read the 17th century. Next year you'll do the 18th." I suppose there are fleeting moments even now when I still want this sense of closure. But really, closing is not what writing (translation) is about. It is in fact about quite the opposite. Which is why, frustrated (but fruitfully so?) and brimming with open questions, my students and I leave each other at the end of each semester with the sense that the writing and the reading have only begun, that almost everything remains to be said, and

NOTES

[1] This essay, which first appeared one year before Herrmann's book was published, is a passionate adjuration to women to *write*, and throughout the text its author makes full use of the ambiguity of precisely those two terms that render *les "voleuses" de "langue"* so difficult a phrase to translate.

Here is the merest glimpse of Cixous:

Flying (stealing) is woman's gesture—flying (stealing) in language (tongues) and making it (them) fly (steal). We have all learned the art of flight (of theft) and its numerous techniques; throughout the centuries we've been unable to possess [language/tongues] except by flying (by stealing); we've lived in flight (in thievery), by flying (by stealth) . . . (49—italics in the original)

And so on. The dizzying play of the central term here (*voler*), pulsing like a strobe between its two meanings (flying/stealing), illuminates woman's doubleness: her duplicity, her necessary stealth, her perpetual flight. But how is the translator to retain the grace—the sheer speed—of the French text, if she gives both meanings of *voler*, as I've done above, each time the term or one of its variants appears? Cixous' original translators solved this dilemma by relegating the second meaning to a footnote and simply translating *voler* as "to fly" (see Marks & de Courtivron, 258). But does this half-translation live up to the original text, give the English reader any real sense of that text at all?

[2] Robert Bly's *The Eight Stages of Translation* offers a fascinating look at how a text might come to mean, in the step-by-step process of being translated.

[3] Which is, in part, what George Steiner means when he says, "To read Shakespeare and Hölderlin is, literally, to prepare to read them" (25). (I believe he means too that every great writer articulates his universe in a new language, hitherto unspoken, which the reader must become fluent in, if s/he is to read it [translate it] accurately.)

[4] The expression "moves" belongs to my former colleague Alex Gold, who used to invoke it not only in relation to the mobility of the text itself, but also to the alternative possibilities the writer faces and must choose between in the course of writing—like the chess player in front of the board.

With regard to the mobility of the text, see John Clifford's "Review: A Response from the Margin" in *College English*, Volume 49, Number 6, October 1987, pp. 692–706. In his thoughtful response to Robert Scholes's *Textual Power*, Clifford comments: "Students in an introductory course might be better served with a less informed interpretation [than Scholes's] of Hemingway, focusing instead on a more rigorous attention to multiplicity, to unresolved ambiguity, to the interrogation and not the resolution of meaning, to the mind's ability to consider simultaneously a range of plausible meanings. Fluidity and engagement seem more potentially empowering than Scholes's univocal semiotic" (703).

[5] By which I do not mean to "replace the concept of originality [in writing] with the concept of misreading or translation," which is what Harold Bloom and

Terry Eagleton wish to do, according to Lori Chamberlain (in "Gender and the Metaphorics of Translation," *Signs*, Volume 13, Number 3 [Spring 1988]: 470.)

[6] See Chamberlain for an enthralling overview and analysis of gender and the metaphorical representation of translation (cited in note 5, above).

Works Cited

Barthes, Roland. *Le plaisir du texte.* Paris: Editions du Seuil, 1973.

Berthoff, Ann E. *forming thinking writing.* Rochelle Park, NJ: Hayden, 1978.

Bly, Robert. *The Eight Stages of Translation.* Boston: Rowan Tree Press, 1983.

Char, René. *Oeuvres complètes.* Paris: Editions Gallimard, 1983.

Christ, Ronald. "An interview with Helen Lane." *Translation Review* 5 (1980): 6–18.

Cixous, Hélène. "Le rire de la méduse." *L'arc* 61 (1975): 39–54.

Faulkner, William. "Faulkner at West Point." In *The Writer's Craft.* Ed. John Hersey. New York: Knopf, 1981.

Flaubert, Gustave. "Letters to Louise Colet." In *The Writer's Craft.* Ed. John Hersey. New York: Knopf, 1981.

Gass, William. "Of Speed Readers and Lip-Movers." In *The Rinehart Reader.* Eds. Jean Wyrick and Beverly J. Slaughter. New York: Holt, Rinehart and Winston, 1989.

Herrmann, Claudine. *Les voleuses de langue.* Paris: Editions des femmes, 1976.

———. *The Tongue Snatchers.* Trans. Nancy Kline. University of Nebraska Press, 1989.

Maier, Carol. "Translation as Performance: Three Notes." *Translation Review* 15 (1984): 5–8.

Mann, Paul. "Translation and Literary Criticism: A Response to Rainer Schulte." *Translation Review* 13 (1983): 8–16.

Marks, Elaine and Isabelle de Courtivron. *New French Feminisms.* New York: Schocken, 1981.

Proust, Marcel. *A la recherche du temps perdu.* 3 vols. Paris: Bibliothèque de la Pléiade, 1954. Vol. 3.

Schulte, Rainer. "Translation and Literary Criticism." *Translation Review* 9 (1982): 1–4.

———. "Translation and Reading." *Translation Review* 18 (1985); 1–2.

Steiner, George. *After Babel.* New York: Oxford U.P., 1975.

Richard Marius

🙂 *Writing Across the Curriculum*

The old prejudice that facts deaden the minds of children has a long history in the 19th and 20th centuries and includes not just the disciples of Rousseau and Dewey but also Charles Dickens who, in the figure of Mr. Gradgrind in *Hard Times*, satirized the teaching of mere facts. But it isn't facts that deaden the minds of young children, who are storing facts in their minds every day with astonishing voracity. It is incoherence—our failure to ensure that a pattern of shared, vividly taught, and socially enabling knowledge will emerge from our instruction.

E. D. Hirsch, Jr. *Cultural Literacy: What Every American Needs to Know*

Now that the distractions of the sixties are over, and undergraduate education has become more important again (because the graduate departments, aside from the professional schools, are in trouble due to the shortage of academic jobs, university officials have had somehow to deal with the undeniable fact that the students who enter are uncivilized, and that the universities have some responsibility for civilizing them.

Allan Bloom, *The Closing of the American Mind: How Higher Education Has Failed Democracy and Impoverished the Souls of Today's Students*

Whatever else they accomplished with the books quoted above, E. D. Hirsch, Jr., and Allan Bloom made the year 1987 a benchmark in dissatisfaction with America's schools and colleges. Both books stayed on the *New York Times* best-seller lists for months, and both continued their popularity in paperback.

Bloom's work is more personal, an anecdotal and impressionistic jeremiad concluding with an appeal to raise a wall of great books to protect culture from the barbarians—among whom he includes most modern college students and most of their teachers. A 19th-century classicist born out of time, Bloom believes that Greek and Roman culture represented the apogee of civilization and that no one is educated who does not know ancient philosophy. He finds little good in contemporary culture, and indeed little good in American letters. He mentions only four American writers—all men—as worthy of anyone's interest.

He sees few flaws in the societies that produced the classical literature he cherishes. And of course he wrote before the stunning collapse of Communism in Eastern Europe and the seeming end of the possibility of the cataclysmic imperial wars once engineered by those national leaders educated in the classical culture he reveres. He writes like a man for whom hope must be a disappointment.

Hirsch's work is more original, more analytical, more hopeful, and more democratic. In different tones, both argue that American students don't know much and that their schools and colleges are failing them. If nothing else their popularity reflects a general public disenchantment with education in general and higher education in particular. Of late that disenchantment has been painfully translated into budget cuts for state schools and much weaker federal support for both public and private universities. The middle class in the United States appears to hold the paradoxical view that a college education is necessary for success but that colleges are not doing a job good enough to merit sacrificial support. This is a serious matter indeed.

Much random evidence confirms a pessimistic view of contemporary education. On a blank map of the world, one third of the entering students of a state unversity of my acquaintance recently located Europe in the middle of Africa. It is not all the fault of the schools. Proverbial wisdom spoke of leading unthirsty horses to water. To many of us in higher education, students seem to bring to our classes little curiosity about what we have to teach them. We complain that we teach a generation that neither reads books nor follows current events.

A couple of years ago I asked how many students in my freshman class of 15 read a daily newspaper; three held up their hands. I asked how many read a weekly news magazine; the same three said they did. One student, exasperated at being asked such a personal question, said, "We don't have *time* to read." I mentioned one day that the most powerful radio voice I had ever heard belonged to Franklin D. Roosevelt. They were astonished that I could recall Roosevelt; I wished I had gone on to reminisce about listening to President Lincoln's Gettysburg Address through the static on our radios.

Their limited sense of past time reminds me of Faulkner's comment in "A Rose for Emily" about the old men at Miss Emily Grierson's funeral, "confusing time with its mathematical progression, as the old do, to whom all the past is not a diminishing road but, instead, a huge meadow which no winter ever quite touches, divided from them now by the narrow bottleneck of the most recent decade of years."

In my writing course taught during the 1988 presidential campaign, I required my students to read the *Boston Globe* and the *New York Times* every day and to write a longish paper on the vision of America revealed by one of the candidates in his public utterances. On their anonymous evaluations at the end of the term, most said they hated the assignment. I doubt that half the class voted in the election.

What is to be done? Today's students are dedicated to many good causes; some 75 percent of Harvard undergraduates do public service volunteer work in Cambridge and surrounding towns. A current of idealism runs strong among most college students. Even so, I fear they do not know much when they graduate and that today's universities offer little more than an important social experience, filtering out the less capable and the less wealthy, and letting the more capable and the more wealthy pass through. Businesses and the professions accept college graduates because graduates have proven that they know how to submit to discipline, obey the rules, work hard, and get along in the middle class—worthwhile accomplishments, certainly. In effect college has become boot camp to the economy, and efficient organizations need boot camps, I suppose. But whether any college graduate knows much or can reason well about data is another question. I don't think most college graduates can reason about data any better than the rest of the population, and I doubt seriously that most of them have any conception of the past that makes even the term "cultural literacy" have any meaning.

The argument in favor of cultural literacy is that we must have a sense of our culture's past if we are to make sensible decisions about life in the present. It also means that to enjoy the past—a Monet exhibit, for example, or a Shakespearean play—we must bring to it some understanding of its principal terms. For several centuries it was assumed by nearly everybody that the purpose of the university was to provide a forum, a meeting place of past and present, and that students entering the forum would for several years have an intensive experience in absorbing a usable past, one that would define them and direct them in the "now" of their lives. One came out of the university knowing a lot and knowing also how to reason.

The ability to reason was always considered essential, whether in the classical Platonic academy or in the scholastic disputations of the middle ages or in the philological and philosophical university curricula of the 18th and 19th centuries. How do we think about what we know? Part of the task of education is to help students approach knowledge with critical insight and with the ability to make sense of it. Until very recently, British and European universities approached this task by having students write papers, take yearly examinations, and stand comprehensive oral and written examinations for their degrees at the end.

American universities, democratically engaged in giving a far larger percentage of our population a college education, have approached the task by segmenting the student's experience into courses. In an earlier time at Harvard, courses were a year long, as they were in British and European schools. Now they are a semester long; in many state universities, courses may be only for a "quarter," a ten-week term of which there are three during the regular academic year and one in summer. In these brief courses, teachers try to stuff as many facts as possible into the heads of factless students. But once students finish the course, they are through with it forever unless they do graduate work in the discipline. The teacher is the only examiner. No board or committee passes on the teacher's evaluation of his own students. Under the name of academic freedom, American college teachers have achieved an independence from one another reminiscent of teachers in 12th-century Paris, where every master set up shop and lived on the fees students paid him—a system the University of Paris soon put aside. In the United States, the communal aspects of teaching have all but vanished, except for its faint and sickly apparition in the so-called interdisciplinary courses that rose for a time in the 1960s. Their ghostly presence has fled with the new day, and our students once again pursue curricula which, in the humanities at least, are so fragmented that students have a hard time relating one thing they know to everything else they know. From my observation, even the best universities are failing in their ancient obligation to teach students to reason in the linear, logical, dispassionate, and reflective way once assumed to be the emblem of the educated person.

The problems I have sketched seem critical. It is neither practical nor desirable to homogenize curricula or to eliminate electives or to condemn the variety in American education. We might make professors more responsible to one another, but we cannot wait for a general restructuring of the course system. We can, however, address the task of teaching students to reason. I believe that the best avenue to this goal lies in having our students write papers with qualities that whole institutions can agree on if faculties are willing to take the time to formulate certain guidelines. And I believe that by making the public aware that we are trying to teach reasoning through writing we may recapture some of the public support that we have lost.

The most important guideline would be to demand in student writing evidence that the writer is thinking, reasoning, reflecting and not merely reporting information collected from other sources. Yes, everyone knows that when we give the same paper to a random group of professors, some will grade that paper an A, some an F, and most in between. I think such results come about because no effort is made beforehand to agree on what readers are looking for. If we make the principal guideline evidence that the writers are thinking for themselves about information they control authoritatively, I think we can shrink the area of disagreement. If faculties and administrations can agree that the highest goal of every student paper is to have that student reason, and if that goal is announced, emphasized, taught in most classes, the effects will surely be better than what the most casual observer sees now. If we can get students to reason about what they know—truly reason and not merely report—they will remember better both the facts and how we teach them to think.

Writing is the supreme tool for learning. When we write, we set our thoughts down in a visible, extended discourse that allows us to compare one part with another, recognize contradictions, test our use of the evidence, and shape our interpretation of reality. But if we take seriously my proposal, we must change the way we teach our courses and the way we evaluate papers. These changes will be difficult because teachers and students alike have a great deal at stake in the present inadequate system of education.

Some anecdotal recollections:

My graduate training at Yale was in history of the Christian Church, especially in the middle ages and the 16th century. I loved my discipline for its drama, its characters, and above all for its connections. Historians are detectives, looking at past events that at first may seem unrelated. Historians discover that there are—or that there may be—binding threads wrapped around the parts. I say "may be" because history is not a neat discipline; the evidence historians rely on has ragged edges and holes. No matter how many facts we pile up, no one can recreate the past exactly as it was, and even if we could, we would still run into insoluble puzzles. Much 16th-century art and literature seems macabre, burdened with images of death and corruption and soaked with melancholy. Did the macabre sense contribute to the outbreak of the Protestant Reformation, and if so, how? There are no simple answers to such questions, but the discipline of posing them and trying to answer them and testing the answers in a community of discourse familiar with the evidence breathes life into the study of dead ages.

Armed with a fresh new PhD in 1962, I set out to teach history, first at Gettysburg College and two years later, at my alma mater, the University of Tennessee, Knoxville. For eight years I lectured, pumping facts into my students like a gardener daily watering his flowers, gave midterm exams and finals, and required a term paper. Students enjoyed my courses; I enjoyed them, too, and I liked my students.

Then doubts set in. Each year at the beginning of my advanced course, I gave my students a ten-question quiz to see what they had retained from my lectures in the western civilization course they had taken from me as freshmen. I asked them to identify historical figures on whom I had spent a great deal of time—Luther, Machiavelli, Henry VIII, and so on. I did not grade the quiz; it was an effort to grade myself. The results were not reassuring. Usually my students recognized no more than three or four names.

The writing of my charges also dismayed me. Some students wrote brilliantly; most made little sense even if they wrote correctly. Sometimes when I marked them down for not making themselves clear, they rushed to my office to explain their papers. More often they told me that what I found lacking in their work was there; I had simply missed it. They would stand over some incomprehensible sentence saying earnestly, "See, I say that right here." When I observed that I could not see "that" right there, they sometimes decided that for reasons beyond their comprehension, I had decided to persecute them. More often they said plaintively, "I *know* it; I just can't *write* it."

In my advanced course I required a term paper. This was a "substantial research project." I worked hard with my students helping them each find a subject. When the papers came in at the end of the term, I worked hard marking them. It puzzled me that most students lost all interest in those papers once they had received their grade. At the end of each term I was left with a pile of papers that they never bothered to pick up. Every year or two I tossed a huge bundle of graded, marked, and unclaimed papers into the garbage, casting a rueful eye on my unread comments in the margins.

The writing of my history students had two common flaws. Primary was knowledge of the facts, the evidence, the sources. They were not good readers, often because they did not read enough but often also because they read too much too hurriedly. They used my lectures as a clue to what they ought to read; if I stressed some point again and again, they could usually reproduce it in a recognizable form on their exams. (A colleague told me he could give his class calesthenics by saying, "This material will be on the exam. The first point is. . . ." At each number—first, second, third—the entire class would bend over to write it down, hence the calesthenics. I tried it, and it worked, my classes bowing like Chinese gymnasts.) My students were not good at reading on their own. Their papers were thin, often clogged with prejudices baldly asserted as eternal truth, what William Golding once called "folk history," assumptions shared by people who pick up a misty oral tradition and pass it on to anyone who listens to them. ("Reconstruction was a tyrannical evil thrust on the defeated South by the North, benefiting only the carpetbaggers and the scalawags who profited from the prostrate South's weakness." "The renaissance was filled with men bigger than life.")

As Hirsch argues, we can understand "culture" only if we command some knowledge of nouns with cultural and historical associations that provide a framework of knowledge on which we can hang our own daily experience, especially the experience that causes us to think reflectively about events, people, and ideas. Real knowledge is connectedness—and the recognition that some links are missing, that there is always a problematic, an area where we must infer, guess, and search. Knowledge for my students was a collection of answers to questions. Reflection, rumination, and exploration had little place in their writing.

My students had a second major problem with their papers. Their prose was vague, convoluted, pointless, incomprehensible. It was boring. This problem seems now commonplace in academe. No one I know ever says seriously, "I'm going to spend a delightful evening grading papers." Most faculty members in the modern university believe that grading student papers is a lower form of labor, a bit like cleaning toilets or mopping kitchen floors, a humiliating toil to be left behind as they move up in academe. In large universities senior professors sometimes do not grade papers at all. They leave that responsibility to their section leaders.

Why do we dislike the task of grading papers so much? Because we often have no idea what our students are talking about. Because papers are disjointed, repetitive, and incoherent. Because what we read is tedious and unoriginal. Because papers have no elegance. Student writing is the hardest reading we do. We must concentrate; we must reread; we must puzzle over the essay as though it were some cryptic and half-deciphered language chiseled into flaking stone. When we read for pleasure, we seek information, but not *merely* information. We read for information presented in such a way that it *means* something in a larger scheme of things, information put together so that we see in it a pattern, a shape, a significance that we might not have known had the writer not given us these facts in just this way. We admire thoughtfulness, pausing to admire a powerful sentence or striking metaphor or combination of telling words. Our short-term memories seldom retain much more than impressionistic fragments about style. We read to see what happens. In much student prose, nothing much happens; and if it does, it is often buried under monotonous or incomprehensible diction.

The two problems are as closely related as Siamese twins. Students who know little strive to make the most of it. They gush unrelated and half-understood facts and opinions, believing that the chief object of writing a ten-page paper is to fill ten pages. No matter that the ten pages make no special point, infer little from evidence, and have no unity or sense of development, no reflection, no exploration. They will give us ten pages.

They do not have an argument because they do not know enough about the material to formulate one; or else they have only half an argument peeking out from behind their words but not quite bold enough to emerge. They do not draw a conclusion because their hold on the evidence is so slender that they do not dare conclude anything or else they have no experience in concluding and leave the papers for readers to make of them what they will. They may conclude by preaching a little sermon, declaring that all right-minded people should do something about the problem—

whatever it is. Student prose is marked by a desperate urge not to say anything *wrong*. Like many of their professors, they have learned that when they are unsure of their knowledge, they can always obfuscate.

As a professor of history, I had to ask myself this question: "Why am I doing this?" I also had to ask, "Why are my students doing this?" As a lecturer, I was performing and enjoying myself; my students said they enjoyed my teaching and rewarded me with faithful attendance and high evaluations in the course guides that started appearing in the 1960s. I tried to tell myself that performance has its values. We attend a concert, and unless we are musicians in a grand manner, we do not leave with the symphony or the concerto committed to memory. We may be able to hum a few bars or even recognize the piece if we hear it again on the car radio as we go home. If we go to concerts, we develop ability to tell the difference between good performances and mediocre ones or bad ones, and we increase the variety of music that we appreciate. In time we may memorize a beloved piece. Even without retaining much of the experience, we find going to concerts entertaining and even uplifting.

Why can't we judge a lecture on history in the same way? A good lecture shows a mind working over problems. It teaches intuitions about acceptable and unacceptable ways of getting at the evidence. It conveys intellectual excitement and stirs interest in the discipline. It may make students pursue historical studies further—just as one stirring concert may turn neophytes into regular concert-goers.

These rationalizations were not satisfying. My students were passive. They expected to be entertained—just as television entertained them. I wanted to please them—and did. I was not teaching them anything they remembered. That hurt.

In 1970 I made a drastic change. I walked into my advanced course that autumn and told my students that I had good news and bad news. The good news was that we would not have a midterm or a final or a term paper. They looked at me with a mingling of astonishment and ecstasy, as if they had all died and waked up in an eternal New Orleans. Then came the bad news: I was going to require an eight-to-ten-page paper from them every two weeks. I would tell them the general subject, lecture about that subject and discuss it with them, and discuss their papers in the class after I had marked them. They did not have to go to the library to look up information; they did have to quote or cite texts from the books assigned to the class. Most of these were anthologies of primary source documents. They had to reflect on what the texts meant to a larger meaning in the time. What did Machiavelli's sense of how the prince should rule reflect about his view of human nature? What did Luther's concept of justification by faith mean for the ethical life? The first paper was due before the drop date; my class quickly dwindled from 55 to 18. My department chair grumbled and worried.

I persevered. My students wrote and wrote. I read and read, making brief comments. Always during the next session after papers came in, I read good papers aloud to the class, explaining why they were good, pointing out where writers were reasoning. I wanted them to know that I could be pleased and that some of their peers were meeting my standards. I showed how a good paper got right to the point, how it used evidence, how it took into account alternative explanations and contrary interpretations of the evidence, how it reasoned to a conclusion. I tried to teach them that there are always some parts of the evidence that do not add up.

Within a couple of years my class enrollments came back to their old level, but this time with a somewhat different constituency. Now I had a fair number of engineers, an occasional person from agriculture, students from the college of business, and a few errant souls from other parts of the university, taking my course not only to learn something about history but also to learn how to write an essay.

In a year or two, I adapted this method to my freshman survey, having those students write four-page papers every ten days and enlisting a couple of loyal graduate students to help me read them. I spent time with those graduate students, carefully teaching them what I wanted them to do and grading with them on the afternoons after papers came in after a morning class. When we came on a problem paper, we discussed it among ourselves.

I learned several things quickly. When I had my students do so much writing, I could not cover as much material as I had when I spent most of the course time lecturing. Teachers protest to me now that if they make students write, they cannot cover the material. But coverage is a false god. We never cover all the material anyway. And what good is it to cover multitudes of facts if students do not remember them six weeks later or cannot do anything with them even while they remember them? My students remembered what they wrote about. Their own thinking processes improved; they were able to judge better the thinking processes of others.

I taught myself what writing teachers nowadays call "holistic scoring." In holistic scoring, one reads papers rapidly, without any effort to mark them line by line. The first aim is to divide them into categories of achievement, to find the best papers and the worst papers and those in between. I read for meaning; papers that I could quickly understand and believe went into the top pile; papers I had difficulty understanding or believing went into the middle pile; papers I couldn't understand or believe went into the lowest pile. I formulated three questions: What does the paper say? Why does it say it? Is it worth saying?

Teachers may hate to grade papers because they think they must slog through them, reading them line by line, correcting every error. In fact a quick scan tells you quickly the most important thing about a paper—what it says. Or doesn't say. The slow, painful readings of papers, pencil in hand, often makes teachers forget the writer's point. It is far more efficient to read a group of papers quickly, compare them with each other, and read them quickly again than it is to read them laboriously one by one. On the second reading one can make some marginal comments, and at the end, one can write a few lines explaining the grade.

Even these marks can be minimal if the teacher carefully discusses the papers in class after reading them. Such discussion is the best way I know to show students what is expected, where they have succeeded, and where they have fallen short in their writing. Most student writing fails not on the level of the sentence but on the level of the essay. Discussing their papers as essays helped my students understand that I wanted them to think and took away their fear that I was subjecting them to some sort of exercise in grammar or that I was requiring them to write with the quiet elegance of George Orwell or that I was interested in piles of facts. Yes, I wanted some facts, but I wanted to know what those facts meant, and I found that I could teach nearly all my students the difference between a compilation and an essay by spending time in class talking about their work. I could not teach them all to write *good* essays. But I felt that it was something for them to recognize the form even if they could not yet master it.

My lectures and discussions became more pointed. I asked myself of every lecture, What will my students get out of this? How can they best use what I have to give to them? I realized that when I had a complicated set of ideas to present, I had to make several different presentations, putting those ideas in different words, illustrating them, repeating them until my students could understand them. My unclarity quickly showed up on their papers. The continual encounter with their minds made me realize how difficult it is for them to grasp some thoughts, especially thoughts removed as far from their experience as the religious and political debates of the 16th century.

Most teachers overestimate the power of students to absorb information about the unfamiliar. A good teacher explains and explains and does not move on to the next level of the course until she is sure that most students have understood the presentation. To read student essays immediately after one has delivered a brilliant set of lectures is usually humbling. We see how little of that brilliance has been translated into the minds of its audience. Hardly any teachers in large universities now permit themselves to have that humbling—and instructive—experience because hardly any teachers read student papers. That job is left to the proletariat among academics—graduate students and adjunct faculty.

We can call on common experience to judge the lecture method of teaching. We know that when someone makes an oral presentation about an important issue in a meeting, managers worth their perks will call for it to be put in writing and studied carefully before any decisions are made about it. In an effective organization, the written proposal is discussed—often by means of written memoranda. Oral presentations are not efficient in themselves as transmitters of information. As Yogi Berra, that great philosopher of the people, said, "Oral contracts aren't worth the paper they're written on." The principle holds true for any oral presentation, lecture or otherwise, intended for future reference. Lectures may introduce ideas; they may stimulate interest; they may provoke thought. But unless they are embedded in a context of writing, they vanish like steam. A business or a government that operated on oral transmission only would collapse in a moment. Universities roll on and on in the inertia of the lecture method. Again and again various college graduates have told me something like this: "I've always been interested in _____ . I wrote a paper on that in college." I have almost never heard even a colleague say, "I'll never forget what Professor Twistov said in his lecture on the Brenner Pass." (Or whatever.) But if lectures and discussions were tied always to writing students were about to do or writing they had just done, both memory and thinking would improve.

My students seemed to enjoy writing for me. They soon realized I would never humiliate them for what they wrote. I made a habit of reading only good papers in class; as people improved, I happily read their work. I never told the class who the author of the paper was; but the authors often privately expressed to me their pride in their papers when I picked them out as exemplary and read them aloud. Several students told me privately that their great aim was to write a paper so well that I would choose it to read to the group. Many who had assumed that good writing was produced only by mythical people who wrote great books realized what was possible for some ordinary-looking students their own age. An added advantage was that with so much writing to do, students kept up in their reading. They realized quickly what I have said earlier in this essay: the more we know about something, the more fluid is our writing about it, and the more we write about a subject, the more we want to know about it.

In 1978 I came to Harvard to direct the Expository Writing Program, heir of the oldest college writing program in the United States. My experiments at the University of Tennessee seem rather primitive now. Thanks to my reading in the field of rhetoric and writing and thanks to the continual experimentation of members of my devoted staff and to continual trial and error on my own, I think I know much more about teaching writing than I did in those years when I was guiding students from Machiavelli to Montaigne.

We all know how dangerous it is to generalize too much from one's own experience. Even so, I think my experience gives me some perspective, and with it I feel pessimism though not despair. In our press we get an almost daily dosage of bitter truth about what students do not know. I am not convinced that graduates know any more. At Harvard as in state universities throughout the United States, large lecture courses flourish. Courses of 500, 600, 700 are not uncommon. At least one Harvard undergraduate course draws 1000 students a year. The usual procedure is the same that I followed at first in my Western Civ course at the University of Tennessee: the lecturer performs twice a week, and students are dispersed for a third hour in "sections" taught by a graduate student or by an adjunct member of the faculty. The quality of the section leaders varies widely; one may even say wildly. Some are splendid; most are acceptable; some are god-awful.

The section leaders try to create a seminar where discussion goes on. The theory holds that the section leaders can tell who is learning and who is not by the quality of the discussion.

We may agree that a rousing discussion of a topic can inform and enlighten. Discussion sections where students try out ideas and brain-wrestle with both their leader and their peers can be memorable. Yet at a certain point writing becomes a necessary adjunct in the measurement of how much students are learning and whether they are reasoning. A glib talker can make himself and others imagine that he is much more knowledgeable and rational than he is; a glib writer can be much more quickly found out. The talker can change the subject ever so slightly when the going gets tough. Others fill in the blanks when the talker falters. "What you mean is . . . ." "Well, I see it this way." But what happens if the participants in a seminar are to make short, written presentations at the beginning of a seminar that might serve as the foundation for discussion in the rest of the period? Or what if participants were required to write a summary interpretation of the discussion afterward, perhaps presenting it for a brief discussion in the next class session? I do not suggest that every student make a written presentation every time, but the habit of writing and the experience of taking a turn at presenting writing to the group for commentary are valuable helps to both memory and thought.

In some graduate seminars, the sessions are shaped around papers presented by students and discussed by the group. "Seminar reports," we called such papers in my day. That sort of experience happens rarely at Harvard, if indeed it happens at all. Does it happen elsewhere? Seldom, I think. Students talk and talk and talk; those who do not want to talk seldom have to talk. In a "good" section, the students seem to have a good time; in a "bad" section, they seem bored. That, at least, is the inference I draw from Harvard's guide to courses published every year by the Committee for Undergraduate Education. I have taught an undergraduate English course at Harvard, meeting for three hours one night a week, dividing my students into two groups, and requiring members of each group to present a short paper on the assignment every other week. The course was fun, and I think I taught something, or that rather my students learned something.

Nowadays large lecture courses may require student papers, although they may not. These are graded by the section leader. If section leaders are carefully trained in groups where the head of the course leads them through many papers and instills in them standards for marking, the grading may be fairly consistent and intelligent across all the sections. Such training is rare, and large variations exist in the standards for grading among teaching fellows of whom I have some knowledge.

Even more variation is found in comments graders make on papers. We see many papers from other courses at our writing center. Some comments are helpful; most are slight and unhelpful. Some are harmful. Many papers have no comments at all. My general impression is that little consistent or constructive attention is paid to student writing in large lecture courses at Harvard. Somebody reads the papers; it is better for students to write even unread papers than to write nothing at all; but the level of commentary on papers at Harvard is generally abysmal. Section leaders believe that their most important task is to assign grades. The grade of B+ is a favorite because, I think, it is a grade unlikely to bring down on the head of the grader much student complaint.

None of this is to suggest that students are driven into these courses against their will. Even in Harvard's Core Curriculum, dozens of courses exist with small enrollments. In the rest of the college, small courses abound. In a recent year, some 1300 courses listed in the catalogue were not given because no one signed up for them. My judgments are impressionistic and not statistical; students appear to love the excitement of a brilliant lecturer—and Harvard has many brilliant lecturers. Students want to be entertained.

Here television has only exacerbated a common human trait. The effect of television may have been to change somewhat the notion of what entertainment is and to raise expectations. I am tempted to draw an analogy from the precipitous decline in minor-league baseball once fans could bring the major leagues into their living rooms. The huge auditoriums now scattered through Harvard and other large schools, the nearly perfect sound equipment, and on occasion, brilliant picture projection make it possible for 1000 students to hear the same lecture that in another age might have been delivered to 50 or 60. Why hear someone less entertaining (less "brilliant," as students usually say) when it is possible to hear a star!

Some students tell me that they like the relative anonymity of these courses. They sink into their seats as though at a movie, knowing that all eyes will be forward and that none will be on them. In a world where they face many demands, internal and external, they know that in a huge auditorium, surrounded by hundreds of their fellows, nothing will be required of them except that they be quiet.

What about the professors? The good lecturers love to speak to the multitudes. They become actors, playing to an audience that often adores them. Andy Warhol said that the time would come when we would all be famous for 15 minutes. College professors in large courses can be famous for 50 minutes twice a week. It's a heady experience, and isolated as they are by the footlights (many of them lecture on elevated podiums like stages), they do not have to suffer the grinding experience of talking to students face to face—or of reading their papers. It has become a mark of prestige to teach a course that has an enrollment of 600 or 700 students. Imagine a pianist who could have that kind of audience twice a week for 12 weeks!

The big lectures not only satisfy professorial egos; they are also much less work. Yes, some professors rework their lectures often, but not many. Most put together some notes that they can revise slightly and use for years and years. They appear, tweedy gods fallen to earth for a brief time; they dispense knowledge, often with entertaining asides and witty illustrations; they may answer a few questions from the audience; and then they disappear, presumably in a sort of temporary baroque apotheosis surrounded by winged muses as they soar into the library or the laboratory to tramp the Elysian Fields of knowledge. To try to get professors long accustomed to this pleasant routine to sit in small groups with students and to read their writing and to comment intelligently on it and perhaps to make them revise it and submit it again reminds me a bit of a recent Russian attempt to change the course of one of the north-flowing rivers of Siberia.

Administrators love these gigantic lecture courses. Students praise them, and administrations in their habitual warfare with students appreciate the relief of offering something that pleases the hordes. To remove the entertaining big lecture would be like canceling the circuses in ancient Rome.

The administrators have a point. A reform movement away from the big lecture might bring on economic catastrophe. No reputable historian of academe has ever to my knowledge suggested that the advent of the big lecture course with its satellite sections came about because someone suggested that such courses would make for splendid teaching and learning. The system became widespread in the 1950s and 1960s solely for economic reasons. The baby boomers landed in college in a crushing wave. Existing faculties could "teach" many more students by the lecture/sections method than in smaller sections. Since many such courses are introductory, the lecturer could teach two or three of them without much strain and still have time to teach an advanced course. And who cared about "teaching" when "credits" became the goal of education?

But in the 1990s educational failure looks us in the face. By every measure, American education is falling behind much of the rest of the industrial world. The writing problem, poorly defined but universally admitted, seems to be part of everyone's agenda. Many schools are beefing up their writing programs and trying to assign more writing in courses in all the disciplines. "Writing Across the Curriculum" is emblazoned on the banner of education because administrators and faculties alike know that student writing is terrible and that it is a shame to American colleges not to do something about it. These are hopeful signs.

I manage to restrain my jubilation when I recall how many forces are working against the prospect of real improvement. The most important immediate task is to re-educate faculty members about their teaching responsibilities and their mutual obligations. Part of this re-education may be to shame them into seeing that they have a responsibility to keep student minds from sinking into a narcotic passivity during their college years. Making students write is an effective means of activating those minds; but if students are going to v. rite, somebody with real knowledge about writing has to respond to their work—and respond adequately enough to teach students something about thinking in the discipline.

Faculty members have to start talking with one another not only across departmental lines but within departments about their teaching and about what they want in the way of writing assignments. Presidents, provosts, deans, and department chairs should lead the way in bringing these discussions about. Only if faculty members talk to one another about teaching issues can general writing issues be effectively addressed.

Assuming they are addressed, I believe the first step in large universities will be to start programs to teach section leaders how to assign and comment upon student writing. Some schools are already using their writing programs to do this work of education. In large universities, section leaders may include both graduate students and adjunct faculty. The writing program can run seminars for these people, perhaps paying them to attend. The seminars work best when professors from the various departments take an interest in them and even participate in them. They would work even better if the university required them of every section leader.

The second step will be to reconsider the general issue of the huge lecture course in the modern university. That will take years—perhaps decades.

To reform education along directions that I am suggesting will require great public support. Maybe that support, translated into public pressure to make teaching more important to higher education, will force administrations to get faculty members to talk to one another about the teaching task and its writing component. Reform will cost a lot of money, and the public will have to provide it. The public will not provide funds unless it is convinced that universities are making a genuine effort to teach. I can think of no better way to make that effort believable than for colleges and universities to require student writing and to develop institutional guidelines for reading those papers and commenting intelligently and helpfully on them.

The popular success of the books by Bloom and Hirsch have demonstrated a swell of interest in America in the issues and a dissatisfaction with what now is. The public is restless, and unless higher education justifies itself more fully in the classroom, public support will dwindle, and universities will wither. If the public perceives that the main task of a university is socialization, discipline, and so forth, it will also perceive that faculties can be even smaller and that those who teach can be paid even less.

A third step would be to recognize writing programs for what they should be—professional departments within the university, requiring a professional staff with the respect and benefits that other faculty members have. Here there are many questions, and the answers are difficult. This step would require changes so sweeping in the university that they go beyond the limits of this essay. But it is necessary if colleges and universities are to have any claim to educational seriousness in the modern world.

Educational reform is a matter of politics. We need leaders who will make support of education a political issue on the level of support for defense. Bloom and Hirsch suggest that education is defense, and with the sudden and dramatic lessening of East-West tensions, we may have a great historical opportunity to put a peace dividend into the service of education. But unless faculties take a greater responsibility for teaching students to reason, for giving graduates the sense that they have indeed been educated as well as socialized, we will reap nothing at all. Without public support for education we are doomed to lose our primacy in the world in both economics and culture. Much evidence abounds that we are losing that primacy quickly.

The pen is mightier than the sword; so runs an old proverb. The ability to write is the ability to think logically in an extended way about reality. The tools for writing have changed from pen and paper to the computer keyboard and the printer, but the need has never been greater.

About the Authors

Sven Birkerts:

Sven Birkerts won the Citation for Excellence in Reviewing from the National Book Critics Circle in 1986. His work is cited in *Best Essays of 1987* and *Best Essays of 1988* (Ticknor and Fields). He has published two books, *An Artificial Wilderness: Essays on Twentieth Century Literature* (William Morrow, 1987) and *The Electric Life: Essays on Modern Poetry* (Morrow, 1989), which received a special P.E.N. Spielvogel-Diamondstein citation. *American Energies: Essays on Fiction* is forthcoming from Morrow. He has taught writing at Harvard for seven years.

Victor Kantor Burg:

Victor Kantor Burg has taught writing to undergraduates at Harvard, and presently teaches literature at M.I.T. and writing/presentations to mid-career Master's students at the Kennedy School of Government. His journalism, reviews and columns have been published in The New York Times, The Christian Science Monitor and The Boston Globe, among other places. His screenplay, *Cause to Hope,* is in development with Robert Geller of Learning in Focus Productions. His plays have been and will continue to be performed in Cambridge, Boston and New York. He is writing a mystery, *The Riddle Soup,* for his son, Hal.

Judith Beth Cohen:

Judith Beth Cohen has published a novel, *Seasons* (The Permanent Press, 1984; Rowohlt Verlag, W. Germany, 1979), as well as short stories, essays and book reviews. She has received a grant from the American Express Fund for Curriculum Development in Ethics (Summer 1988), a Fulbright Summer Fellowship, and the P.E.N. Syndicated Fiction Award. She teaches in the Liberal Studies Division of the Graduate School at Lesley College and is an associate at the Bard College Institute for Writing and Thinking.

Eileen Farrell:

Eileen Farrell is an anthropologist whose articles include "The Poetics of Renunciation: Form and Content in Ritual Fasting" (*The Journal of Psychoanalytic Anthropology* 8 [4], Fall 1985). In addition to courses in social and psychological anthropology, she taught writing at Harvard for eight years. She now teaches writing at Emerson College.

Alex Gold:

Alex Gold has published critical articles and is currently completing a novel. He taught literature at Stanford University and at Boston University before coming to Harvard where he taught writing for eight years.

Pat C. Hoy II:

Pat C. Hoy II has co-edited two collections of modern essays—*Prose Pieces* and *Women's Voices.* His textbook, *Writing and Reading Essays* (McGraw-Hill), will be published in 1991. His articles, essays, and reviews have appeared in *The Sewanee Review, Twentieth Century Literature, South Atlantic Review,* and *the Doris Lessing Newsletter.* He was a Professor of English at the U.S. Military Academy before coming to Harvard, where he has taught for the past three years.

Alex Johnson:

Alexandra Johnson won a 1990 P.E.N. Special Citation for *The Novel Self,* a study of women's literary diaries, currently in progress (Harvard University Press, forthcoming). Her essays and reviews have appeared in: *The New Yorker, The New York Times Book Review, The Saturday Review, Ms. Magazine, The*

Boston Review and *The Christian Science Monitor*, among other national publications. Ms. Johnson, who was the Assistant Literary Editor of *The Christian Science Monitor*, has also written for Public Television in Boston and New York. She has taught writing at Harvard for seven years.

Nancy Kline:

Nancy Kline has published three books: *The Faithful* (William Morrow, 1968; Peter Owen, London, 1969), *Lightning: The Poetry of René Char* (Northeastern University Press, 1981), and *The Tongue Snatchers*, a translation of Claudine Herrmann's *Les voleuses de langue* (University of Nebraska Press, 1989). Her short stories, essays and translations have appeared widely. She won an N.E.A. Creative Writing Grant in 1981, and has been a Finalist in Playwriting and in Nonfiction in the Massachusetts Artists Fellowship Competition. She is Director of the Writing Project at Barnard, where she holds a joint appointment in English and French.

Fred Marchant:

Fred Marchant's poems and essays have appeared in many journals, including *Poetry Northwest, America, Amelia, Connecticut Poetry Review, Harvard Magazine, The Boston Review, The Harvard Book Review,* and *Yankee.* He is an editor of *AGNI* and Associate Professor of Humanities and Director of Integrated Studies at Suffolk University.

Richard Marius:

Richard Marius has published four works of nonfiction: *Luther* (Lippincott, 1974), *Thomas More* (Knopf, 1984 and J.M. Dent, London), *A Writer's Companion* (Knopf, 1984) and *The McGraw-Hill English Handbook* [with Harver Wiener] (McGraw-Hill, 1984). In addition, he has published two nov-

els, *The Coming of Rain* (Knopf, 1969) and *Bound for the Promised Land* (Knopf, 1976). His *Thomas More* was nominated for the American Book Award in 1984. Reviews and articles have appeared in numerous magazines. He has taught for twenty-five years and is now Director of Expository Writing at Harvard.

Lowry Pei:

Lowry Pei has published a novel, *Family Resemblances* (Random House, 1986), as well as numerous critical articles, short stories and book reviews. His fiction has been chosen to appear in *Best American Short Stories 1984* and in *The American Story: The Best of StoryQuarterly (1990)*, and he has been a Finalist in Fiction in the Massachusetts Artists Fellowship Competition. He is an Associate Professor of English and Director of Writing at Simmons College.

Maxine Rodburg:

Maxine Rodburg's short stories have appeared in *The Virginia Quarterly Review, The Michigan Quarterly*, and *Belles Lettres.* She earned her M.F.A. from the University of Michigan, where she received four first-place Hopwood Awards. She has taught writing at Harvard for three years.

Linda Simon:

Linda Simon has published six books: *Gertrude Stein: a Composite Portrait* (Avon, 1974), *The Biography of Alice B. Toklas* (Doubleday, 1977; Avon, 1978; Peter Owen, London, 1978; Editions Seghers, Paris, 1984), *Thornton Wilder: His World* (Doubleday, 1979), *Of Virtue Rare: Margaret Beaufort, Matriarch of the House of Tudor* (Houghton Mifflin, 1982), *Good Writing: a Guide and Sourcebook* (St. Martin's, 1988), and *Contexts: A Thematic Reader* (St. Martin's, 1991). Her book reviews and essays have appeared widely. She directs the Writing Center at Harvard.